MW01289637

AUTHENTIC
SALVATION

AUTHENTIC SALVATION

The Why, the Who, the How, the results,
and the When of True Salvation in Christ

Joseph E. McGee

XULON PRESS

Xulon Press
2301 Lucien Way #415
Maitland, FL 32751
407.339.4217
www.xulonpress.com

© 2020 by Joseph E. McGee

All rights reserved solely by the author. The author guarantees all
contents are original and do not infringe upon the legal rights of
any other person or work. No part of this book may be reproduced
in any form without the permission of the author. The views
expressed in this book are not necessarily those of the publisher.

Unless otherwise indicated, Scripture quotations taken from the
New King James Version (NKJV). Copyright © 1982 by Thomas
Nelson, Inc. Used by permission. All rights reserved.

Printed in the United States of America.

Those who may be interested in receiving a lessons outline with
additional information that may be used to teach this book may
inquire by emailing **drjosephmcgee@yahoo.com**

Paperback ISBN-13: 978-1-6628-0337-6
eBook ISBN-13: 978-1-6628-0338-3

Table of Contents

Acknowledgments

There are so many whom I would like to acknowledge. The first being Robyn McGee, my wife of forty-five years, who encouraged me to write this book. She provided much advice and insight when examining and editing the first draft of each chapter. I feel that it is important to mention Dr. Stan Bronston who, having written his book, provided advice concerning the direction and form of my work. The treasurer of our Baptist association and retired army major, Roger Cain, who helped edit and provided suggestions throughout the work. Much thanks and appreciation for Dr. David Mapes, professor at Luther Rice Seminary, my former supervisor and friend, for his theological advice. He sometimes challenged me but more often suggested appropriate wording. Then there is retired high school English teacher and local writer for our community newspaper, Mary Ann Ellis, who provided much editing. Lastly, I want to acknowledge the excellent editing work of my ministry assistant, Wendy Hipps, for her time and suggestions. Without their dedicated help, I do not believe that I would have ever tried such a monumental task. May God bless them all.

PREFACE

Important To Read

One may ask, "why a book on the topic of salvation?" I will provide a three-part answer based upon my observations. The first observation is my awareness of individuals who have been provided a false presentation, or explanation, of authentic salvation with a follow-up of repeating certain words or phrases along with a prayer and a promise of salvation. The Holy Spirit played no part in the process resulting in the individual living with false hope of salvation. I wrote the first chapter with this in mind by providing many of the misconceptions of authentic salvation. The second observation is that most books previously written concerning the doctrine of salvation either provide such substantial academic information to the point that the average layperson will never comprehend and there are no practical implications for one's daily life. On the other hand, some books are so vague that much information is left out to the point that the reader walks away wanting. The third observation was experienced during multiple worship services. Often when the words "regeneration," "imputation," "Justification," "sanctification," "atonement," "the cross," and many others are spoken or mentioned in the song there is no emotion. To the average believer, such words are nothing but church jargon, and the deep meanings of each word that should move us to shout or cry-out is lost and the church at large misses a blessing. I blame this on the lack of discipleship in many churches. I am not talking about that one hour each Sunday evening that a few of our churches still honor. I am talking about the training of behavior and beliefs that may be taught during that special time or through Sunday school or the messages during church service. When the people of the church understand such words, they will be moved and experience more powerful worship. This is my motivation: That the reader may know if he or she has experienced authentic salvation; That the reader may understand why everyone needs to experience authentic salvation; How that salvation became available to sinful people who have no hope; How an individual may accept that authentic salvation; What blessings and changes should result in one's nature who has experienced authentic salvation; And what is the future for all who enjoy authentic salvation.

I am a linear thinker. Some may ask, "What is a linear thinker?" A linear thinker, or writer, is one who teaches, or relates information to hearers, or readers, by depending on sequential developments. This is accomplished by building foundations before a major point may be readily understood. Speaking of foundations, the reader will notice that I frequently begin a topic with either a short definition of explanation or by providing a quote to afford a basic overview of the subject that may be easier to comprehend and provide a focus that better prepares the reader before developing a much larger or academic exegesis.

I have divided this book into six parts; each part is built on the previous part so that the reader may have a foundation as to readily understand the part he or she is presently reading. The first part explains the meaning of authentic salvation. The reader may note that I not only provide a short explanation of authentic salvation by providing many misconceptions so that the reader may know what authentic salvation is not. Part two explains why humanity needs to experience authentic salvation. I noticed that many books written on salvation fail to acknowledge in detail much of what is written in chapters two and three. Part two ends with humanity in their sins with no hope. Nonetheless, there is a ray of hope for humankind, the coming atonement on the cross. Part three provides much important information concerning the atonement provided by the shed blood of Christ on the cross. Part four reveals the call of one's salvation and how he or she can accept God's grace. Part five explains the many blessings that the believer receives at salvation and the work of the Holy Spirit in his or her life. Lastly, part six discloses the only way one may go to heaven.

The reader may have noticed that I am writing in the first person. I know that a writer is usually expected to write in the third person. But this is more than just information to be read. This is personal to me. I have a fear that many will stand before the Great White Throne Judgment with a realization that they were counting on false hope. As previously stated, I believe that many of the words found in our hymns and praise songs are over-looked and, in some situations, have become meaningless. However, through the study of this book, the meaning of the words may come alive, resulting in a clearer understanding, and appreciation for what Christ accomplished on the cross and exciting and heartfelt worship. May God bless you!

Part One

The What of Authentic Salvation

> Not everyone who says to Me, Lord, Lord, shall
> enter the kingdom of heaven, but he who does the
> will of My Father in heaven. Many will say to Me
> in that day, Lord, Lord, have we not prophesied
> in Your name, cast out demons in Your name, and
> done many wonders in Your name? And then I will
> declare to them, I never knew you; depart from Me,
> you who practice lawlessness. Matt. 7:21-23

This part only contains one chapter that reveals vaguely what authentic salvation is (the major details will be shared throughout this book). In accomplishing the goal of explaining what authentic salvation is the writer will provide many examples of what it is not with a prayer that the reader may examine his or her own salvation experience to have an assurance that he or she is not living with false hope.

CHAPTER ONE

Living With False Hope

Not everyone who says to Me, Lord, Lord, shall enter the kingdom of heaven, but he who does the will of My Father in heaven. Many will say to Me in that day, Lord, Lord, have we not prophesied in Your name, cast out demons in Your name, and done many wonders in Your name? And then I will declare to them, I never knew you; depart from Me, you who practice lawlessness. Matt. 7:21-23[11]

During the 1990s, I participated in the founding of a mission church while providing for my family by selling heat pumps three to four days a week. After the owner of the company decided to sell a new brand of heat pump, the new provider made it mandatory for the company to send a sales representative and a technician for one week of training to Fort Worth, Texas, where each had to pass a test to qualify to sell the provider's product; I was the first to go and was confident that I would pass the test. After all, I had won a contest sponsored by Southern Company by outselling all the competitors within the region. Southern Company invited me to train other heating and air conditioning sales representatives on the selling of heat pumps. Nonetheless, when I arrived in Fort Worth, Texas, I found that the owner had mixed up the training events. It was the week of training for technicians, not for sales representatives. I realized at that moment that when I left for Texas, I had relied on "false hope;" I was not as prepared as I thought.

I write this chapter intending to make the reader pause and ask the questions: "Is my salvation authentic?" "Am I living with the true assurance that I will enter the gates of heaven when I die?" If not, "am I living with false hope?" I know that much of this chapter is nothing new to some who will read it, but it sets the direction and focus of the book. What is authentic salvation? What is it not? Why do we need it? Who provides it? How do we obtain it? What must we do to experience it?

We often hear preachers preach on the "Blessed Hope." This is a reference to the certain expectation of the appearing of the Lord at the Rapture (Tit.2:13). Paul inscribed the Greek word "*elpis*," meaning that a true believer not only desires or believes that Christ will come, but his or her knowledge is an undeniable certainty.[2] The Believer who has truly encountered authentic salvation will experience the "Blessed Hope." Those who pass away before the Second Coming of Christ will one day stand before the Lord at the Judgment Seat of Christ (2 Cor. 5: 9-11). It is here that all true Believers' life work will be evaluated, not for salvation, but for eternal rewards for their works accomplished for Christ and not for themselves.

Nonetheless, the text (Matt. 7: 21-23) is not describing regenerated believers standing before the Lord at the Judgment Seat of Christ. On the contrary, it is non-regenerated individuals standing before the Lord at the Great White Throne of Judgment (Rev. 20:11-15). This judgment is not that salvation:

it is the judgment where the lost will hear their verdict. It is important to note that the Lord's statement in Matthew 7 is not addressing atheists, agnostics, devil worshipers, or pagans. He is addressing lost souls who believed that God's Son existed and had been devoted church members who now realize that they had mistakenly depended on false hope for their salvation. These men and women had spoken the right religious church speak and involved themselves in religious ministries such as prophesying (proclaiming or preaching) and the most mystical ministries such as casting out devils and accomplishing many wonders in Christ's name (7:22). However, they tragically will hear the Lord declare, "I never knew you, depart from Me you who practice lawlessness" (7:23).

Often an English word may have more than one definition. This is true of many Greek words as well. The word "know," or "knew," is often translated from the Greek word *ginosko*. Sometimes the meaning is the possessing of factual knowledge of a person or thing; other times it suggests sexual relations. Nevertheless, in this passage, it is the intimate relationship that God has for Believers.[3] One may claim to "know" Christ (have intellectual knowledge or information of), but it is more important that Christ "know" you (not just an intellectual knowledge of facts, but having intimate heart knowledge). These individuals seem to claim they knew the Lord; they even claimed more than once that their religious works were accomplished "In His name" (7:21-22), a phrase placed before Christ, the judge, for a positive verdict. They are now discovering that simply applying Christ's name is not enough, and they now understand that all they accomplished in His name was for their selfish benefits rather than for Him (Christ). What they achieved in their so-called ministry was hollow, self-serving, and more than likely never heartfelt or motivated by the Holy Spirit.

Mathew 7 divulges that Christ will be the Judge: "Then I will declare to them" (7:23). The same evidence that Christ will be the judge is established in Revelation 20: 11-15. The word "declare" is found in judicial language. It is the declaration of a judge that is serious, public, and irreversible.[4] The judge's verdict "depart from Me" is eternal separation from God. These are not people who were once saved, then lost again. Jesus stated, "I never knew you." How many people think they are saved but have never experienced authentic salvation?

The late Dr. Billy Graham often noted that the greatest mission field is found within our church rolls. This raises a question: How could seemingly dedicated religious people not stand before the Lord at the Judgment Seat of Christ meant for those who are authentically saved but rather find themselves standing before God at the Great White Throne of Judgment to hear their judgment of eternal separation from the Lord, knowing that their destiny was eternal suffering in the flaming fires of hell meant for the devil and his demons? Throughout the rest of this chapter, I will attempt to provide several reasonable answers to this question.

Sacraments (Religious Rituals)

Some religious denominations advocate the practice of sacraments as a means to salvation. Sacraments are often considered a sensible sign by which invisible grace and inward sanctification are communicated to the soul.[5] Many denominations observe all, or some, of the sacraments; we will discuss the seven that are practiced in the Catholic Church:

- **Baptism:** Catholics, as other denominations, understand baptism as the initiation of a new life and union with Jesus Christ and the Christian community. They advocate that baptism forgives sin. Infants are not born Catholic. Nonetheless, Catholic parents will present their newborns to the priests to be baptized (pouring water on the heads of the infants) resulting in the child's union with Christ and the Church. The Catholic Church advocates that some form of baptism in Jesus Christ is necessary for salvation.[6]

- **Confirmation:** Confirmation is observed after baptism and some form of training, thereby resulting in the completion and the maturity of the Christian and the providing of the opportunity to recommit him or herself to a Christian vocation.[7]

- **Eucharist:** The Eucharist is considered the most important sacrament in the Catholic Church. The partaking of the Eucharist unites one with the Lord. It celebrates the Lord's death, burial, and resurrection. It is a reminder that the Catholic must follow Jesus and therefore must live like Jesus. Catholics advocate the idea of "transubstantiation." They express the teaching that the bread and the wine change into the reality of Jesus; therefore, one receives the whole of Christ since He is utterly present in the wine and the bread.[8] Many denominations refer to the Eucharist as the Lord's Supper or communion.

- **Reconciliation:** This is accomplished when the Catholic member acknowledges his or her sinfulness and with a contrite heart confesses with a priest. The priest will then require some form of penance, that is, the enactment of some charitable act, or sacrifice, or the recitation of some prayers. Penance provides evidence that the sinning individual is willing to heal the harm that he or she caused to other Christians and the opportunity for the Lord to change one's life. This process affords forgiveness and salvation.[9]

- **Anointing of the Sick:** Catholics understand that sin and sickness are often related, that sickness and human suffering are effects of original sin. The general human condition needs healing, saving, and redeeming. Therefore, when the sick are anointed and healed, it is in the context of forgiveness of sin.[10]

- **Holy Orders:** This is accomplished with the laying on of hands during the ordination service of men for their clergy service within the Christian community. This suggests a special symbol of the ongoing presence of Christ.[11]

- **Matrimony:** The Catholic Church understands marriage as a sacrament that reminds the participants of the never-ending love that Christ has for the Church.[12]

Please do not think that I am belittling those who practice sacraments. I am only suggesting that one's salvation should never be founded upon sacraments and rituals that are in some fashion established upon works. True salvation is not achieved by works but only through the imputed righteousness of Christ and one's faith, which will be discussed in later chapters. These sacraments are no different from the religious rituals that the Jews practiced during the time of Jesus. They gave alms to the poor, they observed expected religious holy days, they observed all the Jewish rituals, the men were circumcised, and all kept the law. Outwardly, they presented themselves as highly religious Temple-attending Jews. Nonetheless, Jesus claimed that though they were beautiful outwardly like a whitewashed tomb, they were, in reality, full of dead men's bones (spiritually dead). Jesus further stated that they may have appeared outwardly to men as righteous; however, they were inwardly full of hypocrisy and lawlessness (Matt. 23: 27-28).

Those denominations that practice "ordinances" (baptism and the Lord's Supper, and sometimes foot washing) rather than "sacraments" do so not to gain salvation but out of obedience and observance to Christ because of their salvation. It should be stressed that if anyone is relying on the observance of any of the sacraments, ordinances, or any other religious ritual for salvation, that individual should give pause and question the validity of his or her redemption. They are in danger of hearing Christ the Judge declare, "I never knew you, Depart from Me."

Religious Works

The apostle Paul wrote, "For by grace you have been saved through faith, and not of yourselves; it is the gift of God, not of works, lest any man shall boast. For we are His workmanship, created in Christ Jesus for good works" (Eph. 2: 8-10). Paul was merely stating that one is not able to save himself or herself through any Christian conduct, ministry, or works such as tithing, reading the Bible, church attendance or membership, etc. Our salvation is acquired through faith, which the Holy Spirit provides when one is drawn or called (this will be discussed in detail in a future chapter.). Nevertheless, Paul states that there is a place for religious work (v-10); the works motivated out of obedience, love, and thanksgiving for the salvation already experienced.

The Anglican minister, John Wesley, came to this country in 1735 through 1737, preaching the gospel and sharing his teaching of "methods of Christianity." After the Revolutionary War, many of the Anglican churches became Methodist, following his teachings of methods. Although the teachings were that of works, it is not to say that Methodists cannot experience true salvation. Many will be surprised to know that John Wesley was unsaved while ministering in Georgia spreading his methods throughout. Being paralyzed with fear of dying, he questioned his salvation while on a ship returning from Georgia during a terrible storm. During his attack of dread, he noticed some Moravians traveling with the crew singing with joy. In his effort to understand their bravery, he would later seek out one of their leaders and learn of the need for authentic salvation, which he soon experienced on May 24, 1738.[13]

The Great Reformer, Martin Luther, lived in fear of God and the thought of going to hell. He was a Catholic monk who would beat and whip himself to bring his flesh under submission. He rightly believed that his religious works failed him, and he could never be righteous enough. That fear left one day as he was reading Romans 1:17: "The just shall live by faith." Luther learned that all his religious works would never be enough to justify his standing before God. He accepted that he was justified by faith and not by his works or through his own righteousness but by the imputed righteousness of Jesus Christ.

The only works, or righteousness, which can stand before the Divine God of judgment is that of unreserved perfection and purity that steadfastly conforms to the Holy Word of God. It should be strongly noted that according to the Scriptures, no one in the past, present, or future will ever be able to measure up to God's expectation other than our Lord Jesus Christ (Isa. 64:6). The Bible teaches that our righteousness is completely defiled by only one error or sin and that no one, other than Christ, has lived a perfect life: "There is none righteous, no not one" (Rom: 3:10).

The truth of the matter is that without Christ, there would be no hope (Rom. 3:21-23). Although the apostle Paul often declared that believers are justified by faith apart from works (Rom. 3:20-30; Gal. 2:16; 2 Tim. 1:9), there are still countless individuals who essentially believe that as long as one engages in more good works rather than bad ones that he or she will go to heaven. It's as though the person attends and joins a church, worships, give, partakes in the ministry and mission of the church, helps others, all for the sake of appeasing a mighty God in heaven only to hear Him say at the end of life, "Depart from Me, I never knew you" (Matt. 7: 21-23). Those who live by their religious works and not by faith in Christ will tragically discover themselves kneeling before the Lord, the Judge, at the Great White Throne of Judgment, being judged according to their good works only to learn too late that their works were never good enough to meet God's requirement (Rev. 20:12-13).

Social Salvation

On more than one occasion, the apostle Paul confronted the Jewish people regarding their credence, fidelity, and loyalty to God. One such occasion is found in Romans 2: 17-24. Most Jews were very conceited and misguided concerning their standing before God. They visualized themselves as God's people. They were born Jews as their forefathers before them. The Jews had been entrusted with God's laws. God at one time referred to them as His people. Many erroneously believed that as Abraham's physical descendants, they were spontaneously made spiritual descendants. They inaccurately assumed that keeping the law and performing the act of circumcision on newborn male babies made them automatically considered God's spiritual people. Paul rightly noted their living of the law was only a means of boasting (2:17) that the name of God was blasphemed among the Gentiles because of their hypocritical lifestyles (2:24), that they failed as God's people, and that their circumcision was of no avail (2: 25-29). He also stated that most were Jews outwardly, but not inwardly (2: 28-29). Essentially, Paul surmised that being born to a family of Jews did not make one spiritual inwardly nor did it produce a right relationship with God.

Church rolls are often filled with members who have been falsely motivated. Their membership was not motivated by a call from the Holy Spirit, by faith, nor by repentance that resulted in true spiritual regeneration, but rather by something social. Numbers of people rely on the religious affiliation of their parents or grandparents, even though they have not attended church or experienced spiritual regeneration. Often a family may have a history of being a member of one church for generations, and the church has become the "family church." The children of the family live with the pressure and expectation of becoming a member of the "family church." Often the child or young adult confuses church membership with that of salvation; therefore, the incorrect motivation leaves them unprepared to meet God in the afterlife. It should be noted that others are motivated to join a church in hope of obtaining business and political advantages.

I remember in my younger days working for a new business. I had to refuse their insistence that I join the large First Baptist Church to gain some business contacts. There are occasions when some politicians motivated by possible votes may join or rededicate their church attendance. Too often, those who join the church with erroneous motivation may feel comfortable with their standing before God. Nonetheless, many will stand before Christ at the Great White Throne of Judgment and hear Him say, "I never knew you, Depart from Me."

False Gospel Presentation

Evangelical churches place a premium on the Great Commission. Christians are instructed to baptize and to disciple the members (Matt. 28:18-20). It is a great concern that many ministers place the emphasis on baptism and little emphasis on discipleship. We need to take a moment to discuss why this is of great concern! There seems to be glorification placed upon those who baptize the greatest numbers, whether with or without proper motivation. These are the ones who are invited to the religious conference, receive places and positions of honor, and receive great accolades and recognition from their peers; this is not to say that all do not deserve this. Nonetheless, in some areas, the pastors who may only baptize a smaller number are left to feel rejected or inadequate. This glorification of great numbers is often the motivation for prideful ministers to say or do anything to encourage a person to be baptized. They try to convince church members that they are not saved (sometimes this is the truth) so that he might baptize them again. He will provide some simple statements that they can repeat and then proclaim them saved and set a date for baptism while convincing himself that it's all for God; in truth, it's all for his selfish glorification.

There are opposing views relating to the work of the Holy Spirit initiating the salvation experience and man's depraved nature. This does not mean that a man or a woman is all bad. It means that no man or woman can ever be good enough, or righteous enough, to experience the Lord's salvation on their own accord or merit. Therefore, many of the views may disagree upon the degree of depravity, repentance, and faith, most all agree that one's salvation is first instigated through the divine work of the Holy Spirit to convict and draw one to Christ (more of this in chapter ten). The Holy Spirit, with the use of an individual, Scripture, the media, or a gospel tract will initiate the process; without the initiating, or prompting, of the Holy Spirit, one cannot be saved (John 6:44).

Progressive Armenians do not believe that the process can only be initiated or prompted by the Holy Spirit. According to the great revival preacher, Charles Finney, Progressive Arminianism is a denial of original sin or man's sinful nature. He believed that all people were able to respond to the Gospel without any special assistance or prompting of the Holy Spirit's illumination but through enlightenment (intellect) and persuasion, in which the Classical Armenians find vulgarity.[14]

Many pastors and revival preachers challenge and condemn Progressive Arminianism theology, but in reality, in their quest to baptize great numbers practice this hazardous doctrine. Therefore, the following questions should be asked when we hear and read of those who are receiving great accolades for baptizing great numbers: "How many of those baptized were prompted by the Holy Spirit?" and "Was the one performing the baptism doing so for honor and glory to the Lord with authentic love and concern for those being baptized, or for self-serving recognition and accolades?" They are convinced that all they need to do is to share some passage of the Scripture, to persuade them to say yes, and then pray so they can then proclaim the individual saved. Often the unbelievers have not been drawn or prompted by the Holy Spirit. They may be prompted by the one giving a presentation, but the Holy Spirit has been left out.

The truth is that without the prompting and work of the Holy Spirit, there is no regeneration. True salvation is more than believing that God exists. The devil knows that God exists, and he is still going to hell. Just because an individual pronounces someone saved does not obligate God to save him or her. Just reciting a prayer does not save. That is no different from someone saying, "Hocus pocus," now I am saved. There will be many standing before Christ at the Great White Throne of Judgment who hear God say, "I never knew you, depart from Me." They possess no authentic salvation but rather they were living with false hope provided by those who delivered a false presentation. I believe that there will be a lot of vain, glory-seeking preachers who will have to give an account for misleading unbelievers who will find themselves someday in hell eternally.

Psychological Salvation

While serving in the ministry for over forty-five years, I have occasionally offered advice when counseling Christians. Often the root of the trouble is the person's lack of self-esteem, living in denial, or the refusal to accept the reality of his or her sinful state. On one hand, a strong and healthy mind can be beneficial for success and clarity in life. On the other hand, the mind can be disastrous when a person lies to himself or herself and allow the lies to dictate their most important belief concerning eternity. Some may not like what they see when they look in a mirror. The result is low self-esteem regarding their looks or personality. Some do not want to face the reality of their sinful lifestyle and the consequences thereof. They somehow try to convince themselves, and others, that they are not evil. These are the ones that the apostle Paul addressed:

> Because, although they knew God, they did not glorify Him as God, nor were thankful, but became futile in their thoughts, and their foolish hearts were darkened. Professing to be wise, they became fools and changed the glory of the incorruptible God into an image made like corruptible man and birds and four-footed animals and creeping things. Therefore God also gave them up to uncleanliness, in the lust of their hearts, to dishonor their bodies among themselves, who exchange the truth of God for the lie and worshiped and served the creature rather than the Creator, who is blessed forever. Amen.
> Romans 1: 21-25

Paul first referred to these individuals as ungodly and unrighteous who will encounter the wrath of God (1:18). This wrath is not an impulsive outburst of anger but rather a determined response of a righteous God against sin (John 3:36; Rom. 9:22; Eph. 5:6).[15] Paul points out that after these non-believers witnessed and rejected God's general revelation through creation that they were without excuse (1:19-20). Paul further defines these individuals' character and nature as those of homosexuals (1:26-27), debased (v.28), sexually immoral, unrighteous, wicked, covetousness, malicious, envious, murderous, deceitful, evil-minded, whisperers (v.29), backbiters, haters of God, inventors of evil things, disobedient to parents (v.30), undiscerning, untrustworthy, unloving, unforgiving, and unmerciful (v.31). God's judgment upon those who commit such things eternity is hell (v.32).

Paul later wrote his letter to the churches in the region of Galatia (modern Turkey), providing a similar list of fleshly sinful acts with a few additions (Gal. 5: 19-21). He declared that those who practice such atrocities and whose natures are all flesh and not spiritual will not inherit the Kingdom of God.

Nevertheless, Paul describes such people as somewhat religious (vs 21-25). Although their lifestyle is nothing to be desired, they seem to consider themselves religious by worshipping not the God Jehovah in Heaven, but some made-up god of their own invention. They worship a god of their imagination that accepts their sinful lifestyle. Have you ever wondered how some who live a perpetual life of sin, continual lying, stealing, or sexual deviance can proclaim that they have a righteous relationship with God? Many of these individuals have joined a church and may attend regularly. These individuals have experienced some sort of psychological experience, having never been truly spiritually regenerated. They have devised a god that is one of only love, understanding, and acceptance of a sinful lifestyle. Their made-up god does not have the attributes of justice, wrath, and fury against sin and its consequences.

One day, while working in my yard, I was listening to the last CD Johnny Cash cut before he died. One of the songs was entitled, "Personal Jesus." A thought ran through my mind that many who love this song are not thinking about a personal relationship with Jesus. They embrace a personal Jesus of their imagination who is not the Son of God rather than the real Jesus whose hatred toward sin was so great that He gave His life for all who were to experience its punishment in Hell with no possibility of salvation. Their thought is on a Jesus that fits their perception in a way that allows them to live guilt-free.

Many are convinced that if they are good enough, they will enter Heaven's gate when they die. They know that their lives do not meet God's standards. However, when they compare their sinful life against another's more sinful life, they mistakenly believe that they are now righteous enough to go to Heaven. The sad fact concerning all of the above is that they may feel saved (psychologically); nonetheless, when they die and stand before God, they will hear the dreadful words from our Lord, "I never knew you, Depart from Me."

Reliance on Feelings and Emotions

Many individuals' salvation is founded on certain life experiences and feelings. It may be the feeling or emotion that one experiences when he or she hears a spiritual song or hears an awesome testimony or that of an experience of answered prayer or an experience of some type of blessing seemingly from God. Although an experience at times is a good thing, it is vital that no one ever base his or her salvation on such.

One major philosophy of the sixteenth and seventeenth centuries was empiricism. It focused on the idea that knowledge and belief are derived through observance and experience of the five senses (touch, hearing, sight, feeling, and smell). Philosopher David Hume placed much on impressions made during one's experiences of life and those beliefs are developed through feelings from experiences.[16] A religious philosopher who was mainly responsible for incorporating empiricism within religion was Friedrich Schleiermacher (1768-1834), a liberal theologian that held the conviction that religion is not a matter of belief (doctrines from the Scripture) or some form of practice, but that of feelings and experience.[17] Numerous individuals have neither understanding of philosophy, nor any understanding of empiricism whose lifestyle and testimony reflects such a viewpoint.

The question to discuss is how can such life experiences and feelings be confused as proof of spiritual regeneration? I will try to answer this question in two parts. The first part of the answer is that numerous people confuse an adrenalin rush as that of the moving of the Holy Spirit. They experience the euphoria, excitement, and the freshness resulting from one's adrenalin increase, which is mistaken as the moving of the Holy Spirit. It should be noted that the feeling of the adrenalin rush often happens at the same time as that of a spiritual event. I found this fact to be true from my own experience during my early ministry. I was a preacher when I met my wife in high school. Thereby, we did not go to many places while dating that was not some religious meeting. We viewed a few movies at the indoor theater and attended my senior prom and her junior and senior proms. A few years after we were married, it was decided that we would go on a formal date by attending the Broadway play "Cats" at the Fox Theater in Atlanta. I had never experienced anything like it. The show was awesome, especially when a lady dressed as a beaten old cat stood and sang "Memory." I had never heard anything like it. The entire audience was moved to the point that without any prompting, stood and applauded. I was moved by her singing to the point that I almost shouted "amen" when standing. Thankfully, I realized what I was about to do and held back the "amen." I thought on this for a while and concluded that most of my experiences had always been church-related; that I had encountered such feelings when I was moved by a religious song or a powerful message or testimony. Then it occurred to me that often when I felt such powerful feelings that it was not always the result of the Holy Spirit but simply an adrenalin rush. This is why a person may get excited and mistakenly believe that he is feeling the moving of the Holy Spirit when someone sings a song but is not able to hear the words or message of the song. He is responding not to the Holy Spirit but emotions felt in the beat of the music.

The second part of the answer to the question is God's grace. "The grace of God has appeared to all men" (Tit. 2:11). Grace is simply God working on behalf of mankind and is extended to everyone, both believers and unbelievers. Though its intent is salvation, it does not always end with the salvation of sinful people. Rather, it consists of the blessings of God given to all, even the underserved. The Bible discloses this grace: The Lord is good to all (Ps. 145:9). God causes it to rain on the just and unjust and causes the sun to rise on the evil and good

(Matt. 5:45). God's grace sustains all human life (Ps. 36:6). It maintains the moral order of the universe and supplies basic human needs (Ps. 65:9). God's grace allows the unjust to experience the blessings of God for the just. Often when a church member, living with false hope, experiences blessings from God or answered prayers, it may be that he or she only experiences the residual effects of some true believer's answered prayer or the blessing in response to other Christians.[18] Those who rely on their feelings and emotions may very well stand before the Lord at the Great White Throne of Judgment and hear Him say, "Depart from Me."

Much of this chapter describes what salvation is not and those living with false hope and the reasons that are the source of false hope. The remaining chapters of this book will address those looking to participate in the blessed hope. We will first begin by examining, in detail, what changes occurred during the fall of man and why all of humankind needs to experience spiritual regeneration. Then we will discuss how Christ provided redemption through the atonement made on the cross. And lastly, we will examine the work of the Holy Spirit in the initiation of the salvation of the soul so that those who accept and experience spiritual regeneration may look forward to their attendance at the Judgment Seat of Christ.

Part Two

The Why of Authentic Salvation

> Now the serpent was more cunning than any beast
> of the field which the LORD God had made. And
> he said to the woman, "Has God indeed said, 'You
> shall not eat of every tree of the garden'?" Genesis 3:1

Part two consists of five chapters that explain humanity's need to experience true and authentic salvation. This part begins with the participants in the Garden of Eden; God, Satan, and Adam. It provides an overview as to who and what God is that helps the reader understand why God expects righteousness (perfection) from those who would fellowship and worship with Him. This part exposes the danger of Satan, his need to overcome God, and his motivation to destroy humankind's relationship and fellowship with God. The reader will understand who and what Adam was before the Fall. The changes that occurred to Adam spiritually and physically after he sinned and how Adam's failure to obey God brought forth devastated consequences upon all humankind. Lastly, the reader will have a better understanding of sin and its consequences. This part will end with all humanity as sinful individuals with no hope.

CHAPTER TWO

The Fall: the Holy God and the Unholy Satan

> Now the serpent was more cunning than any beast
> of the field which the LORD God had made. And
> he said to the woman, "Has God indeed said, 'You
> shall not eat of every tree of the garden'?" Genesis 3:1

Often, I hear believers trying to explain the experience of authentic salvation to the unregenerate. However, in their quest of sharing the gospel, they frequently fail to explain "why" one needs salvation. To answer this question, we will need to examine the event of the Fall and all the participants in chapters two through six.

The Fall is defined as the cataclysmic event of Adam and Eve who suffered the devastating consequence of a broken relationship with God that affected all future human beings. Whereas, future restoration was predicted that would provide a new relationship with God's people (Gen. 3:15). Each participant of the Fall must be scrutinized for clarity and understanding of future chapters in this book. Please note that this chapter will focus on the persons of the holy God and the unholy Satan.

GOD: WHO HE IS AND HIS RELATIONSHIP WITH ADAM

Our culture has changed dramatically within the last several years. This present culture has made sin appear so acceptable that those things that were once considered deviant are now considered normal. This has resulted in society's low view of God. The same God who wants to intimately know and have a relationship with all people. It is imperative to know much about the only living God who wants to know us. Therefore, I will address information concerning God's nature and attributes that communicates His relationship with men and women.

First, God is a person. When referring to God as a person it is acknowledging that He has a personality. Like any person, God possesses a self-conscious, a will, and is capable of experiencing a relationship with human beings. God has even assigned Himself a name, "I Am" (Yahweh, Jehovah, the LORD, Exod. 3:14). He is not an abstract, inconceivable being, or an anonymous force that is standoffish, impassive, or unconcerned for His creation. He is an eternal living being who does not depend on anyone or anything outside Himself to exist or to rule.[19] Theologian, Millard J. Erickson, suggests several implications of God's personality:

> God is a person (indeed, he is pictured as our Father), our relationship with him has a dimension of warmth and understanding. God is not a bureau or a department, a machine, or a computer that automatically supplies the needs of people. He is a knowing, loving, good Father. He can be approached. He can be spoken to, and he in turn speaks. God

does not simply receive and accept what we offer. He is a living, reciprocating being. He is not merely one of whom we hear, but one whom we need to know.[20]

Second, God is Spirit, "God is Spirit, and those who worship Him must worship in spirit and truth" (John 4:24, also implied in John 1:8; 1 Tim. 1:17; 6:15-16). Since God is spirit, He is not limited as one with a physical body. He is not limited to any particular geography, space, or physical location. Although the Scriptures speak of God in a physical sense. They feature His hands, feet, eyes, etc. The Holy Spirit inspired the writers to incorporate anthropomorphic language in their quest to help the readers to relate to and understand God. Anthropomorphic means to ascribe human form to a being not human. The theologian, Millard J. Erickson, addressed this with the following statement:

> There are, of course, numerous passages that suggest that God has physical features, such as hands or feet. It seems most helpful to treat these anthropomorphisms, attempts to express the truth about God through human analogies. [Erickson continues to explain some temporary account of God in a physical body] There are also cases where God appeared in physical form, particularly in the Old Testament, in theophanies, or temporary self-manifestations.[21]

In John 4:24 the apostle John enlightens the reader that one must worship God in spirit. In a later chapter, I will discuss how God created man with the ability to worship Him in spirit and truth.

Third, God desires to be known. Atheists do not believe in the existence of God. They would suggest that since God does not exist, he cannot be known. Agnostics are not sure of God's existence. Therefore, a God that one is not convinced exists cannot be positively known. Deists acknowledge God's existence and His work of creation. They suggest that God left creation to its own devices; therefore, He does not care to be known. Nevertheless, God is knowable and desires to be known. All knowledge of God is revealed by way of revelation. The word "revelation" implies an uncovering, removal of the veil, or disclosure of what was previously unknown. God bridged the gap between Adam, and later all humankind, and Himself through the process of revelation to make Himself and His will known. This revelation of God is accomplished by way of two different avenues. One avenue is God's general revelation and the other avenue is His special revelation.[22]

General Revelation

God's general revelation is His witness, or revealing, of Himself through His creation and creatures. It is through general revelation that God provides evidence of His existence to humanity. David declared; "The heavens declare the glory of God; and the firmament shows His handy work" (Ps. 19:1). When one perceives the heavens, their surroundings, or the reproduction of life he or she witnesses the evidence of the omniscient, omnipotent Creator. The apostle Paul sheds light on this truth:

> For the wrath of God is revealed from heaven against
> all ungodliness and unrighteousness of men, who
> suppress the truth in unrighteousness, because what
> may be known of God is manifest in them, for God

> has shown it to them. For since the creation of the
> world His invisible attributes are clearly seen, being
> understood by the things made, even His eternal
> power and Godhead, so that they are without excuse,
> because, although they knew God, they did not glo-
> rify Him as God, nor were thankful, but became
> futile in their thoughts, and their foolish hearts were
> darkened. Rom. 1: 18-21

Paul declares that mankind has rejected God's attributes of omniscience, omnipotence, omnipresence, and eternality that are evidenced by His creation of the earth, the universe, and humanity. Although general revelation does not necessarily provide salvation it does afford evidence and cognizance of the existence of an all-powerful Creator who created man in His own image (more of this in chapter three), who created the earth with the oxygen and nitrogen levels for man to exist. God provided the seasons so seeds would germinate and provide sustenance for humanity, and He created man with the capability to procreate. He is the Creator who deserves everyone's worship and glory.

Not all physicists and cosmologists insist that the earth and universe came forth by chance; that something came forth from nothing. Many have acknowledged that creation was not caused by chance; Despite his skepticism concerning God, astronomer Alan Sandage, stated:

> The world is too complicated in all of its parts to be
> due to chance alone. I am convinced that the exis-
> tence of life with all of its order in each of its organ-
> isms is simply too well put together. Each part of a

living thing depends on all its other parts to function. How does each part know? How is each part specified at conception? The more one learns of biochemistry the more unbelievable it becomes unless there is some kind of organizing principle and architect for believers...And all of the conditions were set from the moment of the universe's origin.[23]

The following are additional evidence of God's general revelation other than the creation. One, Human beings possess a conscience or a sense of morals that are attributed to them (Rom. 2:12-16). Two, the observation that God did not create the universe and then leave it alone, but rather He continues to care for it through His providential and sustaining care (Acts 14:8-18). Lastly, God's general revelation is evidenced by humanity's inborn sense of God (Eccl. 3:11; Acts 17: 22-31).[24]

Special Revelation

God provides special revelation to reveal Himself directly, intimately, and in greater detail concerning His nature, attributes, moral laws, promises, means, will, and His salvation. God reveals Himself through:

- His action when He spoke directly to Adam and Eve in the Garden of Eden (Gen. 2 and 3), when He addressed the nation of Israel audibly at Sinai (Deut. 5:4), by His action when He spoke to Moses personally and confirmed His witness through signs and wonders (Deut. 34), and His action through His three vocal confirmations of His Son on three occasions (Matt. 3:17; 17:5; John 12:28).

- Dreams and visions by providing Isaiah a vision of the Son of God in His full pre-incarnate glory (Isa. 6:1-4), by providing such vision of the Son of Man in the Book of Daniel, and by providing the apostle John a vision while in a cave on the Isle of Patmos (Revelations).

- The incarnation of His Son when He, the Creator, took upon Himself the limitations of human flesh and dwelt among His creation (John 1: 1-5, 14), thereby revealing the fullness of God's person to men (John 14: 9-10). Paul describes Jesus as the image of the invisible God (Col. 1:15).

- The form of the Bible (Heb. 1:1). The Scriptures are a fixed written testimony from the Creator to His creatures. The Bible is the inspired Word of God (2 Tim. 3:16 and 1 Pet. 1: 20-21). The special revelation of God reveals that the one and only God is the creator and sustainer of the universe and the redeemer of humanity who desires to be known intimately.

It is important to study the attributes of God (some refer to this as His perfections or character[25]).God's attributes are revealed in Scripture in two categories. The first category refers to His communicable attributes (some refer to them as His moral or goodness of God attributes [26]). The communicable attributes are the characteristics or perfections of God revealed in the Scriptures that He communicates, or shares, with humans who are created in His image. These attributes include wisdom, truthfulness, faithfulness, goodness, love, grace, mercy, patience, holiness, righteous wrath, righteousness, justice, and power.[27]

The second category is God's incommunicable attributes (or sometimes referred to God's non-moral, perfections. or greatness of God attributes) [28]. These characteristics or perfections of God do not communicate or cannot be experienced by human beings. These attributes include God's independence, His immutability (unchangeableness), His eternity, His omnipresence (God exists in all time and geography), His infinity (limitless in time, space, or distance), His omnipotence (God is all-mighty and all-powerful), and His omniscience (all-knowing). The remainder of this section will be an overview (not a detailed study) of His attributes so that the writer may build a foundation that will assist the reader in understanding future topics of this book:

God's Incommunicable Attributes

Following is a shortlist of God's incommunicable attributes that are not part of any man's attribute, but in some fashion relates God to man.

God is Infinite: God is limitless concerning His eternity (God is timeless); His omnipresence (space, Ps. 139:7-8); His omnipotence (God's power and ability, Gen. 17:1; 28:3); and His omniscience (God knowledge, Ps. 139:1-6; Matt. 11:21; Dan. 2:36-43). We now will explore, in greater detail, some of God's incommunicable attributes and how they relate to His infinity. First, God is infinitely eternal (He is not bound or limited by time). This indicates that God has always existed and will always exist. God was before the creation of the earth and universe (John1: 1-2). In his book, *Basic Theology*, Charles Ryrie states, "His Existence extends endlessly backward and forward (from our viewpoint of time) without any interruptions or limitations caused by a succession of events."[29] God's eternity implies His self-existence; God does not rely on any outside force or substance to survive. He only depends upon Himself and will never cease to exist. God's attribute of eternity before and throughout time provides the evidence that God knows and experiences the past, the present, and the future all at the same time. He is from everlasting to everlasting (Ps. 90:2). Second, God is infinitely omnipresence; He has no boundaries or limitations of space. All finite (having limitations or boundaries) individuals or objects have a location somewhere; they cannot exist universally at all times. God, being spirit, can be present everywhere with His entire being at the same moment. Jeremiah states, "God is both near and far away filling heaven and earth" (Jer. 23:23-24). While God is present everywhere, He manifests His presence in diverse ways in different situations, to bless, caution, comfort, rebuke, reward or punish. There is no place one may go to escape, or not be observed by God (Ps. 139:7-10).[30]

Third, God is infinitely omnipotent. God is all-powerful and can accomplish anything consistent with His nature and His will. God's omnipotence is not as much about His physical power but His being, His ability, and the reference to Him as the "Almighty." The name "Almighty" (the mighty one) is probably derived from the verb meaning "to be strong" (Gen. 17:1; 28:3; Isa. 13:6). Because God is Almighty, all things are possible (Matt. 19:26), He created the heaven, earth, and the universe (Gen. 1), He can do all things; nothing is too hard for Him (Ps. 115:3; Matt. 19:26). God has power over nature and all creation. The doctrine of omnipotence becomes the source of great comfort for the believer (1 Pet. 1:5).[31]

Lastly, God is infinitely omniscient; He knows all things present, past, and, in His foreknowledge, the future. He knows all human beings' past, present, and future decisions. He knows all His responses to each of our decisions. God already knows the historical and future world events; therefore, He will never be caught off guard in response to any personal, historical, or future events. God has access to all information and therefore His judgments are always made wisely. God knows all things that exist (Ps. 139:1-6; Matt. 6: 8; 10: 28-30). Since God is also omnipresent and not bound by time, He knows all things in one eternal act. [32] This means that when God created time, "In the beginning" (Gen. 1; 1) God observed and has knowledge of everything in one event, that had happened, that was happening, and that would happen as if it all took place at the same moment.

God's Communicable Attributes:

Holiness: The Hebrew verb *qodes* and the Greek *hagios* in most circumstances are interpreted as holy, sanctified, or consecrate. The Scriptures offer a twofold portrayal of the holiness of God. One portrayal is the notion that God is distinct or separate from everything else. God is portrayed as majestic; His qualities know no boundary and His being is enormously above and separated from His creatures. The second portrayal or sense of the holiness of God is His moral purity and perfection (Ps. 145:17; 1 Sam. 6; 20); which is associated with divine holiness. [33] Since God is pure and perfect, He cannot sin or condone it.

Grace: Humanity was judged guilty and no one can seek salvation through his or her righteousness. All of humanity had no hope. However, God's attribute of grace provided a means by which all could experience salvation. Grace is defined as the unmerited or undeserving favor of God to those who are condemned. God provided the means of salvation through His goodness and generosity that is not based upon anyone's merit or worthiness, or what they deserve, but solely on their need for salvation (Eph. 2:4-10).

Righteous: This is God's holiness applied to his relationship to all other beings. The righteousness of God is the law of God, being a true expression of his nature (character and essence), is as perfect as He is (Ps. 19: 1-9). God's righteousness is His actions that are always perfect, just, and in the agreement of the law, he established.[34] When God judges the world, He will judge it justly and impartially according to His holy standards (Ps. 9:8; 98:9).

Wrath: This expresses several emotions of God, such as; anger, indignation, vexation, bitterness, and fury. It is God's response to apparent wrongness, unfairness, and injustice. Wrath is God's absolute response to sin.[35] The Old Testament regularly pictures God responding to sin with wrath (Exod. 4:14; 15:7; 32: 10-12; Num. 11:1; Jer. 21:3-7). Often the prophets refer to the wrath of God in association with the Day of the Lord as a cosmic, climatic outbreak of judgment. The apostle Paul contrasts God's righteousness with His wrath in Romans, "For the wrath of God is revealed from heaven against all ungodliness and unrighteousness of men, who suppress the truth in unrighteousness" (1:18). Paul addresses the two objects of God's wrath; "ungodliness" and "unrighteousness." "Ungodliness" refers to sins of a moral nature while "unrighteousness" refers to sins of a religious nature. These are those who "suppress the truth of

God." They do not live justly, and they cannot obtain salvation within their righteousness.[36]

Jealousy: God admits to His jealousy, "You shall have no other gods before Me. You shall not make for yourself a carved image, any likeness of anything that is in heaven or above, or that is in the earth beneath, or that is in the water under the earth. You shall not bow down to them nor serve them. For I, the LORD your God, am a jealous God" (Exod. 20: 2-5). God's jealousy is His zeal like passion for the protection of all that belongs to Him, such as; His name (Exod. 34:14; Ezek. 39:25), glory, people (2 Kings 19:31), sole right to receive worship (Exod. 20:5; Duet. 4:24; 1 Kings 14:22) ultimate obedience (Josh. 24:19; James 4:5), land (Ezek. 36: 5-38), and His Kingdom (Isa. 9: 6-7). Those who do not respect His ownership or rights will experience His vengeance (Isa. 42:13: 59: 16-20; Ezek. 5:13; 35:5; Nah. 1:2; Zeph. 3:8).[37] God desires that all humanity choose to love Him, to be their provider and Savior since He is the Creator and Sustainer of all that is in existence and since He alone is worthy, rather than pursuing false gods that are incapable of loving them in return. There is no selfishness in God's jealously, He is like a man who expects fidelity, love, and honor from his wife and protects her from those who would defile her. God's zeal is in only protecting that which is His.

Love: "God is love" (1 John 4:8 & 4:16). God's love, *agape*, is God's deliberate action toward all men and women. God's love involves doing what is best for men and women, not necessarily what they desire. John 3:16 states "For God so loved the world that He gave His only begotten Son." Humanity would have preferred something else, but God provided what they needed. This love is an action more so than a feeling; it is affectionate, sacrificing, and benevolent, and provides salvation for those who accept this love.[38]

Justice: Scripture demands that sin has consequences that must be experienced, whether sooner or later. God warned Adam to not eat from the tree of knowledge of good and evil, if so, he would die (Gen. 2:17). Adam and Eve did eat the fruit from the tree and immediately experienced spiritual death and later both experienced physical deaths. Similar occurrences were experienced throughout Scripture, such as Paul's statement that "the wages of sin is death" (Rom. 6:23). God is righteous. He acts in conformity to His law while administering His kingdom according to His laws. His justice is His official righteousness, as well as His requirement that all individuals adhere to His standard. God's judgment means that he administers His law fairly, without favoritism or partiality. Each person is responsible for his or her action, not that of others or their station in life. In human judgment each is to receive what is due to them, whether good or bad, based upon His holy laws.[39]

SATAN: THE TEMPTER OF ADAM AND EVE

Although this chapter reveals the person of God and the person of Satan it should be made abundantly clear that the two are not equals. Many unconsciously view God and Satan as two equal forces; kind of like the teaching of the yin and yang of the Chinese philosophers that advocate the idea of two dualistic opposite contrary equal forces. Many erroneously comprehend the view of God and Satan in a cosmic battle of right and wrong with equal powers and abilities that end in a climactic confrontation. The reader must understand that unlike God, Satan is not infinite; he suffers boundaries and limitations; Unlike God,

Satan is not eternal. He had a beginning when God created him and he continues to rely on God for life support; Satan, unlike God, is not omniscient, he does not possess the knowledge that God possesses; Satan, unlike God, is not omnipotent; and Satan, unlike God, is not omnipresent, therefore, most of his activity is accomplished through his fallen angels (demons).

Satan's Background: Satan is a created being with freewill that God first purposed to be a righteous high ruling archangel (Ezek. 28: 13 – 14). He was not originally evil; He became the devil (the adversary) when he chose to be evil and rebelled against God his Creator (Ezek. 28:15). Therefore, Satan was subsequently dishonorably discharged from his position and holy service on behalf of God (Ezek. 28:16). Satan is referred to by many names, such as the "accuser" (Rev. 12:10); the "adversary" (1 Pet. 5:8); the "evil one" (1 John 5:19); the "tempter"(Matt. 4:3); the "ruler of demons" (Matt. 9:34, 12:24); the "enemy"(Matt. 13:39); the "father of lies" (John 8:44); the "murderer" (John 8: 44); as "one who deceives" (Rev. 12: 9); and as the "ruler of this world" (John 12: 31;14:30).

Satan's Downfall: It appears that Satan's rebellion began with his pride (1 Tim. 3:6); the Scriptures reveal that "pride comes before destruction" (Pro. 16:18). Pride is the first of the seven deadly sins (Pro. 6:16-19). The Bible provides the insight that pride was the foremost reason for Satan's failure and lost relationship with God.

The first insight is established by the Prophet Isaiah (14: 3-21). This is a lament (an expression of sorrow) for a dead person who has fallen (14:11, 19-20). This prophetic lament mourns the humiliation of a King of Babylon who would enjoy a high authoritative and prestigious position (14: 3-4). This powerful king raised himself above many as a formidable and cruel political figure with undue power and authority who felt a desire to control everyone and everything (14: 4-6, 16-17).[40] He set himself up as a god. Therefore, God responded by humiliating him while further inflicting public suffering and a dishonorable death (14: 8-11). Isaiah further discloses that this king shared the same trait of the sin of pride evidenced in Satan (14:12-15). Three of the Church Fathers, Augustine (354-373), Jerome (345-420), and Origen (184-254), suggest that Isaiah described two individuals within the passage. The first individual was a future King of Babylon who exhibited much wickedness and would die and never enter heaven (14:3-11; 16-21), the second individual is identified as Lucifer (Satan) who never experienced death and had fallen from heaven.[41] The evidence of Satan's selfish pride and his attempt to usurp God's authority and lead a rebellion against God is his five "I will" comments (14:12-14). Isaiah compared the King of Babylon to that of Satan's downfall. Both were guilty of pride; both wanted to be preeminent; both were brought down by God; the King of Babylon was humiliated and died. Satan, on the other hand, was unsuccessful with his rebellion against God, thereby; he had lost his grand position in heaven and was sent to earth. By contrast, the King of Babylon's failure took place on earth, while the failure of Satan took place in heaven. It is possible that by Isaiah comparing the two that it may be suggested that the King of Babylon was influenced as an agent of Satan.

The second insight that pride was Satan's big downfall is revealed by Ezekiel (28:1-19). Like Isaiah, Ezekiel discusses two different individuals. The first person was an actual King of Tyre who was lifted with pride (28:1-5), who was a man

(28:2, 9), and who was humiliated by God and punished with a deplorable death (28:6-10). The second person describes Satan; who was prideful of his perfections, beauty, and wisdom (28:11-13, 17), and Ezekiel revealed he was an angel (anointed cherub) whose dwelling was in heaven before being cast out (28:14-16). Ezekiel depicts Satan as the actual supernatural source of wickedness. Ezekiel, as well as Isaiah, being inspired by the Holy Spirit, provides insight into an event in Satan's life that took place between the creation in Genesis Chapter One and the Fall of man in Chapter Three. The point made by both writers is that Satan was lifted with pride and he desires to have pre-eminence over all creation, including God. It also provides evidence that Satan is still rebelling against God and endeavors to influence both sinners and saints to rebel by disobeying Him (Matt. 16:21-23).

Satan in the Present: After he failed to defeat God in heaven, Satan was cast out, along with the angels that he led in rebellion against God. He presently manages his angels (demons) as the leader of the government of the satanic world (Matt.12:24: John 12:31; Eph. 2:1-2). Satan refuses to accept defeat. He paces seeks to deceive (1 Pet. 5:8), to destroy, to accuse, to tempt, and to usurp the authority of God (2 Cor. 4:3-4). He was bold enough to try to defeat the purpose of Christ with temptations in the wilderness (Matt. 4: 1-12). Satan's present work is widespread and destructive. God permits his evil activity for His purpose for the time being.

Satan's Future: Satan will lead another rebellion in heaven and will be permanently banned (Rev. 12:7-12) then confined to the abyss for a thousand years (Rev. 20:1-30), he will be released for a time and endeavor to overthrow God (Rev. 20:8-9). His final destination is the eternal lake of fire (Rev. 20:10).

God is an infinite spiritual being who is eternal, omniscient, omnipresent, and omnipotent and Satan is not. God created man as an object of His love and affection. He desires to be known by each in an intimate relationship. Satan is prideful and possesses no incommunicable attributes. Satan does not know the future and he believes that he can change his predestined end. He still believes that he can, along with others, rebel against God and overthrow Him. This was his motivation in the Garden of Eden when he approached and tempted Adam and Eve, who will be discussed in the next chapter.

CHAPTER THREE

The Fall: Adam's Original Nature and State

I remember, as a young child, my mother teaching me the story of Adam and Eve. I, as many of the readers, envisioned Adam and Eve as two ordinary people living an extraordinary life in the garden among the animals while God provided all of their sustenance of fruits, grain, and vegetables. God had provided for Adam and Eve so they would continue a contented and fulfilled life with Him. After God finished His creation, He declared that "It is good." Nevertheless, God made a condition that they could eat of every tree in the garden except the Tree of Knowledge of Good and Evil. If so, they would die the day they ate thereof. Nonetheless, after the warning of death, God withdrew for a moment. Satan, the evil one, also known as the devil, in the form of a serpent, took the opportunity to sow his poisonous seed of temptation in the minds of Adam and Eve. They both succumbed to Satan's lies (referred to as the Fall), resulting in rebellion when they freely chose to disobey God by eating of the Tree of Knowledge of Good and Evil (Gen. 2: 17).

When Adam and Eve succumbed to Satan's lies, they immediately realized they were naked and covered themselves with large leaves. Later God confronted them with their disobedience and

39

provided animal skins to cover their nakedness in reaction to their sin, and then later He banned them from the Garden of Eden. Adam now worked in the hot fields by the sweat of his face and Eve would suffer pregnancy pains. The realm of life is full of calamity, because of this great, over-whelming cosmic tragedy in the Garden of Eden. The consequences still vibrate in humanity today.

Often people overlook the fact that Adam and Eve did not physically die that day, but centuries later. So, what did die that day? What was the significance of the animal skins? How did the relationship change between man and God? What was Adam's original state and how did it change? As a child, I did not consider or understand the significance of the above questions. Therefore, as with the last chapter, I will continue to provide a background of all the participants of the Fall that were present in the Garden of Eden to help the reader understand the answer to each of the above questions.

The rest of this chapter will center on three biblical passages (Gen. 1:26-28; Gen. 2: 7-9; 15-25, and Isa. 43:7) to specify Adam's original nature, state, and purpose before the Fall. Please note that one will discover that there are diverse meanings of the word "nature" when referencing to man. On one hand, the meaning has much to do with man's behavior or background. On the other hand, the word nature refers to what a person is made of. While probing Adam's nature, the reader will observe that Adam's substance consisted of immaterial and material aspects, two substances joined together in a union that produced a living person. Adam's nature produces the characteristics of a living nature which are the intellectual capacity of the mind, the emotional capacity of feelings, the volitional (making choices or decisions) capacity of a will, the social capacity of relationships, the moral capacity of conscience, and the causal (to cause an act) capacity of a body[42]. When examining Adam's state, the reader will understand that Adam's state was his standing before God in perfect righteousness. In discussing Adam's purpose, I will help the reader discover the intent and objective of God when He created Adam. It is only after the reader understands this chapter concerning Adam's nature, state, and purpose that he or she may ascertain the immediate and later catastrophic changes that took place in Adam as a result of the Fall. These will be discussed fully in future chapters. Following is the observation from the three previous passages of Scripture:

God created Adam in His Image

> Then God said, 'Let Us make man in Our image, according to Our likeness; let them have dominion over the fish of the sea, over the birds of the air, and over the cattle, over all of the earth and over every creeping thing that creeps on the earth." So God created man in His own image, in the image of God He created him; male and female He created them. Then God blessed them, and God said to them, "Be fruitful and multiply, fill the earth and subdue it; have dominion over the fish of the sea, over the birds of the air, and over every living thing that moves on the earth." Gen. 1: 26–28

The following truths from this passage will provide the reader understanding of the pre-fallen Adam:

Adam was created on the sixth day of creation (Gen. 1:31). After God created the earth to sustain the life of man, Adam was created. The Hebrew *asah* (make) describes a process of construction[43]. This process was to "create" (*bara*; 1: 27). This is unlike Genesis, Chapter one, verse one that indicated that God creates out of nothing (*ex nihilo*; Heb. 11:3), but by contrasting the Hebrew word, *bara*, with the verb, *asah* (make) Genesis, Chapter One, verse Twenty-Six, provides the idea of creating out of existing materials (Gen. 2: 7).[44] Both meanings depict a supernatural instantaneous act of God. Adam's creation was not by the process of evolution.

Adam was created in God's image. The meaning of the Hebrew, *teselem* (image) is established when the reader understands how the Old Testament saints comprehended it. Throughout the ancient Near East, an image was believed to contain the essence of that which is represented. Any idol (image) of a deity such as a false god or king was worshiped since it was believed to contain the false god or king's essence. Therefore, the Scriptures instruct the believer not to worship graven images (Exod. 20: 4; Deut. 7:5; 27:15). God's people are instructed to never put a false god before the true and living God (Exod. 20:3).

There are three existing views of the "image of God:"

1. **The Relational View:** This view suggests that relationship is the image of God. Theologian Millard Erickson states, "Humans can be said to be in the image, or to display the image [of God] when standing in a particular relationship, which indeed is the image."[45] Man's responsibility to love is met as he relates to God and others. The Neo-Orthodox Theologian Karl Barth

understood the image of God as entailing not only the vertical relationship between humans and God but also the horizontal relationship between humans.[46] One of Adam's purposes was to have relations with his wife to produce children to populate the earth. The relational view defines the man's purpose, not what and who he is.

2. **The Functional View:** This view suggests that the image of God is something that humans do. The passages above links the image with ruling and subduing the earth.[47] Erickson suggests that this image is not something present in the make-up of the human, or the experience of relationships, but rather consists of what one does; it is a human function which is frequently the exercise of dominion and rule over the creation.[48]

3. **The Substantial View:** This view has been the most dominant during most of the history of Christianity. The common substantive view of the image of God is a mixture of psychological and the spiritual qualities of God in human nature, especially reason. This view suggests that the image is a part of the man's nature or state. It describes who he is, not what he does or his purpose.[49] This view does not reject the importance of relational and functional views but understands them as a by-product of the substantial nature of man. Some (Mormons) consider the image of God to be an aspect of the physical body since they envision God as physical.[50] Nevertheless, God is not physical in His original form; but Spirit (John 4:24).

There are truths gleaned from all three views of the image of God. Nevertheless, the substantial view is by far the most biblical view of the image of God. On one hand, this view describes how the image of God is inherently structural to man, how the image of God is characteristic within the makeup of man. On the other hand, the relational and functional views are only the consequence of man being the image of God structurally.[51]

We will begin a somewhat intensive study of the substantial view of God beginning with the fact that of all the creatures that God created, man is the only one made "in the image of God." The fact that man is in the image of God means that man, in some narrow capacity, is like God and represents God. However, it should be noted that this does not insinuate the man is or will become a god. Theologian Wayne Grudem explains:

> When God says, "Let us make man in our image, after our likeness" (Gen. 1:26), the meaning is that God plans to make a creature similar to Himself. Both the Hebrew word for "image" (*tselem*) and the Hebrew word for "likeness" (*demut*) refers to something that is *similar* but not identical to the things it represents or is an "image" of. The word *image* can also be used of something that *represents* something else? ... When we realize the Hebrew words for "image" and Likeness" simply informed the original readers that man was *like* God and would in many ways *represent* God... When Scripture reports that God said, "Let us make man in our image, after our likeness" (Gen. 1:26), it simply would have meant to the original readers, "Let us make man to be *like* us and to *represent* us."[52]

The image of God allowed Adam to serve as God's vice-regent and steward with the capacity to be and act like Him by mirroring His communicable attributes.[53] This is what differentiates man from animals. Although both have a soul and a spirit, man, not animals, was created in God's image. As an image of God, Adam had a will that was free with the ability to make choices. Adam possessed a rational mind; therefore, he could think critically and logically. He possessed memory, imagination, and language skills for communicating and understanding others. Adam possessed emotions and feelings, such as fear, anger, guilt, regret, shame, happiness, and joy. Adam was created with the capability to participate in relationships with God and with others.[54]

Erickson suggests that the communicable attributes of God also constitute His image.[55] Adam was faithful and created holy and morally upright. He could demonstrate mercy, grace, and love in perfection. Lastly, Adam was created in a state of righteousness; he lived according to God's law. Therefore, he was innocent and perfect in all his ways and possessed no sin.

God created Adam as a Dualistic Being

> And the Lord God formed man of the dust of the ground, and breathed into his nostrils the breath of life; and man became a living being… Then the Lord God took the man and put him in the Garden of Eden to tend and keep it. And the Lord God commanded the man, saying, "Of every tree of the garden you may freely eat; but of the tree of knowledge of good and evil you shall not eat, for in the day you eat of it you shall surely die." Gen. 2:7, 15-17

This second passage discloses that Adam was created with a body, spirit, and soul. There are several views of Adam's creation from this passage. The first view is referred to as monism, which is primarily advocated by non-believers. This view denies that a human is composed of parts or separate entities (material and immaterial) but rather as a radical unity. The monists propose that it is unthinkable that a human could exist or experience immortality without a body. Therefore, when the body dies, the soul dies. There is no afterlife.[56]

The second view is referred to as the dichotomy view. This is the most widely held view throughout most of Christian history. This advocates the thought that humans are composed of two substances, a material aspect (body) and an immaterial component (the soul and spirit). The body is the physical part of humans, the part that dies, and the spirit is the immaterial part of humans that survives death. Just as a jewel has different facets but is a whole, man, in his material and immaterial aspect, is a whole completed being. It is this immortal nature that sets humans apart from all other creatures.[57]

The last one that we will discuss is referred to as the trichotomy view. This view is like the dichotomy view except it proposes that the soul and spirit are not the same, but rather two separate entities. Although I disagree with their concept, I do respect them. I believe that they have a misunderstanding of the soul. I ask my trichotomy friends how they will respond to Luke 10:27 when Jesus states, "You shall love the LORD your God with all your heart, with all your soul, with all your strength, and with your mind, and your neighbor as yourself." Notice that it might be implied that there are additional entities of the immaterial; "heart," "strength," and "mind." By the same reasoning that the Trichomonist believes in two immaterial parts (soul and spirit), this passage can implicate that man is a quadchotomy or quidchotomy.

During the explanation of the importance of the dichotomy views from Genesis 2;7, I encourage the reader to read this section very slowly and maybe even meditate on some section since I have endeavored to interpret a complex truth into simpler terms. My goal is that the reader retains and understands enough information that he or she will better understand the phrase, "for in the day that you eat of it you shall surely die." (Gen. 2:17). The second goal is that the reader will understand that God made man dualistic (body and soul) so that he may obey, worship, and have fellowship with Him.

The Material Substance of Man

Genesis 2:7 begins with the statement that God "formed man of the dust of the ground." The Hebrew word *yasar* (formed) is used for a potter's activity that molds and fashions pots of clay (Isa. 29:16; Jer. 18:4-6); instead of clay, God used *apar* (dust) from the ground to mold and shape Adam's physical body.[58] This dust made Adam mortal. Later, the penalty of Adam's sin was his body (flesh) being returned to the dust of the earth (Gen. 3:19). It should be noted that the name of the first man was Adam, the Hebrew word for man, *adam*, is closely related to the Hebrew word *adama* (ground). This made Adam perfectly suited for the task of working the ground and caring for God's creation.[59] This material body provides the means of how men and women may be able to carry out God's will on earth physically.

The Immaterial Substance of Man

Spirit

The statement from Genesis 2:7 states that God "breathed into his nostrils the breath of life." The Hebrew words for "breath" or "spirit" is often referred to as *ruach* or *ruakh*, while the Greek is referred to as *pneuma*. Most often the Old Testament Hebrew word *ruach* refers to the meaning of spirit as:

- The vital power of life from God that animates the body (Gen. 2:7; Judg. 15:19; Job 27:3).
- The inner life such as intellect (Gen. 41:8; Ezek. 20:32), spiritual understanding (Job 20:3; 32:8), wisdom (Ezek. 283), will (Dan. 5:20), and emotions (1 Sam. 1:15; Prov. 15:13).
- The openness of the soul to God (Ps. 51:10; Isa. 26:9).[60]

There is a common agreement among Old Testament theologians of the above meaning of the Hebrew word *ruach*. Nevertheless, many Hebrew scholars agree to the meaning of *ruach*, but suggest that the actual Hebrew word used in Genesis 2; 7 was the rare somewhat synonym *nesama*. Adam was divinely formed from the dust of the earth and became a living being when God breathed (spirit) into his nostrils.[61]

Following is Scriptural evidence that the breath of God provided the source of life within man:

> When referring to the results of the flood the Scriptures state: "And all flesh died that moved on the earth: birds and cattle and beast and every

creeping thing that creeps on the earth, and every man. All in whose nostrils was the breath of the spirit of life, all that was on dry land, died." Gen. 7: 21–22

"The Spirit of God has made me, and the breath of the Almighty gives me life."Job 33:4

The New Testament defines *pneuma* as:

- The life force that animates the body and departs at death (Matt. 27:50; James 2:26).
- The self that interacts with God; it often refers to inter-action with God and the spiritual realm (Rom. 1:9; 8:16; 1 Cor. 14:14; Rev. 21:10).
- The Holy Spirit.
- The capacity of humans experiencing a relationship with God.[62]

Soul

The Old Testament Hebrew word for "soul" is *nephesh* and the Greek New Testament is *psyche*. Regarding humans, *nephesh* and *psyche* refer to a person in his or her entirety as a living being (spirit and body). When God breathed (*nesama*) into Adam's nostrils, he became a living being (soul, *nephesh)*.

The term "soul" denotes;

- The whole person, both body and spirit (Matt. 10:28; Acts 2:41; Rom.13:1).
- The seat of personal identity, often concerning God and salvation (Matt. 10:28, 39; Luke 1:46; John 12:25).

- The inner life of the body (Acts 20:10; Eph. 6:6).
- The intellect (Acts 14:2; Phil. 1:27).
- The will (Deut. 21:14; Ezek. 16:27; Matt. 22:37; Eph. 6:6).
- The emotions (Prov. 16:23; Matt. 26:38; Mark 14:34).
- The mind (Gen. 23:8; Deut. 18:6).
- The seat of conscience. This is where the Lord speaks (Ps. 42:1-2; Isa. 29:6).
- The moral and spiritual life (Heb. 6:19; 1 Pet. 1:22; 3 John 2).
- The soul is eternal while the body is not.

At physical death, the soul survives and is immediately in the presence of God (Luke 12:20). John states that when the saints are killed on earth during the trial and tribulation period that they will discover their souls in heaven (Rev. 6:9). The apostle Paul revealed that when the believer's soul is absent from the body it will be in the presence of the Lord (2 Cor. 5: 8).[63] Ultimately, all the souls of saints will be united with imperishable resurrected bodies (1 Cor. 15: 42 – 45). Likewise, it stands to reason that the non-believers will receive an indestructible body since it will not be burned up or be extinguished in the everlasting fire in hell.

It should not come as a surprise that some theologians interpret the terms "soul" and "spirit" as being synonymous. The Bible often refers to them interchangeably to indicate the immaterial nature of man (Matt. 10:28; Acts 2:31; 1 Cor. 5:3; 6:20). Both provide the same general functions (Mark 8:12; John 11:33; 13:21 with Matt. 10:28; John 12:27 also 2 Cor. 7:13; 1 Cor. 16:18 with Matt. 11:29). Further evidence that the terms are interchangeable is that of those who have departed from this life who is sometimes mentioned as "souls" and sometimes as "spirit' (Gen. 35:18; 1 Kings 17:21; Matt. 27:50; John 19:30; Acts 2:27, 31).[64] Theologian, David Mapes explains:

> Soul and spirit have some obvious differences in meaning. For example, spirit can mean wind or breathe, whereas the semantic domain of soul lacks this meaning...When the terms are used in reference to the immaterial part of man's nature, the terms are used synonymously. Spirit is the word which means the whole immaterial part of the nature and soul is another word which means the exact same immaterial part of nature (Isa. 26:9; Job 7:11). Never does the Scripture use spirit to refer to only a part of the immaterial nature while soul is the other part of the immaterial nature.[65]

W. D. Stacey, who agrees that they are often used synonymously, states the difference in these terms: "When reference is made to man in his relation to God *ruach* is the term most likely to be used...but when reference is made to man concerning other men, or man living the common life of men, then *nephesh* is most likely if a physical term is required. In both cases, the whole man was involved."[66] This may not always be the case; however, Stacey did state that "the term most likely to be used."

After defining the flesh, soul, and spirit I will now provide a clearer understanding of the soul. The reader may have noted that most of the definition of the spirit is also found within the definition of the soul. The reader may have also noted that unlike the spirit, the soul also includes the flesh. Therefore, it may start occurring to the reader that the soul is the being, the person that consists of the fleshly body and spirit. David Mapes provides an ontological nature of man (study of what man is made of) chart that simplifies this concept:

Dust (body) + Breath of Life (Spirit) = Living Soul; that is Material + Immaterial = Living Being (Person)

Mapes provided clarity when referring to theologians Friedrich Oehler and J. T. Beck:

> Body + spirit = living soul. According to Oehler, man does not possess a soul, he is a soul. He continued to explain the ontological nature of man by making a distinction that man possesses a spirit, but is a soul. The soul sprang from the union of the spirit and the body and exists continually through it...For Oehler the soul as used in Gen 2:7 referred to the entire man. Oehler is not saying that the joint activity of the body and spirit working together produce a third entity called a soul. Oehler is saying the body/spirit complex is the soul or the whole person.[67]

> Scripture gives no indication that man is anything other than dualistic in his ontological nature. What does it mean to be a human being? It means that he is ontologically composed of two separate, distinct, yet in this life indivisible parts: the body and the spirit. So, the soul is a composition of body and spirit. If either part is lacking, then the soul (person) does not exist. At the same time, it takes

both parts working together with each other to have
a living person.[68]

A little over forty years ago my wife and I purchased our first home. I remember the bathroom had some substance on the wall that was exceedingly difficult to remove. I came up with, what I now know as a dumb idea to mix bleach and ammonia to clean the substance. After a while, I found myself in a dangerous situation because of the mixing of the cleaning agents. My wife had to take me to the emergency room in which the attending physicians informed me that I was most fortunate to not have experienced a more serious attack or even died. It seems that if one mixes bleach and ammonia that it creates a chemical reaction that generates a gas called chloramine (NH_2CI) which is highly toxic. The bleach and ammonia are separate elements and chloramine gas is not an element but a compound that is developed when you mix the two elements (bleach and ammonia). The bleach and ammonia are still present and can be broken back down again under the right circumstance. This is the same as the body and spirit being two different elements and when joined together the results are not a third element, but a new compound referred to as the soul.

I know that my trichotomy friends disagree with my assessment of the dichotomy view. They will contend that the body, spirit, and soul are separate elements. They do not realize that the Scriptures refer to the soul, not only as of the spirit but also the body. The one Scripture that they quote to bring creditability to their view is 1 Thess. 5:23, "Now may the God of peace Himself sanctify you completely; and may your whole spirit, soul, and body be preserved blameless at the coming of our Lord Jesus Christ." The reader must note that the apostle

Paul was not indicating that the immaterial part of man could be divided into two separate elements or substances. When one investigates all New Treatment Scriptures written by Paul concerning "soul" and "spirit" he never referred to a trichotomy view of mankind; this was the only instance where he wrote "spirit" and "soul" in the same passage. The question is why? One of the courses that I teach for two different seminaries is entitled hermeneutics. Essentially, it is the science of interpreting Scripture properly. To do so, one must realize certain facts when interpreting a passage. Why and when was the passage written? What was the customs of those to whom was it written? Who wrote the passage? What does the passage mean in the original language in which it was written? How does the passage fit with the text before or after? These are just a few questions that need to be examined when correctly interpreting Scripture passages. When one studies Bible culture, he or she will discover that the literary styles of one culture and age may be very different from our literary styles. In our country, when a writer is writing a historical subject, he or she will write it in chronological order. This was not always the case of the Middle Eastern men many centuries ago. Their emphasis was not to always write in chronological order, but that of making a point. Therefore, some of the events that took place in the New Testament Gospels did not always seem to be in the same order as that of another book of the Gospels. Paul was not writing a new theology not found in his other writings; he was only making a comprehensive point. To understand the point, I went to one of my most academic commentaries, *The New International Greek Commentary: The Epistles to The Thessalonians*. The writer, Charles Wanamaker, suggests that Paul had made several references to the main topic here; that is the sanctification of the believer (3:11-13; 4:1 – 5:22; and now 5:23). Paul was emphasizing the importance of sanctification to be kept complete, without blame at the *Parousia* (coming) of our Lord Jesus Christ (5:23). Paul was making a comprehensive point of complete sanctification as he referred to the material and immaterial elements of the soul. After all, if the spirit (the immaterial) is sanctified it will affect what one thinks, and if the body (the material) is truly sanctified it will affect what one does. Since the spirit and body are a dichotomy, and if both are sanctified then the soul is truly completely sanctified. Wanamaker stated, "Paul's intention was not to offer an anthropological definition. Rather he sought to emphasize his desire that God would preserve his readers as complete human beings, blameless in the impending judgment of the day of the Lord or Parousia (cf. 3:13).[69]

Adam was dualistic in his nature. There is a clear distinction between the material and the immaterial working in unity forming the soul (being) and neither is capable to exist on the earth independent of the other (James 2:26; Rev. 11:1; Gen. 35:18). Adam's immaterial substance working in unity with his material substances provides the functional nature in which one could have a relationship with God and know His will. Adam's material substance provides the means of how he could accomplish all God had revealed to and instructed him to do. I believe that the human being (soul) consists of the material (fleshly body) and the immaterial (spirit). The immaterial is somewhat a receiver within the soul that is capable to communicate with God to accept Him, to know Him, and to discover His will. While the material (fleshly body), and sometimes the immaterial (spirit and conscience), provides the capability to carry out and to accomplish God's will.

God Created Adam for His Glory

> Everyone who is called by My name, whom I have
> created for My glory; I have formed him, yes, I have
> made him. Isa. 43:7

The last passage suggests that Adam, as all persons are intended, was called by God's name since each belongs to Him and is a part of His family (Deut. 28:10; Jer. 14; 9; Ezek. 36:20). Adam was brought into existence, created, formed, and made, for one purpose: the glory of God. The question may be asked, "How may a person bring glory to God?" To answer this question, one needs to understand the meaning of the actual Old Testament Hebrew and the New Testament Greek words for glory or glorify. The basic Hebrew word is *kabod* (some pronounce *kavod)* which suggests heaviness in weight (1 Sam. 4:18; Prov. 27:3). The verb means "to give weight to, to honor" (Exod. 20:12). It is the recognition of the place of the person of honor in a community. It means to praise and to recognize the importance of another for the weight that he or she carries within a community. The Hebrew word *kabod* also denotes the manifestation of light by which God revealed Himself, whether in lightning flash or blinding splendor. The Old Testament instructs that glory should be given only to God as His divine powers and majesty gives Him importance and weight in the relationship to the worshipping community (Ps.22:23; 86:12; Isa. 24: 15).

The New Testament provides the Greek word *doxa* to define glory, while limiting the meaning to God's glory by indicating His majesty (Rom. 1:23) and His perfections, especially concerning righteousness (Rom. 3:23). This glory of God is made tangible in the person of Jesus Christ since He is the very presence of God (Luke 9:32; John 1:14; 1 Cor. 2:8; Heb. 1:3). The New Testament also carries the Old Testament meaning of divine power and majesty (Acts 7:2; Eph. 1:7).

Divine glory means that humans should only glory in God and not seek selfish glory for themselves from men (Matt. 6:2; John 5:44; 1 Thess. 2:6). Believers should only seek to receive praise and honor from Christ (Rom. 2:7; 5:2; 1 Thess. 2:19).[70]

The question some may be thinking is, "how do we give glory to God?" First, we give glory to God by praising and testifying to all those around us for what He has done and provided (Isa. 42:8). Second, we glorify God by being good stewards of all our possessions (actually His), time, talents, tithes, and offerings. Third, we glorify God by obeying His word and keeping His precepts and commandments (Ps. 103: 17 – 18; John 14:15). We glorify God when we reflect on His communicable attributes (love, justice, mercy, holiness, etc.). Lastly, we glorify God when the world can see Christ in us.

The last question to be considered is, "How did Adam glorify God?" I will answer this by referring to Adam before the Fall. First, Adam, as a sinless person, could do the following: he glorified God by becoming His representative or vice-regent as he represented God in the Garden of Eden. He glorified God by caring for God's creation as a steward. Adam glorified God by accomplishing God's will. He glorified God through his perfect righteousness and his perfect communicable attributes. Lastly, Adam glorified God through his unspoiled relationship with God and his unwavering obedience.

Later, in another chapter, we will discover that Adam's nature, state, and purpose will either be diminished or destroyed as a consequence of the Fall. When one understands all the above information about Adam before the Fall, he or she will be able to comprehend what died the day that Adam and Eve ate of the forbidden fruit. This will provide awareness of how the Fall affected all mankind and why Christ would have to die on the cross so that all may have an opportunity to have a relationship with Him.

CHAPTER FOUR

The Fall: Adam's Temptation

Now the serpent was more cunning than any beast of the field which the LORD God had made. And he said to the woman, "Has God indeed said, 'you shall not eat of every tree of the garden'?" And the woman said to the serpent, "We may eat of the fruit of the tree which is in the midst of the garden, God has said, 'You shall not eat it, nor shall you touch it, lest you die.'" Then the serpent said to the woman, "you will not surely die, for God knows that in the day you eat of it your eyes will be opened, and you will be like God, knowing good and evil." So when the woman saw that the tree was good for food, that it was pleasant to the eyes, and a tree desirable to make one wise, she took of the fruit and ate. She also gave it to her husband with her, and he ate also. Gen. 3: 1–6

I remember, at the age of five, my dad encouraged me to assist him while repairing electrical wiring. This was when a man would teach his son to do what was considered manly things. Experiencing this special event with my dad resulted in a feeling of pride. The truth of the matter was that I knew nothing about electrical wiring. My dad handed me two separate wires while stating, "I am going to let you hold these for me, but under no circumstance do you let them touch, if you do you may get burned, but most definitely you will get shocked and may destroy the Christmas lights." In my innocence, I wondered what my dad meant by "being shocked." I believed that if I were near my dad no harm could come to me. I thought that maybe he was mistaken that the touching of the two wires would destroy the Christmas lights. This was a great temptation for a five-year-old. I was struggling with the idea that if I were to touch them together very quickly, I would find out what it meant to be shocked and it would be too swift to destroy the lights. When my dad looked away, I quickly touched the wires together. There was a loud pop and a spark, I was shocked, and the Christmas lights were destroyed. It scared me and I began to cry, my dad first panicked and soon afterward was upset that I did not obey him. The consequence of my succumbing to temptation brought temporary emotional and physical pain to me and disappointment to my dad; after all, he trusted me! My dad experienced the consequence of my succumbing to temptation. As you can imagine when my mom observed what happened she was upset with my dad. He was not only disappointed in me, he was embarrassed in front of my mom and now regretted that he included me. The consequence temporarily hurt my relationship with my dad. It would be a long time before he would include me in a father-son learning experience, and it also temporarily hurt the relationship between my dad and mom.

There are always consequences when one succumbs to temptation such as emotional, physical, and even spiritual pain or agony. It can destroy relationships with others, and it can affect those around us. The focus of this chapter is the much greater temptation and consequence of Adam and Eve. What does it mean to be tempted? What was the temptation? Who was behind the temptation? Lastly, what were the consequences?

The Meaning of Temptation

One meaning of temptation is "the enticement to do that which is evil with an expectation of pleasure or gain." A second meaning is "a test to determine if one would make the right choice" or "to give evidence of one's obedience and commitment." In the New Testament, The English word "temptation" is often translated from the Greek word, *peirazo*. Greek language scholar, Spiros Zodhiates, defines the good and bad senses of the Greek word. On one hand, the good sense ascertains the character, view, or feelings of someone who is being tested. God is said to try men by adversity to test their faith and confidence in Him (1 Cor. 10:13; Heb. 2:18; 11:17, 37; Rev. 3:10). On the other hand, the bad sense implies a person's virtue is being tested; it is soliciting someone to sin. Satan tempts one to show him or her unapproved.[71] With this thought in mind Adrian Rogers states, "God will test us, but God will not tempt us. God tests us to make us stand. Satan tempts us to make us fall."[72] The Scriptures reveal that Satan is the root of temptation; he entices men and women to do evil in his quest to lead everyone from God's will. Therefore, Satan is known as the tempter (Matt. 4:3; 1 Thess. 3:5). God does not qualify for the second definition of temptation since He never entices anyone to commit evil (James 1:13). Nonetheless, God qualifies for the first definition of temptation by allowing testing for discerning quality of commitment and to increase faith and patience. God tested Abraham (Gen. 22:1; Heb. 11:7), finding him faithful.

God provides a special blessing to those who endure such temptation (James 1:12).

While demonic forces may try to lead the Christian astray, James describes where the real process of temptation lies. James wrote "But each one is tempted when he is drawn away by his desires and enticed. Then, when desire is conceived, it gives birth to sin; and sin, when it is full-grown, brings forth death" (James 1: 14 – 15). James reveals that temptation itself is not sinning, but the yielding to temptation is sin.[73]

How should we confront temptation? We confront temptation through our faith and obedience toward God. Romans 8: 28 states, "And we know that all things work together for good to those who love God, to those who are called according to His purpose." It does not say that we will actually "see" all things working together for our good. No, Paul is only stating that we "know" (faith) that all things will work for the good. Believers live by faith, not by sight. Faith means the surrendering of our wills to God and the obeying of His Word despite our circumstance. One may grow spiritually and emotionally during times of testing and suffering by feeding on God's Word.

The bishop of Milan, Aurelius Ambrosius (340 – 397), historically known as Saint Ambrose, suggests the following concerning temptation; "the devil tempts that he may ruin; God tests that he may crown." And, "The devil's snare does not catch you unless you are first caught by the devil's bait." The Christian author, Erwin W. Lutzer, suggests a similar understanding of temptation. "Temptation is not a sin; it is a call to battle." And, "Each temptation leaves us better or worse; neutrality is impossible."[74]

The Fall of Adam and Eve

During the last chapter, the reader was informed about how Adam and Eve were created to be God's representative. The fact that Adam is a person in the image of God qualifies him to be God's representative. The fact that Adam is a person in the image of God enables him to communicate with God. Adam's entire nature as a single union of parts (material and immaterial) created by God to be in His image qualifies Adam to be God's representative and vice-regent of His creation. Adam and Eve had the capacity to communicate, fellowship, and worship God. As an "image of God" Adam and Eve possessed rational minds, memories, imagination, language skills, emotions, the communicable attributes of God, and free will to make choices. They both lived in a state of original righteousness, which was demonstrated through their moral purity and perfect standing before God. The evidence of Adam's state of righteousness was his honor of walking in the very presence of God, his perfect harmony with God, and his enjoying the presence of God. Originally, Adam and Eve were innocent of any wrongdoing and lived a perfect sinless life. That is until Satan entered the picture.

God's Test (Gen. 2: 8-9; 15-17)

God created Adam and informed him of his work and provisions (Gen. 2: 15-16). It should be noted that the Lord provided a prohibition in verse seventeen; "But of the tree of the knowledge of good and evil you shall not eat, for in the day that you eat of it you shall surely die." I suggest that God provided the tree this designation since it was a test of obedience by which Adam and Eve were tried. Would they be obedient to

God or disobedient? For what other reason would the tree exist? Adam already possessed the knowledge of good by obeying God. The tree provided Adam with a decision that would result in a great consequence of death if he made the wrong choice.

All men and women must make choices daily, whether they be for God, self, or others. They are either selfish or selfless. There are always consequences for our choices, whether they are good or bad. A.W. Tozer once stated, "Men are free to decide their own moral choices, but they are also under the necessity to account to God for those choices."[75] Adam was given a choice. He understood that the wrong choice would cause severe harm. Later the consequence of his choice would entail cosmic consequences to all future humankind.

Some may ask the question, "Why did God test the love and obedience of Adam and Eve?" In chapter two of this book, I identified some of the communicable attributes of God. One of the attributes was God's admitted jealousy, "You shall have no other gods before Me. You shall not make for yourself a carved image, any likeness of anything that is in heaven or above, or that is in the earth beneath, or that is in the water under the earth. You shall not bow down to them nor serve them. For I, the LORD your God, am a jealous God" (Exod. 20: 2-5). Being the Creator and Sustainer of the universe God has a sole right to receive worship, glory, honor, and obedience. Unlike most human jealousy, God's jealousy is not selfish but originates out of concern for His creation. Loving and obeying him produces His blessing and protection, something that false gods are not capable of accomplishing. He is like a man who expects fidelity, love, and honor from his wife and protects her from those who would defile her. God's jealousy is His passion for protecting all that belongs to Him and God desires that all humanity choose to love Him.

The question is, "how do we demonstrate our love toward God?" The answer is through obedience. Gary Chapman wrote a book entitled, *The Five Love Languages*. It describes how spouses may communicate a heartfelt commitment to one another more effectively; they need to discover that each has his or her particular love language. Some spouses respond to the love language of words of affirmation, while others respond to the language of quality time, some prefer the language of receiving gifts, while others respond to the language of acts of service. Lastly, many prefer the language of physical touch.[76]

God has His love language. "If you love Me, keep my commandments." (John 14:15). God's love language is obedience. Adam and Eve had the opportunity to express their love for God through loyalty and obedience.

The Temptation of Satan (Gen. 3: 1–7)

Scripture records that God's "test" of love and obedience was turned into a "temptation" by Satan. Although the term Satan is not mentioned, the Hebrew word *nahas* for serpent is provided (3:1). This same serpent is identified as Satan by the apostle John (Rev. 12:9; 20; 2) and by the apostle Paul (2 Cor. 11:3). Satan appears for the first time in a manifestation in the form of a rebellious serpent. Chapter Two of this book discusses how Satan rebelled against God for the first time after the creation of heaven when God proclaimed all things good (Gen. 1:31) and before the Fall recorded in Genesis 3 (Ezek. 28:11-15). Satan, being a fallen angel, was motivated to challenge God's creation, authority, and His word. In verse one Satan observes

Eve when she is not walking with God and challenges God's goodness and character behind His back. "Has God indeed said, 'You shall not eat of every tree of the garden?'" Satan tempted Eve to be suspicious concerning God's goodness and integrity by raising a question in her mind whether God was dealing thoughtfully and justly with her and Adam. Satan's question was more of a statement in which he feigned shock and disbelief of God's statement. He further proceeded to exaggerate and distort God's prohibition as if God were holding back something. He insinuates that God was spiteful, cruel, jealous, and self-protective. Eve has the opportunity to continue to place her faith in God and His word. She did defend God's statement and to correctly clarify His position. But the temptation begins to take hold on Eve. Satan cunningly moves God from being the beneficial provider in Eve's mind to that of a depressing oppressor.[77]

One may observe Eve's reaction in verses two and three: Note that she listened to what he was saying and responded by repeating what God told her husband earlier (Gen. 2:17). Nevertheless, after stating God's words she proceeds to embellish them with an additional prohibition; "nor shall you touch it, lest you die." Eve watered down God's prohibition, by changing God's very words from, "you shall surely die" (Gen. 2:17), to "lest you die." Could she have played down the consequences of God's prohibition? After all, God has been her loving benefactor; would He allow them to die? This is similar to what some claim today, that God would not allow someone to go to hell!

At this point, Satan has successfully planted seeds of doubt into Eve's mind. Is God holding something back? Is God treating them fairly? Is God telling the truth? Satan responded with a fictitious expression of surprise as he made a severe allegation against God's word and prohibition in verses four and five: He lied when he declared God was not truthful and further made a categorical denial of God's earlier statement when he insisted that "you will not surely die." Satan implied that God's promise of repercussions was not death but they're receiving a special blessing of being like God by knowing good and evil. Satan told them a partial truth (Gen. 3:5). It was true that they would know good and evil, but Satan did not tell them about the pain, suffering, separation, and death that they will experience through their sin. The temptation was in three areas, the lust of the flesh, the lust of the eyes, and the pride of life (1 John 2:16; Matt. 4:1-11).

Eve should have trusted God and utilized her faith and obedience in Him. Nonetheless, she allowed the temptation of Satan to shift her commitment to God and gave preference to her own will and desires. God's will and word was now irrelevant. Her new self-autonomy displaced her submission and obedience to God.

In verse six, Satan presented three desirable features to Eve. The fruit was physically appealing (good for food). The fruit was visually attractive to the eyes (pleasant to the eyes). And the fruit was desirable with knowledge (desirable to make one wise). Eve coveted wisdom, even if it was forbidden by God. Eve wanted to be like God in knowledge (3:4). This is one of man's weaknesses, to be his or her own god. It seems that Adam was nearby (her husband with her). Notice that she did not try to tempt him. Maybe he noticed that she was still alive; we do not know. Nonetheless, she merely offers the fruit to him, which he ate. This action finalized the first human sin.[78] They failed God.

They were no longer innocent. Their relationship with God would, for a moment, be ruined. Much about their nature was now corrupted, and at some point, their bodies would die. This is part of the reason why this is referred to as the Fall of Man.

The apostle Paul was implying Adam's Fall in Romans 5: 18 – 19; "Therefore as through one man's offense judgment came to all men, resulting in condemnation, even so through one Man's righteous act the free gift came to all men, resulting in justification of life. For as by one man's disobedience many were made sinners, so also by one Man's obedience many will be made righteous." Here Paul is comparing the temptations of Adam and Christ (The obedient Man). Both were expected to obey God's word. Both were tempted by Satan; Adam in the Garden of Eden and Christ after fasting and walking in the wilderness for forty days and nights (Matthew 4). Adam had lived in comfort with a full belly before his temptation by Satan. Christ on the other hand had lived in the wilderness, in the sun without comfort, and had not eaten for forty days and forty nights. Adam was offered a bit of fruit, which he could not refuse. First, Christ was offered a stone and challenged to turn it into bread to prove He was God in the flesh.

Secondly, Satan challenged Him to prove that He was the Son of God by jumping from the pinnacle of the temple and calling on the angels to save Him. And lastly, He was offered the kingdoms of the world if He would only bow down to Satan. Adam failed his temptation while Christ was victorious. It is interesting to note that Satan's temptation dealt with the temptation of pride, pride for Christ to prove Himself as the Messiah, pride to prove His power, and the pride to receive His power to rule immediately, rather than on the Father's time. Yet, pride was Satan's downfall.

Did God Create Sin? Did He Plan the Fall?

I have often heard people ask the question, "Where did sin come from?" "Did God predetermine sin?" And, "Who is responsible for sin and the Fall?" These are honest questions and no one should be embarrassed or feel guilty for asking them. In answering the questions, I will take a moment to quote from well-learned Christians.

Apologist Norman Geisler shares in his book, *The Big Book of Christian Apologetics,* that Church history discloses that some of the early Christian theologians approached these questions. If one would sum up the writing of Augustine (354 – 430), bishop of Hippo, and Thomas Aquinas (1225 – 1274) they would find the following:

1. God is absolutely perfect.
2. God created only perfect creatures.
3. One of the perfections God gave some of His creatures was the power of free choice.
4. Some of these creatures freely chose to do evil.
5. Therefore, a perfect creature caused evil.[79]

Geisler also shared his thoughts on the matter. He agreed with Augustine and Aquinas but added more detail by stating that the good creatures misused their free will by introducing evil into the universe. He agreed that evil arose from good, "not directly but indirectly, by the abuse of good power called freedom." Geisler further emphasized that "Freedom in itself is not evil. It is good to be free. But with freedom comes the possibility of evil. So, God is responsible for making evil possible, but free creatures are responsible for making it actual." He continued to suggest that "God is not responsible for the exercise of the free choice to do evil. God does not perform free action for us. Human free choice is not a mere instrumental cause through which God works. God produces the "fact" of free choice, but each human performs the act of free choice."[80]

Geisler sheds additional light on the subject with his book, *If God, Why Evil?* The reader is reminded that Lucifer was a created archangel who was the first to sin when he led a third of the angels to rebel with him against God. He then reminded the reader of the account of Adam and Eve's temptation and their falling into sin. He states that before these events there was no sin in the universe. There is a perfect God, perfect heaven, with perfect creatures called angels. He then asks the questions, "How could sin arise under such perfect conditions? Who caused Lucifer to sin?" Satan was not tempted by anyone. God did not create him with an evil nature that provided him an inclination to sin. The Bible informs us that God does not tempt anyone (James 1:13). Geisler provides answers to the two questions and some new ones. "What caused Lucifer to sin?" No one did. He is the cause of his sin. Sin is a self-caused action, one for which we cannot blame anyone or anything else." "Who causes the first sin? Lucifer, how did he cause it? By the power of free choice, which God gave to him." He continues with the suggestion that some claim that the meaning of free will is "doing what we desire" while claiming that "God must give one the desire to do good, otherwise, by our fallen nature, we do only what is evil." Geisler exposes the flaws of this thought with the following: "Why would God give only some, not all, the desire to do good? By this definition, all persons would do good if only God gave them the desire. Further, Lucifer had no fallen nature, so this definition of *freedom* would not explain his evil choice. Surely, no one who believes in an all-good God, who wants all to do good, could consistently claim that God gave Lucifer the desire to rebel against Him. Perish the thought."[81]

Some readers are thinking, "Why could not God create everyone with the free will to do good? Here, I will try to address this by quoting Alvin Plantinga:

> A world containing creatures who are significantly free (and freely perform more good than evil) is more valuable, all else being equal, than a world containing no free creatures at all. Now God can create free creatures, but He can't cause or determine them to do only what is right. For if He does so, then they aren't significantly free after all; and they do not do what is right freely. To create creatures capable of moral good, therefore, He must create creatures capable of moral evil; and He can't give these creatures freedom to perform evil and at the same time prevent them from doing so. As it turns out, sadly enough, some of the free creatures God created went wrong in the exercise of their freedom; this is the source of moral evil. The fact that free creatures sometimes go wrong, however, counts neither against God's omnipotence nor against His goodness; for He could have forestalled the occurrence of moral evil only by removing the possibility of moral good.[82]

It should be understood that when evil things happen one should never blame God. God has provided humankind with free will. Evil should be blamed on Satan and evil people. Yes, God will indeed test our faith and when we willfully sin, He may be responsible for our chastisement (Heb. 12:5 – 11). Nevertheless, He should never be blamed for evil. Satan holds superior responsibility for sin and evil.

Satan was the first to fail, Adam and Eve followed his temptation. Their sin would affect much pain and heartache. They will experience several separations, such as separation from God's fellowship, separation from the Garden of Eden and the Tree of Life, and eventually their spirit being separated from their body when they experienced death some centuries later. These are the consequence of sin that will be discussed in the next chapter

CHAPTER FIVE

The Fall: The Meaning, the Nature, and the Consequence of Sin

"For all have sinned and fall short of the glory of God...
For the wages of sin is death." Rom. 2:23; 6:23a

"You shall not eat, for in the day that you eat of it you
shall surely die." Gen. 2:17

Previously, the reader viewed the participants in the Garden of Eden (Chapters two and three). The most current chapter examines Satan's temptation and Adam's failure to honor and trust God's Word. This was man's first sin and the expectation of immediate death. Adam and Eve did not die physically on that day; so, what did die? What would be the consequences of this action? These questions will be addressed in this chapter. We will define sin, its nature, and all its consequences; including what died that day and what would die in the future.

While writing about sin I could not help but remember over twenty years ago when I was pastoring a church in Middle Georgia. I had just finished my message and while standing at the front door shaking hands with the members and guests, I noticed a middle-aged woman eyeballing me as she stood in line; she seemed very upset. When she stood in front of me, she let me have it. She claimed that I was speaking about her from the pulpit; my being confused would be an understatement. She very rarely attended church, so I knew very little about her. All I knew for sure was that I had preached a message defining several sins and their consequences. She was guilty of one or more. Hearing this, one of our older mature deacons quickly spoke up. He called her by name, and then shared with her how I preached expository messages. He further explained that while I preach the whole counsel of God through this method that I would eventually preach some message that was directly meant for someone in the audience; he went on to say that the preacher did not select and choose, but instead preached each thing as it came. He gazed into the eyes of the woman and stated, "we all have had a turn at being hit by one of the pastor's messages; it was just your turn today." The woman now being corrected was embarrassed. She then recognized how her outburst revealed to the whole church that she was guilty of one or more of the sins of which I had preached. After she left the old deacon placed his hand on my shoulder and said, "Preacher, everyone wants the preacher to preach on sin; but not their sin."

To realize that one is a sinner, he or she should understand sin, its meaning, its nature, and its consequence. In the last chapter, we observed how Adam was tempted and disobeyed God. Sin is disobeying God. Adam and Eve learned by experience that God is holy and righteous and hates sin. Therefore, sinners must be reprimanded. The Bible is filled with painful events where sin ruined relationships and fellowship with others and most importantly with God. God would later take drastic measures to restore that relationship. To understand the event in the Garden of Eden, one must understand the concept of sin.

THE MEANING OF SIN

When I was a child my mom took it upon herself to provide religious instruction. Each night we would pray and then she proceeded to teach me the Lord's Prayer and Psalms, chapter 23. She was convinced that I should have a concept of sin. In Essence, evil was bad, and good was not bad. In her misguided attempt, she tried to clarify the concept of sin by suggesting that every time I sinned I would receive a black mark on my heart and if I was not careful, my heart would turn black and I would not be able to go to heaven. I know that her motive was right, but her theology was way off base. She scared me to death. A young preschooler does not understand such metaphors. I took it literally that my physical heart was turning black while lying in my bed at night convinced that I was going to hell. One thing for sure, I knew I was a sinner. Every unbeliever needs to realize that he or she is a sinner before they may experience salvation. Therefore, so that the reader may understand the vileness and destruction of sin in the Garden, I will share a few quotes in my quest to define sin.

- **The Reformer Martin Luther:** "Sin is essentially a departure from God."[83]

- **Seventeenth-century author and preacher, John Bunyan:** "Sin is the dare of God's justice, the rape of His mercy, the jeer of His patience, the slight of His power, and the contempt of His love."[84]

- **Millard Erickson:** "Any act, attitude, or disposition that fails to completely fulfill or measure up to the standards of God's righteousness. It may involve an actual transgression of God's law or failure to live up to his norms."[85]

- **Baptist theologian and author, Gregg R. Allison:** "Any lack of conformity to the moral law of God. Such nonconformity applies to one's (1) being: the "sin nature" or tendency to sin; (2) actions: evil deeds like idolatry and murder; (3) attitudes: wrong mindsets like envy and pride; (4) words: inappropriate communications like gossip and slander; and (5) motivations: disoriented purposes like self-glorification and people-pleasing. Elements included in sin are unfaithfulness, disobedience, pride, rebellion, deception, indifference, and hopelessness."[86]

There are many Hebrew and Greek words that describe sin that will be discussed during the next section of this chapter. Nonetheless, for this section, I have chosen to discuss two Greek words that are clarified by Greek scholar, William D. Mounce. The first Greek word is *hamartano*. Mounce explains that this word "gives the sense of missing the mark, losing, or falling short of the goal" (Rom. 3:23). He further explains that generally the meaning "refers to sins or sinning against oneself or another person" (Luke. 17: 3 – 4; Matt. 18: 15 – 21; Acts 25: 8; 1 Cor. 6:18).

The second Greek word is *hamartia*, which is normally translated as "sin." It refers to the transgression of the law. Thereby, *hamartia* is used to denote one's sin against God. "Apart from the atoning blood of Jesus Christ, *hamartia* results in death"

(Rom. 6:23).[87] I believe that most readers are beginning to understand the meaning of sin. It is important to now describe the nature of sin.

THE NATURE OF SIN

I will endeavor to provide an overview of the nature of sin by identifying the following titles and divisions of sin provided by Millard Erickson:

Terms Emphasizing the Cause of Sin

- **Ignorance:** The New Testament Greek word *agnoia* and the Hebrew word *sh^e ggh* often are translated as ignorance or "to err." The word is frequently used in settings where it means innocent ignorance (Rom. 1:13; 2 Cor. 6:9; Gal. 1:22). On one hand, some sins of ignorance are overlooked by God (Acts 17:30). On the other hand, people are made culpable for sins committed out of ignorance (Eph. 4:18). Nonetheless, during the high priest's annual visit to the Holy of Holies to offer sacrifices, he offered them for both himself and "for the sins the people had committed in ignorance" (Heb. 9:7). Erickson stated, "These errors or ignorance were such that the people were liable to punishment for them. This was willful ignorance – the people could have known the right course to follow but chose not to know."

- **Error:** The primary Old Testament Hebrew words *shagah* and *shagag* are often translated as "to err." Erickson suggests that "In its literal sense it is used of sheep that stray from the flock (Ezek. 34: 6) and of drunken persons stumbling and reeling (Isa. 28:7)...the verb form generally refers to an error in moral conduct. The context indicates that the person committing the error is liable for the action." The verb and related noun *sh'gagah* seem to refer to human weakness and the propensity to err (Gen. 6:3). Penalties are assessed for these sins and range from insignificant to severe since the individuals should have known better. Another Hebrew word *ta'ah* is repeatedly translated "to err or wonder about." It is frequently used to describe someone who is intoxicated (Isa. 28:7), or one who deliberately errs in spirit (Isa. 29:24). This term refers to those who deliberately err rather than by accident.

The New Testament Greek word *planomi* and the passive form *planao* denote sin as an error. It commonly emphasizes the causes of going astray, namely, being deceived (Mark 13: 5 – 6; 1 Cor. 6:9; Gal. 6:7; 1 John 3:7). This may be by evil spirits (1 Tim. 4:1; 1 John 4:6), other humans (Eph. 4:4), or it could be one's self (1 John 1:8). Regardless, those who are led into error ought to have recognized the deception. Erickson states:

> In most cases, however, what the Bible terms errors simply ought not to have occurred: one should have known better and was responsible to so inform oneself. While these sins are less heinous than the deliberate and rebellious type of wrongdoing, the individual is still responsible for them, and therefore penalty attaches to them.[88]

- **Inattention:** The New Testament includes two Greek words. The first word is *parakoe* which is commonly translated, "to hear amiss or incorrectly." It often "refers to disobedience as a result of negligence (Rom. 5: 19; 2 Cor. 10:6)." Similarly, the verb *parakouo* means to "refuse to listen." (Matt. 18:17) or to ignore (Mark 5:36). In any case, it is the failure to listen and to take heed to God's voice, which is a serious offense.[89]

Terms Emphasizing the Character of Sin

- **Missing the Mark:** This is the most common concept that stresses the character and nature of sin. The Old Testament Hebrew word is *chata'* and the New Testament Greek word is *hamartano*. This word suggests more than just missing the mark but an implication of a conscious effort to fail, a voluntary and culpable mistake. Erickson quotes Ryder Smith:

> The hundreds of examples of the word's *moral* use require that the wicked man 'misses the right mark *because he chooses* to aim at the wrong one' and 'misses the right path *because he deliberately* follows a wrong one' – That is, there is no question of an innocent mistake or the merely negative idea of failure."[90]

The word refers to one's action concerning other human beings and God. "This sin is a sin against God since it is a failure to hit the mark, He has set His standards of perfect love of God and perfect obedience to Him.

- **Irreligion:** This is a unique word and to explain it we will observe three New Testament Greek words. The first word is *sebe,* which is interpreted as "to worship" or "to reverence." However, when the Greek letter "alpha (a)" is placed before the word it becomes an antonym. Therefore, the Greek word *asebe* becomes "irreverence" and is often found in the Books of Romans, 2 Peter, and Jude.

  The second Greek word *dik* means "righteousness." Nonetheless, the placement of the Greek letter alpha before the word (*adik*) changes the meaning to "unjust" or "unrighteousness." The Greek word *dik* was originally the justice of a court of law. Therefore, *adik* is in contrast to the court of law. The word is used in 1 Cor. 6:9.

  The last Greek word is *nomos,* which means "law." When the Greek letter alpha is placed in the front of the word it becomes *anomia* which means "lawless." It is about breaking the law of God (Matt. 7:23; 13:41; 23:28; 2 Thess. 2: 1 – 12; 1 John 3:2, 4).

- **Transgression:** The Old Testament Hebrew word *'abar* is often interpreted as "to cross over" or "to pass by." Frequently the word involves the ides of transgressing (The overstepping of the limits of God's law). The transgressing of a command or going beyond an established limit (Esther 3:3) and is used of transgressing the Lord's command (Numbers 14: 41 – 42). Adam and Eve transgressed God's command by eating of the forbidden fruit (Gen. 3: 4 – 6). The New Testament Greek word *parabasis* (transgress) implies the breaking of some law of God (Rom. 4:15; Gal. 3:19; Heb. 23:2; 9:15).

- **Iniquity or Lack of Integrity:** The primary Old Testament Hebrew word *'awal* suggests the basic concept of deviating from the right course or path. It carries the idea of injustice, failure to fulfill the standard of righteousness or lack of integrity (Heb. 19:15). The lack of integrity is the failure to fulfill or maintain the law of God, resulting in disunity in the individual.

- **Rebellion:** Many Old Testament Hebrew words depict sin as rebellion. The most common is *pasha'* and its noun form *asha'*. The root meaning is "to rebel" (Isa. 1:2). Another Hebrew word *marah* is translated "to rebel" (Isa. 1:20). The New Testament Greek words, *apeitheia* (Heb. 3:18), *aphist mi* (1 Tim. 4:10, and *apostasia* (2 Thess. 2:3) have the meaning and sense of disobedience and rebellion against God and His word. Erickson states: "All persons are assumed to be in contact with the truth of God, even the Gentiles, who do not have His special revelation. Failure to believe the message, particularly when openly and specifically presented, is disobedience or rebellion. Anyone who disobeys a king is considered an enemy. Likewise, the multitudes that disobey God's word."

- **Treachery:** Treachery is closely related to rebellion. It is the idea of sin as a breach of trust. The Old Testament Hebrew word is *ma'al* (Num. 15:12; 27); which references a woman's unfaithfulness to her husband. Often, the New Testament Greek words *parapipto* and *paraptoma* suggests treachery as a "falling away." The words often focus on the bond or covenant between God and His people. It is the sin of betrayal of or infidelity to that trust which is appropriately labeled treachery.

- **Perversion:** When in use in the Old Testament, the Hebrew word *awah* often is interpreted "to bend or twist" It also means, "to be bent or bowed down" (Isa. 21:3 and 24:1). Sometimes it refers to one with a "warped mind" (Isa. 21:3). It speaks to the nature of one whose sins have caused them to become twisted or distorted from the original image of God (Prov. 12:8).

- **Abomination:** The Old Testament Hebrew words *shiqquts* and *to'ebah* describe acts that are particularly reprehensible to God (Deut. 7: 25 – 26; 12:31; 18: 9 – 12; Lev. 18:22; 20:13). This depiction of sin as an abomination seems to have special reference to God's attitude toward sin and its effects upon Him. The term indicates that these sins are not merely something that God irritably objects to, but rather that which produces revulsion in Him.[91]

Terms Emphasizing the Results of Sin

- **Agitation or Restlessness:** The Old Testament Hebrew word *reshe'* is usually translated as "wickedness." It has been suggested that the concept was original of tossing and restlessness. The root of the Hebrew words means "to be disjointed, ill-regulated, abnormal, and wicked." The Scriptures suggest that the wicked are seen as causing agitation and discomfort for themselves and others as well. They live in chaotic confusion and bring disorder into the lives of those around them.

- **Evil or Badness:** The Old Testament Hebrew word *ra* means evil in the sense of badness. Therefore, it can refer to anything harmful or malignant, or a dangerous animal. It also carries the meaning of distress or adversary (Jer. 42:6). The word binds together the act of sin and its consequences.

- **Guilt:** The Old Testament Hebrew word *asham* is often interpreted as "to do wrong, to commit an offense, or to inflict injury." It suggests that a wrong has been committed for which the perpetrator should be held accountable and make restitution (Num. 5:8). The New Testament Greek word *enochos* suggests that one is liable for punishment (Matt. 5: 21-22; 1 Cor. 11:27; Jam. 2:10). Guilt is not looked upon as a feeling but as a judgment. A person is found guilty before God as convicted by the Holy Spirit and God's Word.

- **Trouble:** The Hebrew word *aven* literally means "trouble." Most often in a moral sense. Trouble is what a sinner reaps as a consequence of his or her sinful actions. (Prov. 22:8). It brings forth a weariness or fatigue to the sinner.[92]

Lastly, Sin Brings forth death: This will be discussed during the next section.

Sin is the displacement of God; it is simply a failure to give God prominence. Millard Erickson states that "It is placing something else, anything else, in the supreme place which is His [God]. Thus; choosing oneself rather than God is not wrong because self is chosen, but because something other than God is chosen. Choosing any finite object over God is wrong. No matter how selfless such an act might be."[93]

THE CONSEQUENCE OF SIN

The writer of the Book of Hebrews discloses both the consequence of sin and its purpose (Heb. 12: 3–11). This passage provides an over-view of discipline in the life of a believer. The Christians were experiencing hardship from two directions: One was torments and troubles experienced through the hostility of unbelievers (12:3). The second was troubles and chastisement brought on by their sinful conduct. Both were opportunities for corrective discipline in the life of the believer. Believers who abuse their free will and allow sin to reign in their life will experience chastisement. Chastisement is a discipline event and punishment which is intended to instruct, to mature, and to change the behavior of erring Christians. It provides a teaching lesson that sin has consequences in which I will provide an overview of the consequences of sin concerning spiritual death, physical death, and lastly eternal death. It is interesting to note that a person who confesses to being a believer who continually lives in sin and does not experience God's chastisement there is evidence of his or her lack of salvation (12:8).

The Consequence of Sin in the Garden of Eden (Gen. 3: 7 – 24)

After Adam and Eve disobeyed God's Word and ate of the forbidden fruit they immediately experienced the consequences of their sin. First, their eyes were opened and for the first time, there was recognition of nudity. This was part of the new knowledge that was gained. Their former healthy relationship had then become something unseemly, shameful, and embarrassing. Their innocence was lost.

God walked in the garden and called out to Adam. He and Eve were attempting to alleviate the situation by making aprons of leaves to hide their nakedness (self-atoning). They had an opportunity to admit their sin to God but decided to try to hide from Him (Gen. 3: 7 – 8). However, God, being omniscient, knew where Adam was hiding. The call, and later the questions, were for Adam's benefit. This allowed Adam an opportunity to come clean and acknowledge his disobedience. Adam and Eve were shameful, remorseful, and guilty. They feared God and were unsuccessfully hiding from God. Hiding from God is impossible (Ps. 139: 1 – 12). When confronted by God, Adam admitted to being naked. God asked two questions: "Who told you that you were naked?" And "Have you eaten from the tree of which I commanded you that you should not eat?" Again, God being omniscient already knew the answers; however, this provided both Adam and Eve the opportunity to confess their sin of disobedience (Gen. 3: 9 – 11).

Instead of repenting of their sin, Adam and Eve attempted to justify their action by passing the buck of responsibility. Adam first blamed Eve: he even tried to implicate God. "The Woman You gave to be with me, she gave me of the tree, and I ate" (3:12). Eve responded by trying to lay the blame on Satan. "The serpent deceived me, and I ate" (3:13).

After hearing the oral argument of the guilty, God passed judgment on Adam, Eve, and Satan.

God declared the serpent's and Satan's judgment in verses fourteen and fifteen. The serpent will crawl on his belly and eat dust for his part in tempting Eve. God then turned from the curse of the serpent to the curse of Satan. This curse provides the first prophetic message of redemption and the enmity between "your seed" (Satan) and "her Seed" (The coming Savior). Although Satan and his followers will cause great pain and trouble by striking Christ's heel, God has predicted that "her Seed," the coming Savior, will bruise the head of Satan. The apostle Paul recounts this; "And the God of peace will crush Satan under your feet shortly" (Rom. 16: 20). This was accomplished at the cross.

God declared several judgments concerning Eve (Gen. 3:16). She placed the blame on the serpent, which was partially true (1 Tim 2:14). Nonetheless, she was not absolved from the responsibility for her distrust and disobedience toward God. Eve would conceive children and give birth in agony. Her relationship with Adam would change so that she would be subjective unto him.

Adam suffered judgment for his disobedience (Gen. 3: 17 – 19). There was a change in the soil resulting in much physical effort to maintain (3:17). Thorns and thistles will have to be removed from around the plants resulting in pain (3: 18), Adam will work by the sweat of his face (3:19a), and lastly, Adam will one day experience physical death (3:19b). The apostle responds with, "For the wages of sin is death" (Rom. 6:23), and "death came into the world through sin" (Rom. 5:12).

Adam and Eve were removed from the experience of comfort and beauty and the eternal sustaining life provided by the Tree of Life in the Garden of Eden (3: 22 – 24). After God drove them out, He placed an angel with a flaming sword to guard the way to the Tree of Life.[94] And as God told Adam earlier, "In the day that you eat thereof, you shall surely die" (Gen. 2:17). Adam and Eve ate of the Tree of the Knowledge of Good and Evil resulting in death.

I have questioned, just like many of you who are reading this book, why did God allow Satan to exist? I know God could take Satan out of the picture at the snap of a finger. One day, while reading Erwin Lutzer's book, *The Serpent of Paradise*, I realized the answer. In the introduction he quotes Martin Luther, "The devil is God's devil."[95] Then it hit me. Satan, even though he is evil and rebellious, is still used for God's purpose. I shared in a previous chapter that we demonstrate our love toward God through our obedience to Him and His Word. God has given us free will to choose; we are not forced to obey God. God allows Satan's existence to provide us a choice to obey or disobey. Adam's free will made it possible for him to sin apart from Satan. Satan just sped up the process.

DEATH: THE GREAT SEPARATION

In our culture, the term "death" is an unpleasant subject that implies the permanent cessation of all vital biological functions of the body, the end of life. Some envision death not only as of the cessation of the biological function (material) but that of the inner function (immaterial). Therefore, some believe that when he or she dies that the future anticipates nothingness. The way death was understood by the biblical Hebrew culture differs from our modern usage. The biblical meaning of death, in some cases, is defined as the cessation of the biological functions of the body. However, for one to truly understand biblical death he or she should note that the word at times denotes a physical implication, but most often it implies a relational function; that of separation. Oswald Chambers, referring to death, states, "Our Lord makes little of physical death, but he makes more of moral and spiritual death."[96]

John MacArthur suggests that death, in its truest sense, is not the result of natural processes stemming from a random and chance universe. But that is the cause of sin. The death happened because the first man, Adam, sinned against God and death was the consequence.[97] William Dyer continues with MacArthur's thought, "Were it not for sin, death had never had a beginning, and was it not for death sin would never have had an ending."[98] When one analyzes death, he or she will discover that the Bible speaks of three deaths; spiritual death, physical death, and eternal death.

Spiritual Death (Gen. 2: 17)

When Adam and Eve sinned, physical death did not occur immediately. Adam lived for 930 years (Gen. 5:5). Nevertheless, spiritual death occurred instantly. Spiritual death is defined as "the state of spiritual alienation (separation) from God." Spiritual death is never defined as the actual death of a human being's spirit since his or her spirit, as part of the soul, never dies (Matt. 10:28). The individual can be physically alive while being spiritually dead. As a result of Adam's sin, all human beings are conceived and born in a state of spiritual separation (spiritual death) from God (Ps. 51:5; Rom. 5: 17 – 21).

Spiritual life is the antonym of spiritual death. One of the Greek words that reflect "life" in the biblical language is *zoe* or *zoepoiein*. There are several definitions of this Greek word, such as a manner of life, conduct, in moral respect (Rom. 6:4; Eph. 4:18); A godly life (2 Pet. 1:3); A blessed and satisfying life. However, *zoepoiein* (spiritual life) like spiritual death is relational. It is the quickening (making alive relationally of the soul) of the indwelling Spirit of God (Eph. 2:5).[99] Unlike spiritual life, spiritual death is the separation or alienation of the soul from God. This deadness renders unregenerate individuals unresponsive to spiritual truths (Rom. 8: 7 – 8; 1 Cor. 2:14; 2 Cor. 4; 4; Eph. 4: 17 – 18). Adam experienced spiritual death immediately after his sin. He lost his innocence and righteous standing before God and his communicable attributes of God were now defiled. Adam's nature was now depraved. However, Adam experienced the quickening of the Spirit and his soul was made spiritually alive (1 Cor. 15:45), but he continued to suffer the consequence of his sin.

Physical Death

As God judged Adam and Eve as recorded in Genesis 3, He did not impose physical death on Adam and Eve immediately. But the process of physical death that began when Adam sinned gradually and ultimately became reality. Adam surely died. The judgment of God's decree against Adam in Genesis 3:24 "In the sweat of your face you shall eat bread till you return to the ground, for out of it you were taken; for dust you are, and to dust, you shall return " was irrevocable. God removed them from the Garden of Eden and the Tree of Life (Gen. 3:24) resulting in the subsequent deterioration of their bodies which eventually led to physical death when major organs such as the brain and heart cease to function. Physical death is the temporary cessation of the person's material substance body.

One of the consequences of sin is that all men will die physically, the Bible states, "As it is appointed that all men to die once but after this the judgment" (Heb. 9:27). This is a reference to the first bodily, physical death. Unless the rapture takes place, all men have been appointed to experience physical death and all will stand before our Lord, either at the Judgment Seat or the Great White Throne to be judged.

The Intermediate State of the Unbeliever: Physical death (separation of the body from the soul) is the beginning of eternal death for the unbeliever; it is somewhat like the pretrial detention of a lawbreaker. He or she is held there until the trial. However, unlike a lawbreaker in this age who stands before the judge to hear a guilty or not guilty judgment, the unbelievers have already been found guilty for rejecting Christ (John 3:18). They will only stand before the Lord to hear his or her verdict of guilty (Matt. 7: 21 -23; John 12:48; Rev. 20: 11-15).

The Biblical languages for some references of hell and the grave are (Gk. *Hades*) and (Heb. *Sheol*). Luke provides a glimpse of the grave in his parable of Lazarus and the rich man (Luke 16: 19 -31). Some argue that this was not a parable but rather an actual event since, unlike other parables, the Lord provided names of some of the main participants. The glimpse of the realm of the dead (often translated as "the grave") took place before our Lord died on the cross and was resurrected. This passage of Scripture is a revelation that those who are not believers will suffer. The rich man died, and his material body was buried (16:22). Nonetheless, his immaterial spirit was in hades. There the rich man was in agony. He thirsted and was tormented in the flame (16: 24 -18). He exhibited a conscience and memory evidenced by his concern for his brothers. I believe that the unbelievers will somehow re-live their life through their memory and weep over the opportunities they had to accept Christ as their Savior. Some may even remember that they were warned that someday they will stand before the Lord at the Great White Throne Judgement; the initiation of eternal death (the second death).

The Intermediate State of the Believer: Physical death for the righteous is the separation of the fleshly body from the soul. Once their righteous die their souls will be in the presence of the Lord (1 Cor. 5:3). The righteous shall one day stand before God at the Judgment Seat of Christ (Rom. 14:10). Every name of those standing before Christ, the Judge, will be found in the Book of Life. This is not a judgment of judicial guilt but one of the rewards for works that have been tested for the right motivation, reason, and obedience to Christ. (Rom. 14:10; 2 Cor. 5:10; Phil. 1:22-24). The believers will live a conscious, peaceful existence in heaven immediately after physical death.

Some erroneously teach that a believer will experience "soul sleeping." This is a false view that suggests that when a person dies, he or she ceases to exist until Jesus returns and his or her body is resurrected. Nonetheless, the Bible provides ample evidence that believers in heaven will be able to hear and speak (Rev. 6:11), they will wear clothes of white robes (Rev. 6:11), they can be seen, which suggests some kind of form (Rev. 6:9). All believers will receive a glorified body at the rapture (1 Cor. 15:44; Phil. 3:20-21).

The present intermediate heaven, where the saints live after physical death, is not their final destination. They will have to return to earth for a time during the millennial reign with Christ (Rev. 5:10). The believers' final state will be in a new heaven (2 Pet. 3:13; Rev. 21:1).

Eternal Death (or State)

Adam temporarily experienced spiritual death, and several centuries' later, physical death. Nonetheless, there is another death that Adam will not experience. The Scriptures refer to this as the Second Death (Rev. 20:6, 14; 21:8). This is the abode for those who physically die while being spiritually dead. Those who die in unbelief will suffer in the lake of fire forever (Rev. 20: 11 – 15) banished from God eternally. Jesus refers to this hell as *gehenna*. Jesus uses a word picture so that His listeners understood that the death of the non-believer is not a cessation of life but, instead, eternal torment. "*Gehenna*" originally referred to the Valley of Hinnon near Jerusalem. The residents sacrificed their children by fire to the god Molek (2 Chron. 28:3; 33:6) which was an abomination. At some point, the Hebrews made the city into a garbage dump in which they cast dead animals and sometimes deceased non- Jews, along with the trash to burn it. There was a perpetual fire. Jesus used this term to describe hell as an enveloping, unquenchable fire (Matt. 18:8-9; Mark 9:42-43, 48), a place where the worm does not die (Mark 9:48). Therefore, the unbelieving dead must receive some type of physical body that will be able to burn for eternity and yet never be consumed or burnt up. This will be a place of weeping and the pain will be so unbearable that there will be "gnashing of the teeth" (Matt. 8:12). Eternal death does not result in the cessation of existence; it is considered a death since it involves everlasting ruin, punishment for sin, and most importantly, the separation from God's grace, mercy, and presence forever. Those who experience physical death but are spiritually alive will escape eternal death, or eternal existence in the everlasting fire of hell forever.

The beginning of eternal death starts at The Great White Throne judgment where those who had previously relied on false hope (this was discussed in chapter one) will stand before the Lord. They had relied on some sort of works for their salvation. In Revelation 20:15, John reveals that the Books of Works (the books) will be open. Each individual's thoughts, actions, good works, and sins will come to light. It is stated that another book will be opened which is the Book of Life. It is a reminder that only individuals named and who had responded in faith and repentance when convicted by the Holy Spirit will be found in that Book and will escape the everlasting death. The names of those present at this judgment will not be found in the Book of Life. They now realize that all the accomplishments of their life listed in the Books of Works were never enough. They are not standing before the Lord waiting to hear if they will go to heaven or hell. That judgment was made when they refused God. Their judgment is a profound "guilty" and their punishment is eternal hellfire separated from God. The torments of death in the grave (the realm of the dead) are different from that of the eternal flames in hell.

The Anonym of Eternal Death is Eternal Life.

Some erroneously believe that at some point all men and women will go to heaven. This belief is usually referred to as "universalism." The most popular view of universalism was proclaimed by Origen (born around A.D. 185 or 186). He taught that the punishment of the wicked in which the Bible speaks will not be some form of eternal suffering, but temporary internal anguish occasioned by their sense of separation from God. He conjectured that the purpose was that of purification and that at some point the condition would come to an end, and all things will be restored to their original condition, thereby that individual would experience universal salvation.[100] Allison defines universalism as:

> The position that if not in life, then after death, all people will ultimately embrace salvation... Universalism fails to respect death as the point at which human destiny, based on one's faith in Christ during one's lifetime, is fixed (Heb. 9:27) The church's historic position, that only believers will be saved, has always included a denunciation of universalism. [101]

Some falsely believe that God's love would not allow a person to suffer for eternity. They refuse to accept that God's justice requires it. Only individuals who have experienced God's authentic salvation before physical death will spend eternal life with God in heaven.

Heaven is the abode and realm of God in His complete glory. It is in heaven that God manifests His supreme majesty and is worshipped for His glorious revelation. Heaven is a real place for believers to fellowship with God for eternity (Rev. 21). Heaven is not only a real place filled with God's presence, it is also an emotional state where God's people will experience eternal blessings and happiness (Rev. 21). There will be a new heaven after the millennium (Rev. 21: 1). It will be there that believers will spend eternity with God (eternal life).

The day that Adam and Eve ate of the forbidden fruit, they died spiritually and required the quickening of the Holy Spirit. Later Adam would experience physical death and be in the presence of the Lord. In the next chapter, we will observe how Adam's sin affects all mankind and how the consequences relate to each individual.

CHAPTER SIX

The Fall: The Importance of Imputation

Therefore, just as through one man sin entered the world, and death through sin, and thus death spread to all men, because all have sinned (For until the law sin was in the world, but sin is not imputed when there is no law. Nevertheless, death reigned from Adam to Moses, even over those who had not sinned according to the likeness of the transgression of Adam, who is a type of Him who was to come. But the free gift is not like the offense. For if by one man's offenses many died, much more the grace of God and the gift by the grace of the one Man, Jesus Christ abounded to many. And the gift is not like that which came through the one who sinned. For the judgment which came from one offense resulted in condemnation, but the free gift which came from many offenses resulted in justification. For if by one man's offense death reigned through the one, much more those who receive abundance of grace and the gift of righteousness will reign in life through the One, Jesus Christ. Therefore, as through one man's

offense judgment came to all men, resulting in condemnation, even so through one Man's righteous act
the free gift came to all men, resulting in justification of life. For as by one man's disobedience many
were made sinners, so also by one Man's obedience
many will be made righteous. Moreover, the law
entered that the offense might abound. But where
sin abounded, grace abounded much more, so that
as sin reigned in death, even so grace might reign
through righteousness to eternal life through Jesus
Christ our Lord. Rom. 5: 12–21

Some years back I was watching a World War II movie that
was the focus of a German prisoner of war camp. In the
movie a man and his teenage son, who had been part of a
civilian army, were captured and marched into the POW camp.
When the teen son marched by the prison's commanding officer
made some sort of smart-alecky comment resulting in the commanding officer forcing the teen out of line and having him
placed on his knees to be executed. The father of the son ran
to the commanding officer begging him to not shoot his son.
He asked the officer if he had any children, to which the officer
replied "Yes." The father further asked the officer if he would
be willing to give his life for his children in which the officer
nodded in the affirmative. The father, almost begging, asked the
officer to take his life so that his son may live. The officer looked
upon the man in admiration and nodded yes. The son watched
as his father was executed for something that he, the son, was
guilty of committing. The father was completely innocent; his
only crime was the love of his son. This is an example of the
imputation of Christ's righteousness where the innocent take
responsibility, the culpability, and the punishment for one who

has been rightly judged guilty. Christ gave His life so that others would not have to die an eternal death (separated from God for eternity). This chapter is the foremost chapter of this section of the book (Chapters two through six). It answers the question, "Why are all human beings in need of salvation?" We will understand the answer by reviewing the meaning and importance of imputation after we review some of the former chapters.

I have presented the following main storyline of the Bible in the last several chapters. God wants to be known and to have an intimate relationship with all humankind. While detailing His communicable attributes the reader was made aware of God's attribute of righteousness. As God, who is righteous, He must bring the sin of the guilty person into account. I revealed how Satan's goals were first to plant seeds of discontent in the mind of Adam and Eve so that they might be separated from God, and second, cause God to destroy His creation. Satan was successful with this first goal when Adam and Eve succumbed. However, Satan failed his second goal which was to cause God to destroy His creation. I shared how man was made in God's image and as His viceroy, man is His representative.

Before the Fall, Adam was created in a state of righteousness and lived a life of perfection. In chapter four the reader observed the temptation of Adam and Eve by Satan. They both succumbed to the temptation and their nature became depraved, therefore they lost their righteous perfection and innocent state before God. They both experienced spiritual death immediately and several centuries' later, physical death. God shed the blood of innocent animals to provide clothing and spiritual life. In the last chapter, the reader observed the consequence of sin. This chapter will detail how the sin of Adam and Eve affects all of humankind and what it means to all. The reader will have a full understanding of his or her plight and recognize how Adam was the federal head of mankind and how that knowledge helps him or her to see why he or she needs Christ as Savior.

Afterward, I will define imputation, and then follow-up with that which was imputed to all men from Adam and what needed to be imputed unto Christ and what He imputed to all who believe.

The Transmission of Adam's Sin

Some may ask, "How does Adam's sin affect all born after him?" Scholars often refer to this reality as "original sin." In one sense, original sin refers to the first sin committed by Adam. However, original sin also incorporates the sinful state and condition of all humankind because of their relationship with Adam. Later, I will discuss how this is the reason that all people possess a depraved and tainted nature. The reader may note that while there is a connection between Adam's sin and the sinfulness of his descendants many have a false notion, or view, as to what the connection may be. Note the following views:

- **Unexplained Solidarity View:** This view suggests that there is vague solidarity between Adam and every human being born after him that cannot be explained or ever known.[102] The problem with this view is that the Scriptures provide much information on the subject.

- **Bad Example View:** This view suggests that Adam's sin was a bad example. That he provided a precedent that others should not follow. They submit that humans are not guilty for Adam's sin, nor have they inherited a sinful nature from him. They suggest that no transmission of sin exists between humankind and Adam. This view was first proposed by Pelagius (354 AD – 420), as a British monk, who taught in Rome, he rejected any doctrine that taught that all humans possess a sin nature or that man experiences death as a result of sin. He submitted that every soul was created innocent and unstained. His beliefs are contrary to the Scriptures, such as Man dies because of sin (Rom. 6:23) and man does have a sinful nature (Rom. 3: 19-18).[103]

- **Inherited Sin Nature View:** This view confirms that all humans inherit a sinful nature from Adam, resulting in every human being conceived with a disposition that is bent toward sin. This view expresses the fact that Adam passes on a corrupt nature to the human race. However, this view denies that Adam's "guilt" was placed upon all humanity. John MacArthur states, "Some who hold this view acknowledges that the inherited sinful nature is enough to render a person condemned by God as a sinner, but they maintain that such condemnation is not on account of Adam's guilt being imputed or reckoned to his descendants."[104] Jacob Arminius (1560 – 1609) was a Dutch theologian who taught that men and women were not considered guilty because of Adam's sin. He believed each individual had to voluntarily and purposefully choose to sin and until that decision was made, they were capable to live righteously.

Although this view affirms that all humans have a corrupt nature from Adam, it does not recognize total depravity (more on this later) nor does it go far enough to recognize that Adam's sin directly brings guilt to all people (Rom. 5:18). It is like baking a cake without the ingredient of sugar, it may look like a cake, but it most definitely does not taste like a cake.[105] The inherited sin nature view lacks the ingredient of Adam's guilt.

- **Realism or the Augustinian View:** This view asserts that all humanity was physically present in Adam when he sinned. As the first man, Adam collectively embodied human nature, of which all his descendants are part. John MacArthur, who does not accept this view, states, "This means that Adam's descendants were in Adam's loins participating in his sin. And since everyone participated in Adam's sin, all people are morally guilty and condemned for doing so. Thus, both the corrupt nature and guilt are passed down naturally from Adam."[106]

Augustin (A. D. 354 – 430) taught that all humanity was "seminally present" in Adam when Adam sinned and therefore all humanity participated in the sin. Although this view provides the truth that guilt and condemnation are deserved because all have sinned,[107] this view is weak in that it suggests that all humanity was "present" when Adam sinned. However, it is my understanding that I was not "present" with Adam but rather represented by Adam. MacArthur provides another shortfall of this view:

> The union between Christ and His people is not a seminal union, for Christ fathered no physical children. Rather, it is a legal union. As our representative,

Christ's obedience is counted – legally imputed or judicially reckoned – by God to be our obedience. [We will discuss imputation in more detail later]. For the parallel between the first and last Adam to hold together (Rom. 5:12 – 21; cf. 1 Cor. 15:45), Adam's sin must be transmitted in the same manner as Christ's righteousness is. Therefore, because Adam was the representative of all humanity, his disobedience is counted – legally imputed or judicially reckoned – by God to be the disobedience of all who were with him. Those who would charge that such imputation is wrong, or inappropriate, because not everyone actually participated in Adam's sin show their inconsistency when they do not make the same charge against the imputation of Christ's righteousness.[108]

- **Federal or Representative Headship View:** This acceptable view asserts that Adam is seen as the "federal head" or "representative" of the entire human race. Federal headship means that the action of a representative is determinative for all members united with him or her. Therefore, when Adam sinned, he represented all humanity, resulting in his sin being reckoned (imputed) to his descendants. Paul Enns explains in detail, "As a result of Adam's sin, since he was the representative of the human race, his sin plunged the entire human race into suffering and death. Through the one sin of Adam, sin and death are imputed to all humanity because all humanity was represented in Adam."[109] This view further affirms that a corrupt nature is passed down to all humanity from Adam and that Adam's guilt is all humanity's guilt.[110]

Evidence for the Federal Headship View: The Scriptures provide examples of federal headship. In Joshua chapter seven, Israel's defeat was attributed to Achan for his disobedience to God when he confiscated silver and gold for himself. Achan alone was responsible for his disobedience, yet his sons and daughters bore his punishment when they were executed with him (Josh. 7: 24 – 25).

First Corinthians 15: 21 – 22 provides conclusive evidence that Adam "represented" all mankind. Paul attributes all death to Adam, noting that death came through one man (Adam). Yet, Paul suggests, that the work of another man (Christ) provides resurrection from that death.

Additional Evidence of Adam's representing of all humankind is provided from Romans 5:12 – 21. Paul begins this passage by presenting the facts of death entered through one man (Adam). This death was the judgment placed upon Adam in which every human being suffers (Rom. 5:12). To fully appreciate verses thirteen and fourteen it helps to understand the Jewish customs of that day. The Mosaic Law enabled God to record, for the first time, sin as a violation of His specific commands and violations. Paul was not denying the personal responsibilities of Adam's descendants before the law. He knew that the Jewish inter- preters agreed that Adam brought sin into the world, but they also suggest that each of Adam's descendants made their own choice to follow in Adam's footsteps.[111] MacArthur explains, "This verse explicitly teaches that Adam's offspring did not commit Adam's sin. So, Adam relates to his offspring as their representative head, and thus the act of Adam is imputed to others, even though the others did not commit the sin that Adam did."[112]

Paul reveals that by one man's sin (Adam) many died (Rom. 5:15). What does Paul mean by "the many?" Greek language scholar, William Mounce, suggests that the Greek word is *hoi polloi*. Mounce suggests that Paul is drawing a contrast between "the one" and "the many." "The many" here has the nuance of "all in a group," for just as "the many/all" became sinners through the one man Adam and are subject to death (Adam's guilt), so also through the one Man Jesus, the offer of salvation by grace "goes out" to "the many." Mounce furthers explains that Paul is careful not to suggest that the same number who are dead in Adam will be saved by Christ, but only those who have a relationship with Jesus by faith. If it was the same number, then Paul would be teaching universalism. Mounce states that the passage in the Biblical Greek language "the many" who are saved in Christ is a more limited number than "the many" who are condemned in Adam.[113] Who are "the many" that are condemned in Adam? Every individual born after Adam makes up the many; "for all have sinned and fall short of the glory of God" (Rom. 3:23). "For God so loved the world [all of the universe] that He gave His only begotten Son" (John 3:16).

The following is evidence of Adam's headship before the Fall suggested by David Mapes:

- Adam was created first. Paul uses this line of reasoning in 2 Timothy to establish the male-female roles in the church.
- Headship was assigned by God (1 Cor. 11).

- Eve was taken out of Adam. Adam is the only being created from "scratch." All other people come from Adam. Therefore, this makes Adam the head of the human race.
- Eve was Adam's helpmeet.
- Adam named the animals and had dominion over them. He even named Eve demonstrating his headship over her.
- Eve sinned first, but it was Adam who was held accountable (Romans 5:12).
- God holds Adam accountable for all mankind. Adam is the head of the human race which means that whatever Adam does, his actions will stand for all humanity.[114]

The Meaning of Imputation

The word "imputation" means "to regard, reckon, or credit something to someone that comes from another." Suppose someone owed a large debt and found that there was no way of ever paying on time. Then another person takes the debt upon himself or herself and pays the debt for them. This is an example of imputation. Biblically, this may be a positive or negative experience. Humanity experiences the negative of imputation when Adam's depraved nature and guilt was placed on each individual. However, those who are believers can experience the positive when they enjoy the imputation of Christ's righteousness.

The Scriptures reveal that all humankind has inherited the consequences of Adam's sin through the imputation of Adam's Guilt and his nature.

The Imputation of Adam's Guilt

The apostle Paul explains the imputed guilt of Adam in the following way: "Therefore, just as through one man [Adam] sin entered the world, and death through sin, and thus death spread to all men because all sinned" (Rom. 5:12). Sin and guilt may sometimes seem similar in meaning. But there is a distinction between the two. Often, guilt is thought of as a feeling of remorse. However, Biblical guilt is defined as a legal verdict or judgment. Legally before God, all men and women have been judged guilty as a result of Adam's sin. In clarifying the difference, sin is a violation of God's divine demands or Word (this is what a person does, or does not do), whereas guilt is the resulting state, or one's "legal status (what a person has become as a result of their sin), in essence, one commits sin and becomes guilty (Hab. 1:11).[115]Paul is indicating that through Adam's sin, the judgment on all humanity is death; "because all sinned." The punishment for our guilt is death; physical (soul and spirit separated from the body) and eternal (living external separation from God in torment). Paul further illuminates this thought, "Therefore, as through one man's offense [Adam] judgment came to all men, resulting in condemnation" (5:18). Paul expresses the fact that since Adam represented all humankind that all of humanity is condemned as a result of his sin. The penalty of sin is legal guilt resulting in condemnation. Wayne Grudem clarifies it this way:

> The conclusion to be drawn from these verses is that all members of the human race were represented by Adam in the time of testing in the Garden of Eden. As our representative, Adam sinned, and God counted us guilty as well as Adam. (A technical term

that is sometimes used in this connection is *imputed*, the meaning "to think of as belonging to someone, and therefore to cause it to belong to that person.") God counted Adam's guilt as belonging to us, and since God is the ultimate judge of all things in the universe, and since his thoughts are always true, Adam's guilt does belong to us. God rightly imputed Adam's guilt to us.[116]

The Imputation of Adam's Nature

In addition to the legal guilt that has been imputed to all human-kind because of Adam's sin, everyone (past and present) has inherited a sinful and depraved nature. This nature is referred to by several different terms; "original pollution," and "inherited corruption." David provides a Biblical foundation for this sinful nature; "Behold, I was brought forth in iniquity, and in sin, my mother conceived me" (Ps. 51:5).

Our nature includes a temperament, or disposition, to sin. Paul affirms this:

> And you He made alive, who were dead in trespasses and sins, in which you once walked according to the course of this world, according to the prince of the power of the air, the spirit who now works in the sons of disobedience, among whom also we all once conducted ourselves in the lusts of our flesh, fulfilling the desires of the flesh and of the mind, and were by nature children of wrath, just as others. Eph. 2: 1 -3

Paul was referring to true Believers who were spiritually dead but now have been made alive by Christ when they believed (v-1). Before their authentic salvation, they lived according to the dictates of the world (society) and that of Satan (prince of the power of the air). The past disposition and temperament were that of conducting one's lifestyle according to the lusts and desires of the flesh and the mind. Those who are now believers previously lived according to the desires of their depraved nature. Later, Paul confesses that this inherited depraved nature came from one man's sin: Adam (Rom. 5:12).

I do not suggest that this inherited, and depraved tendency to sin means that human beings are all evil. I only suggest that no one in the past, present, or the future could ever be good enough to stand righteously before God. Paul admits, "But sin taking opportunity by the commandments, produced in me all manner of evil desire" (Rom. 7:8a), and, "For I know that in me (that is, in my flesh) nothing good dwells (Rom. 7:18a). Paul informs young Titus, "To the pure all things are pure, but to those who are defiled and unbelieving nothing is pure, but even their minds and conscience are defiled" (Tit. 1:15).

In earlier chapters of this book, the reader was informed that when Adam sinned in the Garden of Eden that his communicable attributes had been defiled and that his state of righteousness before God had been destroyed. One sin destroys righteousness; no one on his or her own can ever make it whole again. The prophet Isaiah made it plain, "But we are all an unclean thing, and all our righteousness are like filthy rags" (Isa. 64:6). Isaiah was confessing that all humankind is utterly unworthy to be in the presence of God.

This imputed condition of humanity is rightly referred to as total depravity. This means that every element of human nature is thoroughly infected with sin. Every aspect of the intellect, mind, reason, feelings, sentiments, will, motivation, and purpose experiences the devastating influence of the corruption of sin.[117] This is not to say that unbelievers cannot perform good works in society. However, they cannot accomplish spiritual good or be good in terms of a relationship with God. One must stand before God righteous. Unbelievers are spiritually dead and possess a darkened understanding of God and are alienated from a life of Godliness. Speaking of the unbelievers, Paul writes, "Having their understanding darkened, being alienated from the life of God, because of the ignorance that is in them, because of the blindness of their hearts" (Eph. 4:18).

Because of the inherited sinful nature that has been passed down from Adam, no man or woman could do anything that will please God or have the ability to come to God in his or her personal strength. Paul makes this point, "So then, those who are in the flesh cannot please God" (Rom. 8:8). So, where does that leave us?

This is a devastating and chilling meaning! First, all humanity has been judged and found guilty; the penalty is physical death in this world, and eternal death in the flames of hell separated from God in the next. Second, because of our depraved nature and unrighteousness, there is absolutely nothing that humanity may do that will save us from the judgment and wrath to come. It is entirely hopeless! Nonetheless, though no one may save themselves, there is another who can bring salvation from the wrath to come. That someone is Jesus. He alone may bring redemption from the guilt of sin. There is no other name in which a person may be saved (Acts 4: 12). Jesus, the Christ, provided salvation and redemption while on the cross-making atonement for our sins. In doing so He provided imputation for all who believe by faith.

The Imputation of Christ

The good news of the Gospel is that God can declare a believing person righteous by imputing Christ's righteousness to those who believe. Paul wrote, "Abraham believed God, and it was accounted to him as righteousness." (Rom. 4:3). Paul clarifies:

> But to him who does not works but believes on Him who justifies the ungodly, his faith is accounted for righteousness, just as David also describes the blessedness of the man whom God imputes righteousness apart from works: "Blessed are those whose lawless deeds are forgiven and whose sin are covered. Blessed is the man to whom the LORD shall not impute sin." Rom. 4:6 – 8

Paul reminded the believers that no one can make himself or herself righteous before God (Rom. 1:18; 3:20) and that all have sinned and fall short of God's glory (Rom. 3: 23). Nonetheless, every believer is justified freely by grace through the redemptive act of Christ Jesus (Rom. 3: 24). Christ's righteousness became ours when we believed. It became the free gift of righteousness (Rom. 5: 17). God declares us (the unjust) as just and righteous not based on our actual non-righteous condition but rather based on Christ's perfect righteousness which God considers as belonging to the believers after it was imputed to each. The moment a person trusts Christ an amazing thing takes place.

The sin guilt that was imputed to all men from Adam is now imputed onto Christ when we believe. Christ has taken our guilt upon Himself.

But how did this happen? How did Christ make atonement for our sins? This leads us to the next section of the book which answers the question of how Christ made atonement so that we might experience His imputation of righteousness and what the results of this atonement were?

Who Made Atonement for Sin?

> Being justified freely by His grace through the
> redemption that is in Christ Jesus, whom God set
> forth as a propitiation by His blood, through faith,
> to demonstrate His righteousness, because in His
> forbearance God has passed over the sins that were
> previously committed, to demonstrate at this present
> time His righteousness, that He might be the just
> and justifier of the one who has faith in Jesus. Rom.
> 3: 24 – 26

Part two consists of three chapters. Although part three left
the reader with no hope, part four provides hope for all who,
by faith, believe in Christ. The writer examines the necessary
atonement of Christ; the meaning, nature, extent, and the
atoning work of Christ on the cross.

CHAPTER SEVEN

The Atoning Work of Christ on the Cross

Being justified freely by His grace through the redemption that is in Christ Jesus, whom God set forth as a propitiation by His blood, through faith, to demonstrate His righteousness, because in His forbearance God has passed over the sins that were previously committed, to demonstrate at this present time His righteousness, that He might be the just and the justifier of the one who has faith in Jesus. Rom. 3: 24 – 26

A few months after I had begun my ministry as an Associational Missionary, my wife, who was my office assistant at the time, put out one of her first newsletters. One Easter article dealt with the death and resurrection of Christ, so she thought it would be fitting to include a picture of Christ on the cross to remind the readers that He had risen. However, one of the pastors was quick to give her a piece of his mind. How could she print, as he described, a Catholic cross in the newsletter? He made the false allegation that Baptists only presented an empty cross since Christ had arisen from the dead.

Yes, in most situations the cross that is presented in Baptist Churches has no image of Christ. Nevertheless, I have witnessed many churches that have presented Christ dying on the cross (sometimes live reenactments) during the Easter events. My question is this, "what is wrong with the average church member being reminded of the atoning work of Christ on the cross?" After all, when we partake in the ordinance of baptism are we being reminded not only of Christ's resurrection but His death? When we participate in the Lord's Supper (some denominations refer to this as the Eucharist), isn't it a reminder of Christ's shed blood and torn flesh? Throughout the rest of this chapter I will address the definition of atonement, its use in the Old Testament including the importance of shedding blood and its use in the New Testament, discussing the necessity, the suffering, the shame, and the grace of the cross.

The Definition of Atonement

The word itself is relatively recent. It was an innovation of William Tyndale in 1526 when he substituted the Latin word *reconciliation* when translating the first New Testament English translation printed by the printing press. He combined two words, "at" and "onement," to capture the deeper significance of the work of Christ on the cross.[118]While speaking of the definition of atonement, Oswald Chambers states, "When we are filled with the Holy Spirit, He unites our body, soul, and spirit with God until we are one with God even as Jesus was. This is the meaning of atonement – at-onement with God."[119]Gregg Allison defines it as, "The death of Christ on the cross, and what it accomplished. Because of human fallenness, a sacrifice for sin is necessary to avert condemnation and restore people to God. Old Covenant sacrifices made provisional atonement, looking forward to the work of Christ: His death brought propitiation, expiation, redemption, and reconciliation."[120]

There are several incorrect views concerning the atonement in which I will endeavor to provide a summary.

The Atonement as an Example View: This is found among the Unitarian belief system. They propose that God is not a God of retribution or justice and therefore requires no satisfaction from sinners or someone on their behalf. They insist that Jesus was just a man. Although His death was the supreme act of His devotion to the Father, it was simply what mankind experiences in a sinful world. His death, according to them, was not to be looked upon as an offer of a substitutional sacrifice for sin, but only as an example of the type of dedication that should be characteristic of everyone's life.[121]

The Moral Influence View: This theory places much emphasis on the love of God and therefore, according to this view, the death of Christ on the cross was only an expression of God's love of humanity, rather than His holiness. This theory rejected any idea that God demanded any form of compensation for sin.[122]

The Ransom View or the Atonement as a Rescue from Satan View: This view advocates that Satan holds people captive as a victor in war. Therefore, a ransom must be paid to Satan rather than God. The fallacy of this view is that it is God's holiness, not Satan's that was offended; thereby, payment was to be made to God to avert His wrath against the penalty of sin. It should be noted that Satan has no power to free anyone. God alone has this power.

The Government View: David Mapes best explains this incorrect view with the following statement:

> God is ruler over this world and has established certain laws by which His creation must follow. To break these rules makes one liable for punishment... God... is a ruler and must act in a way to uphold the interest of a moral government. Therefore, He must punish sin. The death of Christ was a demonstration of the justice of God. God demonstrated His hatred for sin through the death of Christ. When a person sees what Christ had to suffer for sin, it ought to deter us from continuing to sin and cause us to come to God and receive forgiveness for our sins. Christ did not take our punishment, for only the guilty party can rightly be punished.[123]

This view denies the imputation of one's sin upon Christ and the imputation of His righteousness when one believes by faith. There are many other incorrect views which we will not cover. Nonetheless, David Mapes points out how one's view of the atonement is often shaped by his view of God:

> One's view of the atonement is shaped by his or her theological view of God, Christ, and man. If God is like your kindly grandfather, then he will not require much from you and will be willing to overlook sin. If God is love, then surely he will not demand a payment that we cannot pay. If God is holy and just, then mankind has a problem with sin. If Christ is just a man, then whatever Christ does is simply an example for us. However, if Christ is

God the Son, then He can do what no man can do. If man has not been affected by Adam's fall, then all he needs is encouragement or an example by which he can come to God. On the other hand, if man is totally depraved, then he is going to need help to come to God.[124]

The Penal Substitutional Views of the Atonement: This is the correct biblical view of the atonement. It advocates the position that sin is the breaking of God's law, therefore deserving of physical, spiritual, and eternal death (Rom. 6:23) since all have sinned (Rom. 3:23), and in the context of the wrath of God against sin (Rom. 1: 18), that Christ freely offered Himself to suffer and die on the cross to bear the full penalty for sin in the place of all sinners who would accept His free gift of salvation.

Atonement in the Old Testament

The atoning death of Christ is better understood from the background of the Old Testament sacrificial system. Before the Lord's atoning death, sacrifices needed to be offered to compensate for sin, which inherently deserved punishment and needed to be set right.

The Hebrew word most often used is *kaphar* and its derivatives. The word means "to cover." Millard Erickson states, "One was delivered from punishment by the interposing of something between one's sin and God. God then saw the atoning sacrifice rather than the sin. The covering of the sin meant that the penalty no longer had to be exacted from the sinner."[125]

Sacrifices were offered to appease God (Job 42:8) and as a substitute for the sinner. It bore the sinner's guilt. For the sacrifice to be effective there had to be some connection or commonality between the victim and the sinner for whom it was offered. Erickson provided the necessary factors for the sacrifice to accomplish its intended effect:

> The sacrificial animal had to be spotless, without blemish. The one for whom atonement was being made had to present the animal and lay hands on it: "You must present it at the entrance to the tent of meeting...You are to lay your hand on the head of the burnt offering, and it will be accepted on your behalf to make atonement for you" (Lev. 1: 3-4). This bringing of the animal and laying hands constituted a confession of guilt on the part of the sinner. The laying on of hands symbolized a transfer of guilt from the sinner to the victim. Then the offering or sacrifice was accepted by the priest.[126]

The Old Testament pictures with clarity the sacrifice and substitutional character of Christ's death on the cross. There is an established connection between the Old Testament sacrifices and Christ's death found in Isaiah 53. This chapter describes the person of the Messiah and indicates the nature and the extent of the sinners' iniquity, "But He was wounded for our transgressions, He was bruised for our iniquities; the chastisement for our peace was upon Him. And by His stripes, we are healed. All we like sheep have gone astray; we have turned every one, to his own way; And the LORD has laid on Him the iniquity of us all" (Isa. 53: 5 – 6).[127]

The Day of Atonement

There is much that one can learn concerning the atonement that was provided by Christ on the cross from the Old Testament's "Day of Atonement," found in Leviticus, chapter 16. Only once a year the High Priest would enter the inner sanctuary of the temple; any other time would result in his death. On this day he would cleanse and purify himself and put on a holy linen tunic and trousers along with some other holy garments so that he could make reconciling sacrifices for his and his family's sin and for the sins of the entire nation of Israel in which he represented Lev. 16: 1 – 5).

In preparation for the sacrifices, he was instructed to gather a young bull to be utilized as a sin offering and a ram for a burnt offering (v-3), and two kid goats, one for the use of a sin offering and the other for the use of a scapegoat (v -5). Aaron used the bull as a sin offering to make atonement for himself and his family (v-6, 11). Aaron took some of the blood of the bull and sprinkled it with his finger on the mercy seat and before the mercy seat seven times (v – 14). After Aaron prepared himself ritually with the bull's shed blood, he proceeded to make atonement for the nation by presenting the two kid goats before the LORD at the door of the tabernacle of meetings (v-7). Aaron was instructed by God to cast lots between the two kid goats to decide which one would be presented before the LORD as a sin offering and which one would be presented as a scapegoat (v – 8–10). Aaron laid one hand on the head of the goat signifying the imputation of the nation's sins and then presented it as the sin offering to the LORD by slaying it and offering its blood behind the veil. The blood was sprinkled before and on the mercy seat and the horns on the altar for the atonement for the people of the nation Israel (v- 15 – 18).

After the sin offering was presented Aaron was instructed to take the scapegoat (the live goat) and placed both hands upon the head of the animal signifying that all of the sins of the people were now imputed, or placed upon the goat (v-20). The goat was led into the wilderness, or uninhabited land, and set loose, signifying that all the sins and guilt were removed and separated from the people (vs- 21 – 22).

Year after year these sacrifices were offered on the Day of Atonement. Every year the sins of the people of Israel came before God. Every year these sins had to once more be covered by offering the same kind of offering they offered the previous year. Later, we will discover that the New Testament writer would point back to the Day of Atonement as symbolic of the atonement of Christ on the cross (Heb. 13: 11- 12; 2 Cor. 5: 21).

Why Blood?

The Old Testament provides the importance of blood sacrifice. "For the life of the flesh is in the blood, and I have given it to you upon the altar to make atonement for the soul" (Lev. 17:11). Blood transmits life-sustaining elements to all areas of the body; therefore, it represents the essence of life. Because of this importance, the Jewish people were forbidden to eat blood (17, 10 & 12). Blood is the source of life. Mark Rooker explains the meaning of this verse:

> Blood and life are associated...and thus under-
> stood as parallel in meaning...Because of this close

association blood is considered the source of life, and because blood represents life (Gen. 9:4; Deut. 12:23), it may expiate [recompense or atone] for life. Because the life of a creature is in the blood, blood makes atonement for one's life. One life sacrificed for another. The shedding of substitutionary blood on the altar makes atonement since the blood of the innocent victim was given for the life of the one who has sinned.[128]

Atonement in the New Testament

The New Testament illustrates the atonement in the context of the Old Testament sacrificial system. The New Testament asserts that the animal sacrifices of the Old Testament pointed to Jesus' sacrificial offering of Himself on the cross. Isaiah identified Christ as the Suffering Servant as he described the Messiah as a guilt offering (Isa. 53:10). John the Baptist emphasized the sacrificial nature of Christ by referring to Him as the "Lamb of God who takes away the sins of the world" (John 1:29). When referring to His sacrificial offering, Jesus stated, "I am the good shepherd, the good shepherd gives his life for his sheep" (John 10:11). The apostle Paul alludes to Christ as "our Passover," relating the atoning work of Christ to the sacrificial lamb (1 Cor. 5:7). Additionally, Paul provides Old Testament sacrificial language referring to the atonement of Christ as a "sweet-smelling aroma" offered to God (Eph. 5:2) as Peter uses such imagery of the believers being purchased by the "precious blood" of Christ (1 Pet. 1: 18-19).

The Book of Hebrews probably provides the best examples of the sacrificial nature of the atonement provided by Christ on the cross. The writer asserts that the shedding of the blood of animals was never sufficient to eradicate the guilt and sin of any human forever, although the person found forgiveness for his or her sin through the sacrifice (Rom. 4: 7 – 8) because God overlooked the sin until His Son came and paid for it (Rom. 3:25). In other words, the individual who came to God by faith was forgiven for his or her rebellion against God while one's still present sins were overlooked based upon the future work of Christ. Concerning the believing Old Testament saint's sin was not actually paid for; it was merely covered until the sacrificial death of Christ. The guilt of sin remained on the forgiven believer's account in the Old Testament. God patiently overlooked this guilt knowing that His Son would pay for those sins of the believing person upon His death (Heb. 10:4; Rom. 3:25). The writer did not stop there but provided hope for those who had no hope. The crucifixion of Jesus Christ was the ultimate sacrifice that permanently dealt with sin once and for all, thus ending the sacrificial Old Testament System (Heb. 10: 11 – 12). Christ, as Priest, offered His sacrificial blood for the sins of the people who accepted His free gift as a once-for-all sacrifice (Heb.9:11 – 28). Christ's resurrection from the grave and death is the proof that God accepted His sacrifice (Heb. 5:7).[129]

The Blood of Christ

"The blood of Christ" was often referred to in the New Testament as an expression of the physical blood of Jesus shed on the cross as a sacrificial offering that affords full atonement for those who, by faith, accept God's free offer of salvation. A reference to the blood of Christ includes the reality that Jesus literally bled on the cross and died for sinners. This "blood" has the power to atone for all the sins of innumerable believers throughout the ages.

The actuality of "the blood of Christ" as a means of atonement (at-oneness) for sin has its origin in the Mosaic Law, especially in the "Day of Atonement" found in Leviticus 16 (previously discussed). Once a year, the high priest presented an offering of the blood of bulls and goats on the altar of the temple, for his and his family's sins, and that of the sins of all the people. In preparation, all things had to be cleansed with blood, for without the shedding of blood there is no forgiveness (Heb. 9:22; Lev. 17:11). The offerings were to be pure with no spot or blemishes on the outside. However, this blood offering was limited in its effectiveness and had to be offered annually again and again. Jesus's blood was perfect. Unlike Adam who had sinned and brought death into the world, Christ, the second Adam, never sinned but brought forth grace (Rom. 5). While the animal sacrifices were spotless outside, Christ was spotless on the inside; He was faultless. Therefore, the blood offered by Christ on the cross was "once and for all" and would never be shed again (Heb. 7:27).

The blood of Christ is the foundation of the New Covenant. On the night before Jesus went to the cross, He presented the cup of wine to His disciples and said, "This cup is the new covenant in My blood, which is shed [poured out] for you" (Luke 22:20). The wine symbolized the blood of Christ which would be poured out for all who would ever believe in Him. When Christ shed His blood on the cross, He discontinued the Old Covenant requirement for the continual sacrifices of animals. The blood of goats and bulls was not sufficient to cover the sins of the people, except temporarily, because sin against a holy and infinite God requires a holy and infinite sacrifice. The writer of Hebrews stated, "But in those sacrifices, there is a reminder of sins every year. For it is not possible that the blood of bulls and goats could take away sins" (Heb. 10: 3 -4). While the blood of bulls and goats was a "reminder" of sin, "the precious blood of Christ paid in full the debt of sin we owe to God, and we need no further sacrifices for sin.

The Cross of Christ

When speaking of the cross, David Watson provides a great picture of its importance, "The cross is a picture of violence, yet the key to peace, a picture of suffering, yet the key to healing, a picture of death, yet the key to life."[130] The Crucifixion was a Roman form of capital punishment of suffering and shame that was most painful and degrading; an agonizing death on the cross. The capital punishment began with the victim being scourged with a whip of nine tails, consisting of leather straps that had pieces of metal and bone attached to the ends that would rip the flesh of the body. The victim was then forced to carry the crossbeam to the execution site. A sign would be placed around the neck of the victim or fastened to the cross detailing the victim's crime. The victim would be stripped of his clothing and placed on the cross so that nails may be pounded into both his wrists and often one nail through his feet. The victim would have to force his body upward by pushing, in great agony, with his feet so that his body would rise, as to be able to breathe. In most cases, death was caused by the loss of blood circulation and coronary failure. Often this could take days before the victim would succumb to the agony. Sometimes the soldiers would break the victim's leg so that he could not push up to breathe to quicken the death.

Matthew shares additional suffering and shame placed upon our Lord. The guards mocked Him by putting a robe on Him and by placing a crown of thorns on His head and a reed in His right hand as a mock scepter. They continued to mock Him by saying, "Hail King of the Jews!" and proceeded to slap Him, spit on Him, and hit Him on the head with the reed (Matt. 27: 29 – 31). These thorns were exceptionally long.[131] The reed, or stick, was then used as a club when the guards repeatedly struck our Lord as the thorns were driven in His head like a spike.

Luke adds that Jesus was blindfolded while the guards struck Him and mocked Him by encouraging Him to prophesy as to who was hitting Him. John adds that the soldiers pierced Jesus' side with a spear resulting in blood and water pouring out of His body. The suffering and shame were so abysmal that Jesus prayed before the event that if it was possible let this cup (sacrifice) pass from Him (Matt. 26:39). Nonetheless, Jesus was obedient and was willing to suffer through the crucifixion for us. Today the cross is the source of our salvation (Rom. 3: 24 – 25; Eph. 2:16; Col. 1:20).

The writer of Hebrews spoke of the shame of the cross, "Looking unto Jesus, the author and finisher of our faith, who for the joy that was set before Him endured the cross, despising the shame, and has sat down on the right hand of the throne of God" (Heb. 12:2). The public shame of crucifixion did not deter Jesus from the cross. F. F. Bruce clarifies the shame of the cross:

> To die by crucifixion was to plumb the lowest depths
> of disgrace; it was a punishment reserved for those
> who were deemed most unfit to live, a punishment
> for those who were subhuman. From so degrading

a death Roman citizens were exempt by ancient statute; the dignity of the Roman name would be besmirched by being brought into association with anything as vile as the cross. For slaves, and criminals of low degree, it was regarded as a suitable means of execution, and a grim deterrent to others. But this disgrace Jesus disregarded, as something not worthy to be taken into account when it was a question of His obedience to the will of God.[132]

The atoning cross of Christ was a cross of suffering, a cross of shame, but more importantly for mankind, the cross was a cross of grace. When referring to the grace of God, John Newton stated: "I am not what I might be, I am not what I ought to be, I am not what I wish to be, I am not what I hope to be; but I thank God I am not what I once was, and I can say with the great apostle, By the grace of God I am what I am."[133] John Stott suggests that "Grace is love that cares and stoops and rescues."[134] According to Millard Erickson, the simplest definition of grace is, "God's dealing with humans in underserved ways; it is simply an outflow of God's goodness and generosity."[135] The apostle Paul references the importance of grace:

But God, who is rich in mercy, because of His great love with which He loved us, even when we were dead in trespasses, made us alive together with Christ (by grace you have been saved), and raised us up together, and made us sit together in the heavenly places in Christ Jesus...For by grace you have been saved through faith, and not of yourself it is the gift of God.Eph. 2: 4 – 8

John explains the extent of God's love. "For God so loved the world that He gave His only begotten son" (John 3:16). Let me remind you again that all humankind was spiritually destitute when it came to righteousness. Paul stated that "all have sinned and fall short of the glory of God (Rom. 3:23). He further stated that the "wages of sin is death" (Rom. 6:23). Isaiah reveals the magnitude of our unrighteous nature, "But we are all like unclean things, and all our righteousness are like filthy rags" (Isa. 64:6). I stated previously and will remind the reader again. All humankind was destined for hell; there was nothing that anyone could ever do to possess such a righteous nature so that believers may stand before God righteous. When Christ atoned for sin on the cross it was a pure act of grace.

Often the cross is worn as jewelry or as decoration. Some believe that wearing a cross makes them somewhat spiritual. Some even use the cross for advertisement in hope that it would cause Christians to use their products. Some see the cross as a symbol of unity. Nonetheless, many who wear or use the cross do not understand its true meaning. If so, they would be scandalized. The cross is a symbol of indescribable cruelty and death that God was willing for His Son to endure for all who would believe. Erwin Lutzer sums it up:

> Such people miss the central message of the cross; it is not just that Jesus died for us, but how He died that is important. The cross was not merely a cruel form of death, but it humiliated its victims; it was used to execute those who were most cursed. The procedure with all its torture ended with the victim naked, with no rights, no reputation, and no recourse. Thus the cross not only proves the gracious love of

God toward sinners but also the depth of our sin and rebellion against Him.[136]

The apostle Paul sums it up:

> Let this mind be in you which was also in Christ Jesus, who, being in the form of God, did not consider it robbery to be equal with God, but made Himself of no reputation, taking the form of a bondservant, and coming in the likeness of men. And being found in the appearance of man, He humbled Himself and became obedient to the point of death, even the death of the cross. Therefore God also highly exalted Him and given Him the name which is above every name, that at the name of Jesus every knee shall bow, of those in heaven, and of those on earth, and that every tongue should confess that Jesus is Lord, to the glory of God the Father. Phil. 2: 5–11

John writes, "For God so loved the world that He gave His only begotten Son, that whoever believes in Him should not perish but have everlasting life" (John 3:16). If God was willing for His Son to experience the suffering and shame of the cross, what do you think He will do to those who refuse the sacrifice made? Adrian Rogers asked the same question, "God did not spare His own Son from the cross. What makes you think He will spare you from rejecting the cross?"[137]

The hymn, "The Old Rugged Cross," written by George Bernard, sums up the meaning of the cross:

On a hill far away, stood an old rugged cross,
the emblem of suffering and shame:

And I love that old cross where the dearest
and best for a world of lost sinners were slain

In the old rugged cross, stained with blood so divine,
a wondrous beauty I see;

For t'was on that old cross Jesus suffered and died,
to pardon and sanctify me.

Chorus
So I'll cherish the old rugged cross.
Till my trophies at last I lay down;

I will cling to the old rugged cross,
and exchange it someday for a crown.

Though the word "atonement" is not native to biblical tradition, the notion of the atoning work of Christ is pervasive and in the next chapter we will observe five of its results: The atonement is sacrificial, it is redemptive, it is substitutional (vicarious), and it reconciles man with God.

CHAPTER EIGHT

The Message and Nature of the Atonement

Now all things are of God, who has reconciled us to Himself through Jesus Christ, and has given us the ministry of reconciliation, that is, that God was in Christ reconciling the world to Himself, not imputing their trespasses to them, and has committed to us the word of reconciliation. Now then, we are ambassadors for Christ, as though God was pleading through us: we implore you on Christ's behalf, be reconciled to God. For He made Him who knew no sin to be sin for us, that we might become the righteousness of God 2 Cor. 5: 18 – 21

For all have sinned and fall short of the glory of God, being justified freely by His grace through the redemption that is in Christ Jesus, whom God set forth as a propitiation by His blood, through faith, to demonstrate His righteousness, because in His forbearance God had passed over the sins that were previously committed, to demonstrate at the present time His righteousness, that He might be

just and the justifier of the one who has faith in Jesus.
Rom. 3: 23–26

S ince 2002 I have had the opportunity to teach men and women who are interested in the Gospel ministry. For several of those years, I served as a Director of a Luther Rice Seminary extension center teaching undergraduates. I was able to teach some courses for the Continuing Education Department of my Baptist State Convention. For the last few years, I have taught for Leavell College, which is the undergraduate college of New Orleans Baptist Theological Seminary. Most students take the work very seriously and endeavor to make an "A." Nevertheless, some only want the paper diploma. They do not take the work seriously. They are content to accomplish only enough effort to pass. This short-cut approach results with deficient information and details that are most helpful in ministry. Therefore, they are cheating themselves out of the success and spiritual enhancement that they could otherwise achieve.

Because of the deficiency of discipleship, many churches are spiritually anemic. This short-cut mentality and spiritual anemia have affected God's people. Often, many Christians do not recognize when the words they hear, or sing, are not theologically sound. Thereby cheating themselves out of moving spiritual worship when the rich meaning of biblical words are no longer understood and goes right over their heads.

Do such people understand Christ's substitutional death on the cross when they sing Isaac Watts' *At the Cross?*

Alas and did my Savior bleed and did my Sovereign die?
Would he devote that sacred head for sinners such as I?

Was it for crimes that I have done, He groan upon the tree?
Amazing pity, grace unknown and love beyond degree!

Chorus
At the cross, at the cross where I first saw the light
and the burden of my heart rolled away.

It was there by faith I received my sight,
and now I am happy all the day.[138]

I love the Vertical Church band's version of the *Lamb of God*
that speaks of the sacrificial, vicarious, propitiatory atonement
that brings forth reconciliation. Note a few of the verses:

You came from heaven's throne acquainted with our sorrow
To trade the debt we owed, Your suffering for our freedom

The Lamb of God in my place,
Your blood poured out, my sin erased
It was my death You died, I am raised to life,
Hallelujah, The Lamb of God.

This is just a sample of words that have to do with salvation
and the nature of the atonement that needs to be examined so
that each one may come to the Scriptures and worship with full
understanding and with enrichment.

THE MESSAGE OF THE ATONEMENT

Before we begin to examine the nature and the extent of the
atonement, I want to articulate the message of the atonement.
The central message of the Scriptures is the atoning work of

God in Christ. Paul states, "But we preach Christ crucified, to the Jews a stumbling block and to the Greeks foolishness" (1 Cor. 1: 23). The foundation of Paul's message was "For I delivered to you first of all that which I also received: that Christ died for our sins according to the Scriptures, and that He was buried, and that He rose again the third day according to the Scriptures" (1 Cor. 15: 3 – 4).

The message of Christ's atonement on the cross reveals to all races, all ethnicities, all genders, and all national boundaries His saving love (Eph. 2: 11 – 22). Christ came not to condemn the world, since the world was already condemned, but because of the love of God Christ came to sacrifice His life so that all who would believe could be saved from the condemnation (John 3: 16 -17).

The message is that every sinner must recognize that he or she is already condemned and has no hope and is destined for hell eternal. The message of the gospel (the good news) is that Christ died in our stead. He paid the penalty for our sins by His suffering and shame on the cross; His grace set us free. Once we accept Him as our Lord and Savior, by faith, we are no longer at enmity with God but rather now experience peace with God (Phil. 3: 9).

THE NATURE OF THE ATONEMENT

When referring to the nature of the atonement I am denoting the inherent, essence, or basic constitution of the atonement. My goal is to assist the reader in the understanding of the nature of the atonement by explaining that the atonement was sacrificial; that the atonement was vicarious (meaning substitutional);

the atonement was propitiatory in nature; and importantly' the atonement reconciled men and women to God who by grace through faith, believe.

The Atonement was Sacrificial: I have already noted much about the sacrificial nature of the atonement in the last chapter. Nevertheless, I will provide a recap and supplemental information shared by Millard Erickson:

> In Hebrew 9: 6 – 15 the work of Christ is likened to the Old Testament Day of Atonement. Christ is depicted as the high priest who entered into the Holy Place to offer sacrifice. But the sacrifice Christ offered was not the blood of goats and calves, but His own blood (v. 12). Thus He secured "eternal redemption." A vivid contrast is drawn between the sacrifice of animals, which had only a limited effect, and of Christ, whose death has eternal effect. Whereas the Mosaic sacrifices had to be offered repeatedly, Christ's death was a once-for-all atonement for the sins of all humankind (v.12).[139]

Erickson continued by comparing the sacrifice in the Old Testament to the sacrifice of Christ Jesus on the cross from The Book of Hebrews. He noted that instead of a burnt offering, the fleshly body of Christ was the instrument of sacrifice (v. 10:5), that instead of a daily or annual offering made by a priest in the Old Testament that the sacrifice of Christ was offered once and for all (v. 10: 11). He further comments on Hebrews, chapter 13 that equates the death of Christ to the sin offering in the Old Testament. Christ's atoning work on the cross sanctified the believers through His blood.

The exceptional fact about Christ's sacrifice is that our Lord was both the victim (sacrifice) and the priest (the sacrificer) who offered the sacrifice.[140] By the shedding of His blood and the experience of the suffering, shame, and death on the cross, Jesus became the ultimate sacrifice, the spotless and unblemished Lamb of God who redeemed us from guilt and sin and cleansed us from all unrighteousness as an expression of His love for us. Through our Lord's atoning sacrifice, we may come boldly before the throne of God, since he is our Advocate. The blood of the Lamb has been shed, and the price for our eternal redemption has been paid once and for all (Heb. 9:26).

The Atonement of Christ was Vicarious: A simple explanation of the vicarious atonement of Christ is the involvement of one individual (Christ) acting in the place of another or for the sake of another (humankind). Christ's sacrificial atonement on the cross was a substitution for the death and guilt that all humanity deserved as compensation for their sins. The apostle Paul refers to the Lord's vicarious atonement when he states, "He who did not spare His own Son, but delivered Him up for us all" (Rom. 8: 32), making Christ "who knew no sin to be sin for us, that we might become the righteousness of God" (2 Cor. 5:21). Previously, Paul explained that believers were reconciled to God in verses eighteen through twenty (more on this later in this chapter). However, in verse twenty-one, Paul reveals how believers are reconciled. First, God sent Christ, His sinless Son, to provide salvation to all who would believe. "But when the fullness of the time had come, God sent forth His Son, born of a woman, born under the law, to redeem those who were under the law, that we might receive the adoption as sons" (Gal. 4: 4 – 5). "Seeing then that we have a great High Priest who has passed through the heavens, Jesus the Son of God, let us hold fast our confession. For we do not have a High Priest who cannot sympathize with our weakness, but was in all points tempted as we are, yet without sin" (Heb. 4: 14 – 15).

Second, Christ was sent to become sin for us. God, using the principle of imputation (5:19), treated Christ as if He was a sinner, although He had never sinned, and had Him to die as a substitute to pay the penalty for the sins of them who believed in Him. "Christ has redeemed us from the curse of the law, having become a curse for us ("Cursed is everyone who hangs on a tree" Gal. 3: 13). One must note that Christ did not become a sinner on the cross but remained perfect and holy. Christ was only treated as if he were guilty of all the sins committed by all who would believe, though He committed none. The wrath of God was satisfied and concluded on Him when the just requirement of His law was met for those whom He died.

Third, Christ has substituted (imputed) His righteousness to those who would believe. This was discussed in another chapter. Every man or woman born can never be righteous enough to provide salvation for themselves. One sin will destroy the righteousness of any human and they are not able to make it right. Therefore, the believer can only rely on the imputed righteousness of Christ.

The atonement was propitiatory in its nature: In a very simple definition of "propitiation," when concerning Christ's atonement on the cross, it means that Christ appeased the wrath of God against all sinful humanity with the very event of presenting Himself as a substitutional sacrifice for all who would believe. Christ not only presented the sacrifice to the Father; He was the sacrifice. Webster defines propitiation as to cause to become favorably inclined; to win or regain the goodwill of; to appease or conciliate; to make atonement.[141]

John MacArthur defines propitiation as follows:

> Scripture represents Christ's death not merely as a sacrifice but as a *propitiatory* sacrifice. That is to say, by receiving the full exercise of the Father's wrath against the sins of His people, Christ satisfied God's righteous anger against sin and thus turned away His wrath from us who, had it not been for our substitute, would bound to suffer it for ourselves.[142]

David Mapes suggests the following:

> Propitiation means that Jesus has satisfied the righteous requirements of God's justice in that his death provided a sacrifice with the potential to remove the offense of sin. Because a sacrifice has been made which can take away the sins of the world, this sacrifice has made it possible for God to extend salvation to every individual. To be sure this possibility only becomes actual for a person who believes.[143]

The Scripture first develops the idea of propitiation from the Old Testament (Num. 7: 1, 89). John MacArthur suggests that the Old Testament Hebrew word *kapher* has a range of meanings, such as "forgive (Lev. 4:20 – 31; 19:22), "to cleanse (Lev. 14: 18 – 31; 15: 19 – 30), and to "ransom" (Exod. 30: 11 – 16; Num. 35: 29 – 34). However, several passages define *kapher* as "propitiation," the act, or concept, of averting God's wrath.[144]

Leviticus 16: 12 – 19 provides a great example of the meaning of "propitiation." The High Priest was instructed to present the blood of the sacrifices that he had already slain and enter the Holy of Holies where God would appear in the cloud upon the mercy seat (vs. 2). There he would place the blood on the horns of the altar and sprinkle the blood on the mercy seat with his finger (vs. 19). This event actualized "propitiation;" appeasement with God by satisfying His righteous requirement of justice.

The New Testament Greek word, *hilasterion* or *hilasomia* is often used for "propitiation" (Rom. 3: 24 – 25; Heb. 2: 17; 1 John 2:2; 1 John 4: 10).Nonetheless, the same word refers to the mercy seat of the ark (Heb. 9:5).[145] Mapes explains, "The New Testament equates Jesus with the mercy seat on the ark. Jesus is the place where God meets with mankind."[146]

The first use of "propitiation" in the New Testament is Romans 3: 25. "Whom God set forth as a propitiation by His blood, through faith, to demonstrate His righteousness, because in His forbearance God had passed over the sins that were previously committed." Previously, Paul detailed the wrath of God against the sins of humankind, both the Gentiles (Rom. 1: 18 -32) and the Jews (Rom. 2: 1 – 3:20). Paul warned how each was storing up wrath when God's righteous judgment would be revealed, "But in accordance with your hardness and your impenitent heart you are treasuring up for yourself wrath in the day of wrath and revelation of the righteous judgment of God" (Rom. 2:5), "But if our unrighteousness demonstrates the righteousness of God, What shall I say? Is God unjust who inflicts wrath? (I speak as a man.) Certainly not! For then how would God judge the world" (Rom. 3:5). The tread of divine wrath is woven through the opening section of Paul's letter to the Romans. If Paul would have stopped writing before chapter three, verse twenty, all humankind would be devastated to learn that everyone ever born would have to one day face the wrath of God with no possibility of salvation:

> But now the righteousness of God apart from the law is revealed, being witness by the Law and the Prophets, even the righteousness of God, through faith in Jesus Christ, to all and on all who believe. For there is no difference. For all have sinned and fall short of the glory of God, being justified freely by His grace through the redemption that is in Christ Jesus, whom God set forth as a propitiation by His blood, through faith, to demonstrate His righteousness, because in His forbearance God had passed over the sins that were previously committed, to demonstrate at the present time His righteousness, that He might be just and the justifier of the one who has faith in Jesus.Romans 3: 21–26

MacArthur states:

> We see precisely that in Romans 3: 21 – 26: God has put forward His Son, the Lord Jesus Christ, "as a propitiation by his blood to be received by faith" (Rom 3:25). God has satisfied his wrath against sin by the sprinkling of the blood of the spotless lamb on the mercy seat of the heavenly altar (Heb. 9: 11 – 15, 23 – 24). He has punished the sins of his people in a substitute, and thus his wrath has been turned away from them.[147]

The significance of propitiation, according to MacArthur, is that it identifies Christ's work as a wrath bearing sacrifice. Sin has been dealt with by the sacrifice Christ made on the cross.[148]

The Atonement Actualized Reconciliation: Reconciliation is set against the backdrop of enmity. "Because the carnal mind is enmity against God; for it is not subject to the law of God, nor indeed can be" (Rom. 8:7). Greek scholar, Spiros Zodhiates suggests that the Greek word for enmity is *echthra*. It may also be translated as enemy, hatred, or hostility.[149]

God instructed Adam to not eat of the Tree of the Knowledge of Good and Evil. If so, the day that they ate they would surely die! (Gen. 2:17). As discussed in previous chapters Adam and Eve ate of the tree and immediately suffered spiritual death; separation from God. Not only were they separated from God they received a sinful and depraved nature. The reader may recall that Adam's immediate instinct after sinning was to hide from God and avoid His fellowship (Gen. 3:8). Since that day, all men and women were born with a nature that is hostile toward God. This is not an implication that all hold contempt for God or outwardly attack God or His Word. It means that no one may ever stand before His presence righteous and therefore experience true fellowship with Him. Sinful humanity is opposed to God and all that is of God. The sinful nature disobeys God's law and works contrary to God's purpose while disbelieving the gospel. There is a void or separation, that must be bridged before one can have a relation and fellowship with God. There must be reconciliation where the enmity (hostility) between God and man, namely the guilt of sin and the punishment of God's wrath is removed and satisfied, thus establishing peace with God.

Christ's atoning death on the cross brought reconciliation. Christ bridged the gap between man and God with the cross to all who would believe. Paul notes:

> For if when we were enemies [one hostile to God] we were reconciled to God through the death of His Son, much more, having been reconciled, we shall be saved by His life. And not only that, but we also rejoice in God through our Lord Jesus Christ, through whom we have now received the reconciliation. Rom. 5: 10–11

Sometimes, when two nations are rattling their swords at one another and peace has been shattered, some neutral third nation may intervene and invite the two warring countries to attend a peace accord, or summit, to establish peace and reconciliation. All humankind was separated and alienated from God and needed restoration of a relationship between them and God. This reconciliation occurred when Christ became the third party over two thousand years ago at Calvary. Through the sacrifice of His blood, He provided a reconciliation with God for all who would believe.

Recapping this chapter, we remind the reader that the message of the gospel is that all humankind is condemned to spend eternity in hell separated from God. However, God loved His creation and sent His own Son to make atonement through His suffering and shame on the cross. The atonement was sacrificial, it was vicarious, it provided propitiation, and reconciliation for all who believe.

Before I can discuss the call and acceptance of salvation, I need to discuss the extent of the atonement since so many disagree with the call or drawing of the Holy Spirit.

CHAPTER NINE

The Extent of the Atonement

Theological groups embrace diverse interpretations regarding the extent of the atonement. While some suggest the extent of the atonement is intended for all who believe, others hold to the notion that the extent of the atonement was intended for a select few (the elect). Some teach that the work of the atonement is rather forced on an individual with a call that is irresistible while others suggest that everyone has free will to receive or reject God's work of atonement. First, I will discuss how Godly Christians can read the Bible with differing interpretations. Second, I will give an overview of the most prevalent three philosophical-theological systems. Lastly, I will discuss a few foundational terms to assist the reader in the understanding of how Godly Christians can have a difference of opinion when interpreting the Scriptures.

I have had the opportunity to teach a few courses on the subject of hermeneutics for two different Bible Colleges. In both cases, the book *Grasping God's Word*, written by J. Scott Duvall and J. Daniel Hays, was the main text. One of the most enlightened sections in their book is Chapter 7, "What Do We Bring to the Text?" The authors discuss how each one brings his or her personal baggage to the text when interpreting. They state at the beginning of the chapter:

> One context that is often overlooked is the context of the reader —- the world from which the reader approaches the text. We as readers of the Bible are not by nature neutral and objective. We bring a lot of preconceived notions and influences with us to the text when we read. Thus, we need to discuss and evaluate these "pre-text" influences, lest they mislead us in our search for the meaning of the text.[150]

The authors continue to address these notions and influences by discussing two that shape one's interpretation of Scripture, Preunderstanding, and Foundational beliefs.

Preunderstanding

Preunderstanding denotes all of an individual's preconceived ideas and understandings that are brought to the text before he or she actually studies the text in detail. This preunderstanding includes the specific experiences and encounters in life resulting in one's assumption that he or she understands the text's interpretation. Preunderstandings are fashioned by both good and bad influences that may be accurate or inaccurate. These influences may come from Bible study, preaching, singing hymns and praise music (some are not theologically sound), watching a biblical Hollywood movie, reading theological study tools which may or may not contain accurate biblical truths. There are outside influences that may fashion one's preunderstanding. It may be the community in which one lives, the assembly that one fellowship, one's culture, one's race, or just the worldview of the individual.

A dangerous aspect of preunderstanding surfaces when he or she approaches a text having their theological agenda already formulated. Therefore one, if not careful, may slant the meaning of the text to fit his or her preconceived interpretation. Some are even prone to skip over the text lightly without studying the text properly.[151]

When teaching a course on hermeneutics I explain the difference between exegesis and eisegesis when interpreting a text of Scripture. Exegesis is the drawing out the meaning of a text by using grammatical and historical tools to understand how the people understood the text in the generation and culture in which it was written, rather than reading one's preconceived notion into the text. Eisegesis is the practice of reading one's preconceived idea into the text rather than drawing out the accurate meaning.

Foundational Belief

Total objectivity may be impossible for any reader of the text. However, while striving for objectivity in biblical interpretation one must not abandon his or her faith or adopt the methods of the unbelievers. There are several foundational beliefs that evangelical Christians must stand on when interpreting a text from the Scriptures:

- The Bible is the Word of God, which is inspired by the Holy Spirit.

- The Bible is authoritative and one hundred percent trustworthy and true.
- God has entered into human history; thus, the supernatural does occur.
- The Bible is not contradictory; when properly studied; it is unified, yet diverse.

While it is important to believe the Bible is God's Word, it must be the final authority in life. Many authorities compete for first place in one's decision-making, such as; the academic authority, the authority of traditions, the authority of our society (the world) including that which is deemed politically correct, and the authority of one's feelings (the flesh). Scripture must always be the final authority in one's life when developing his or her ideologies, beliefs, and precepts. We must allow our preunderstandings to change when necessary while reading and interpreting the Scripture. We must read the Scripture in faith. While one's preunderstanding may change, foundational truth, if correct, should never change.[152]

I am sure that some readers are wondering why I wrote the last segment. I am making the point that there is a divergence of opinions and views concerning the extent of the atonement. Some are Calvinists, in one form or another. Some hold to a form of Arminianism. Then there are many, whom I will refer to as Traditionalists, which deny some of both views. All groups adhere to the same foundational belief that the Bible is God's inspired and inerrant Word and must be the final authority. The disagreement of their philosophical theology is the result of their diverse preunderstandings; preunderstandings that are primarily formed by Calvinists and Arminians books they have read.

In the theological world, one word or short phrase is often utilized to define a large theological concept. One may claim to be a pre-tribulation, premillennial believer. Many Christians can understand this concept without the believer spending an hour describing it. Now, that same adherence to the pre-tribulation premillennial view becomes the believer's philosophical understanding when he or she reads the Bible and interprets each passage along with the pretribulation premillennial view. Whether one's theological view is Arminian, Calvinist, or Traditional the view becomes the philosophical idea or system that is engaged to interpret Scripture; it becomes their preunderstanding. This does not mean that one group is evil, should be demonized, or disfellowshipped. All love God and His Word. We just disagree with an interpretation of Scripture. Before moving to chapter ten concerning the call and acceptance of salvation, I must discuss the biblical views and systems of the Calvinists, the Arminians, and the Traditionalists concerning the extent of the atonement.

Arminian Philosophical Theology

In defining the Arminian Philosophical Theology accurately, I decided to start at the beginning of the movement named after James Arminius (a Dutch seminary professor). One year after his death in 1610, his followers drew up the following Five *Articles of Faith* that were based upon his teachings.

- God elects [to save one] or reproves [to allow one to go to hell] based on one's "foreseen faith" or "unbelief."
- Christ died for all every man [and women], although only believers are saved.

- Man is so depraved that divine grace is necessary unto faith or any good deed.
- Grace may be resisted.
- Whether all who are truly regenerated will certainly persevere in the faith is a point that needs further investigation. It should be noted that the last article was later altered to teach the possibility of the truly regenerate believer's losing his faith and thus losing his salvation.[153]

David Mapes provides additional information:

- Since man is depraved, God provides prevenient grace that makes it possible for a man to respond to God.
- Arminians believe in conditional election, meaning that God chooses people because of something He saw in time. That the individual would choose Him as Savior then He elected him or her for salvation. Therefore, salvation is conditional on the decision.
- Arminians believe in unlimited atonement. It is available to who-so-ever-will.[154]

Calvinist Philosophical Theology

The term *Calvinism* was derived from the French reformer John Calvin (1509 – 1564). Many of his followers met during the Synod (council) of Dort in 1618 to examine the views of the Armenians.[155] They proposed an alternative to the Armenians with their own *Five Points of Calvinism*. While defining the five points we will use the acronym **T.U.L.I.P.**

- **T**otal Depravity: The entire human race, past and present, is affected as a result of Adam's fall; all humanity is dead in trespasses and sins. Man is incapable of saving himself. Therefore, if God is to speak to a person, he or she has to first experience regeneration.

- **Unconditional Election:** Because man is dead in sin, he has no free will or ability to initiate a response to God's call; therefore, at the beginning of creation God elected [chose] certain people to salvation. Election and predestination are unconditional [election is not based upon any condition of man's effort]; they are not based on man's response and freewill because man is unable to, nor does he want to. The reason for a person's salvation (or election) is only known to God.

- **Limited Atonement:** Because God predetermined that certain ones should be regenerated as a result of His unconditional election, He determined that Christ should die for the pre-chosen elect alone. Only those individuals whom God has elected and for whom Christ died will experience salvation.

- **Irresistible grace:** Those whom God elected He draws to Himself through irresistible grace. God "makes man willing" to come to Him. When God calls, "man has no choice but to respond."

- **Perseverance of the Saints:** Those whom God has elected and drawn to Himself through the Holy Spirit will persevere in faith. None whom God has elected will be lost; they are eternally secured.[156]

Traditional Philosophical Theology

Many believers do not fit either the Arminian or the Calvinist mold. They may believe a few points of one or both but still have over-all doubt. Some even refer to themselves as a moderate, or modified Arminian, or Calvinist since they do favor two or three of their points. Think about how they identify with a group that he or she only accepts 40 – 60% of the theology. If you only accepted 40% of the Mormon or Jehovah's Witness doctrine would you refer to yourself as a moderate Mormon or Jehovah's Witness?

Many of the individuals who do not subscribe to either Arminianism or Calvinism may have at one time been somewhat accepting of the Arminian position. But after additional study, they began to doubt the Arminian particulars. Others may have previously leaned toward the Calvinist five points system but later, after a time of reflection and questioning parts of it, discovered that they could never confirm all the points of Calvinism. They ascertained that they believed a few points from both philosophical-theological systems. Much of their problem is their reliance on preachers, groups, theological dictionaries, and commentaries spoken and written by those who were slanting all meaning toward Calvinism or that of the Arminians. In their endeavor to discern biblical truth they mistakenly believed such sources while interpreting the Calvinist and Arminian definitions and meanings of certain words and phrases such as God's sovereignty, God's Foreknowledge, predestination, and relating Scriptures.

Most of the readers who have experienced doubt with both groups will find themselves in a third group. After some research,

I have discovered that some theologians refer to biblical information about a group with no name that is neither Arminian nor Calvinist. However, after reading several blogs and other material I discovered this group is often referred to as Traditional. One of the reasons for this terminology is because of the multitude of writings from the Church Fathers concerning the extent of the atonement that gives evidence for today's traditional philosophical theology (you will see throughout the remainder of this chapter). These writings were in existence many centuries before the Arminian and Calvinist philosophical theology systems. I discovered that within this system two main groups; one that I will refer to as the Free Grace group who are somewhat similar to Arminianism and the second group I will refer to as the Romans Five group whom I most identify. Following is the basic concept of Traditional Philosophical Theology. Note, the primary information concerning the Romans Five view will be provided from the information from the seminary course taught by Dr. David Mapes, entitled, Systematic Theology II:[157]

The five points of the Romans Five model is based upon the text of Romans Five, verses 12 – 19:

> Therefore, just as through one man sin entered the world, and death through sin, and thus death spread to all men, because all sinned – For unto the law sin was in the world, but sin is not imputed when there is no law. Nevertheless, death reigned from Adam to Moses, even over those who had not sinned according to the likeness of the transgression of Adam, who is a type of Him who was to come. But the free gift is not like the offense. For if by one man's offense many died, much more the grace of

God and the gift of grace of the One Man, Jesus Christ, abound to many. And the gift is not like that which came through the one who sinned. For the judgment which came from one offense resulted in condemnation, but the free gift which came from many offenses resulted in justification. For if by one man's offense death reigned through the one, much more those who receive abundance of grace and of the gift of righteousness will reign in life through the One, Jesus Christ.

Therefore, as through one man's offense judgment came to all men, resulting in condemnation, even so through one Man's righteous act the free gift came to all men, resulting in justification of life. For as by one man's disobedience many were made sinners, so also by one Man's obedience many will be made righteous.

- **Total Depravity:** The apostle Paul makes it undeniably clear that all human beings are depraved, that there is no effort afforded to any humans whereby he or she may produce the righteousness that is essential for one to have a relationship with God (Rom. 3: 10 – 18). Paul is essentially stating that all human beings, left alone by God, would go to hell. This is not suggesting that everyone is wicked but rather none may ever be righteous enough by him or herself to fellowship with God (Rom. 5: 17 – 21).

- **Conditional Election:** The Free Grace group and the Romans Five group differ on this point. The Free Grace group suggests that when God foresaw the future and was able to determine who would and who would not respond to the calling of the Holy Spirit that the very act of those who responded with belief was the condition that made them part of the elect. On the other hand, the Romans Five groups suggest that that the condition of one's election was not the act of believing but the results of believing based on Ephesians 1: 3 – 14: Note how often Paul writes the phrase "in Him."

> Blessed be the God and father of our Lord Jesus Christ, who has blessed us with every spiritual blessing in the heavenly places in Christ, just as He chose us in Him before the foundation of the world that we should be holy and without blame before Him in love, having predestined us to adoption as sons by Jesus Christ to Himself, according to the good pleasures of His will, to the praise of the glory of His grace by which He made us accepted in the Beloved. In Him we have redemption through His blood, the forgiveness of sins, according to the riches of His grace which He made to abound toward us in all wisdom and prudence, having made known to us the mystery of His will, according to His good pleasures which He purposed in Himself, that in the dispensation of the fullness of times He might gather together in one all things in Christ, both which are in heaven and which are on earth – in Him. In Him also we have obtained an inheritance, being predestined according to the purpose of Him who works all things according to the counsel of His will, that we who first trusted in Christ should be the praise

of His glory. In Him you also trusted after you heard
the word of truth, the gospel of your salvation; in
whom also, having believed, you were sealed with
the Holy Spirit of promise, who is the guarantee
of our inheritance until the redemption of the purposed possession, to the praise of His glory.

The Romans Five group, as well as the Free Grace group, suggests that God's work of predestination took place after His
foreknowledge that each would respond to the Holy Spirit's
calling or drawing. We will discuss this later. According to the
apostle Paul, immediately after a person believes and trusts
in Christ, God places that person "in Christ." The moment a
person believes (i.e. is saved), he is placed into Christ by the
Holy Spirit where acts associated with salvation such as adoption, justification, and sealing take place. When the believer
is placed "in Christ" he or she not only receives salvation but
obtains an inheritance (1: 11) and the individual is sealed with
the Holy Spirit who is the guarantee of the believer's inheritance (1: 13 – 14). The Free Grace Traditionalist suggests that
one's salvation is a combination of the work of God and the
work or action of the person when he or she believed. The
Romans Five traditionalists suggest that the belief was not the
work or action that saves but that which leads to the act of God
placing the believer "in Christ." Salvation is first initiated by
the calling or drawing of God the Holy Spirit who encourages
the non-believer that he or she is a sinner that only Christ can
save if they fall upon their face before Him. The unregenerate
that repents and believes is provided a new position in Christ.
Therefore, God the Son, Christ Jesus, is the author and the finisher of one's salvation (Heb. 12:2).

The Traditional system is contrary to the Calvinists' idea of total depravity who suggests that for God to speak to a person he or she must experience regeneration first. They offer that if belief provides salvation for a lost soul, then the lost soul's salvation is based on the works of belief. The Traditionalists' response is that belief is not considered works by explaining Romans 4: 1 – 5:

> What then shall we say that Abraham our father has found according to the flesh? For if Abraham was justified by works, he has something to boast about, but not before God. For what does the scripture say? "Abraham believed God, and it was accounted [imputed] to him for righteousness." Now to him who works, the wages are not counted as grace but as debt. But to him who does not work but believes on Him who justifies the ungodly, his faith is accounted [imputed] for righteousness.

Note that Paul does not equate belief as works but only consent to God's calling. According to Greek scholar William Mounce, the biblical word for believe is *aman* which in the context of Romans four means to agree with and trust, "trusting that God is powerful enough to accomplish His word and that what He says is absolute truth and certainty.[158] Therefore, when the Holy Spirit draws and convicts an individual of his or her sinful state and their need for salvation, He reveals that God sent His Son to die on the cross for their sins and is the only remedy. He encourages the acceptance of what Christ accomplished on the cross by repenting and by faith. Through this enlightenment of the Holy Spirit, the individual has the capacity to agree with and trust God. Nonetheless, this opportunity to agree with God is not considered an act of works; it is just an act of agreeing with God. Therefore, belief is not works but consent and an agreement with God.

- **Unlimited Atonement:** The atonement was not meant to be experienced by just a few since Christ died for all humanity (John 3:16). Paul makes this clear in Romans chapter five when he states that by one man's sin (Adam) many died (5:15). What does Paul mean by "the many?" William Mounce, suggests that the Greek word is *hoi polloi* and Paul is drawing a contrast between "the one" and "the many." "The many" here has the nuance of "all in a group," for just as "the many/all" became sinners through the one man Adam and subject to death (Adam's guilt).[159] But note that through one Man, Jesus, the offer of salvation by grace "abounded" (went out) to the "many" although not all the "many" received it. The question may be asked, "Who are the many here?" This group of many refers to all humanity! For "all" have sinned and fall short of the glory of God (Rom. 3: 23), "For the wages of sin is death" (Rom. 6:23a). "For God so loved the "world" [all of the universe] that He gave His only begotten Son" (John 3:16).

- **Resistible Grace:** In Romans 5: 15 -17 the apostle Paul suggests that God's grace may be resisted. Through the one Man, Jesus, the offer of salvation by grace "abounded" (goes out) to "the many," For if by one man's offense [Adam] many died [all humanity], much more the grace of God and the gift by the grace of the One Man, Jesus Christ, abounded [goes out] to many [all human beings]" (Rom. 5: 15). Note that Paul is not suggesting that the same number who are dead in Adam (all of humanity) will be saved by Christ, but only those of another group who have received the grace of God by faith. If it were the same number, then Paul would be teaching universalism. Paul clarifies this, "For if by the one man's offense death reigned through the one, [note carefully here] much more those "who receive" abundance of grace and of the gift of righteousness will reign in life through the One, Jesus Christ" (Rom. 5; 17). Since the grace goes out (abounds) to all, but only those who receive the same grace and righteousness offered by Christ to all are regenerated, it is logical that the individuals who did not receive the grace and righteousness offered must have the ability to resist the grace.

• **Perseverance of the Saints:** This is an area of contention between the two Traditional groups. The Romans Five group may quote verse seventeen, "For if by one man's offense death reigns through the one [Adam], much more those who receive abundance of grace and of the gift of righteousness will reign in life through the One, Jesus Christ" (5: 17). I have to admit that this verse is open to interpretation. On one hand, many Free Grace Traditionalists believe that once a person has been truly born again that his or her salvation is eternally secured. On the other hand, some Free Grace Traditionalists question the eternal security of the saints. Nonetheless, those who are of the Roman's Five persuasions believe in the eternal security of every believer. They refer back to Ephesians, chapter one. Paul reminds the reader that in Him (Christ) we have redemption through His blood and the forgiveness of sins (1:7). That in the dispensation of the fullness of time that God will gather together in one all things "in Christ" (1: 10). That the believers have received (presently) an inheritance in heaven after he or she trusted the gospel of salvation and was sealed by the Holy Spirit of promise (1: 12 – 13). But note verse fourteen, "who [the Holy Spirit] is the guarantee of our inheritance until the redemption of the purchased possession, to the praise of His glory." The moment the believer is placed "in Christ" by God his or her salvation was sealed by the Holy Spirit who guarantees each one's salvation until the day of redemption.

Issues of Disagreement

Following is a shortlist of terms that are interpreted differently based upon one's preunderstanding and philosophical theology system of interpretation. Space prevents me from exegeting each philosophical-theological position; therefore, I will only provide a general overview of the theological terms.

SOVEREIGNTY OF GOD

The root of Calvinism is their understanding of God's sovereignty. Millard Erickson defines God's sovereignty as, "A reference to the fact that God's choices and decisions are in no way constrained by factors outside himself; also, God's right to choose without being answerable to anyone or anything outside himself."[160] To this David Martin Lloyd-Jones responded, "God does not stop to consult us."[161] Ted Dorman defines God's sovereignty as follows, "God is eminently *free* in that God does whatever pleases Him" (Ps. 115:3; 135:6). God is eminently powerful, or *omnipotent*, in that there is nothing consistent with

His character that He cannot do (Luke 1:37). On the other hand, God cannot lie (Titus 1:2) or deny Himself (2 Tim. 2: 13), two things that people all too often do."[162] God is perfect in holiness and justice. Therefore, He would never go against His nature and attributes when He exercises His sovereignty.

These definitions are the basic meaning of the sovereignty of God without any bias. If one were to merge all the above definitions, they will observe the following points:

- God's choices and decisions are not constrained by outside factors; no one over-rules God.

- God is free and has all right to choose and to decree as He pleases without being answerable to anyone outside Himself. The question is how does God exercise His rights? Arminians and Traditionalists believe that God's sovereignty is compatible (working together) with Man's freewill (We will discuss this in detail when we define predestination.)

- God is eminently powerful (omnipotent) and there is nothing consistent with His character that He cannot do.

- Since God is holy, pure, and perfect He cannot go against His nature, Word, and attributes when exercising His sovereignty.

The Traditional View of the Sovereignty of God: Since being the first and oldest view of the atonement I will begin with the Traditional Philosophical Theological View with quotes from the Early Church Father, Tertullian:

> So far as a human being can form [write] a defini-
> tion of God, I adduce [present] one that the con-
> science of all men will also acknowledge – that God
> is the great supreme, existing in eternity, unbegotten,
> unmade, without beginning, without end. Tertullian
> (155 – 220 AD)[163]

The word "sovereignty" really did not come into existence until the fourteenth century, more so in the sixteenth century. Therefore, the Early Church Fathers provided words like omnipotent, supreme, and all-powerful in describing God's sovereignty. An example may be found with the writing of Tatian:

> Such a resourceful God is obviously Omnipotent, or
> all-powerful. Even while affirming that "nothing is
> impossible for the Omnipotent, Origen [184 – 254
> AD] warned not to take the unlimited ability of
> God too far; otherwise, one could end up affirming
> absurd things about him: "God can do everything
> that is possible for him to do without ceasing to be
> God, and good, and wise...so neither is God able to
> commit wickedness, for the power to do evil is con-
> trary to his deity and omnipotence.[164]

Tatian (120 – 180 AD) affirms that God's sovereignty and man's free will is compatible (worked together without conflict).

Traditionalists reject any form of fatalism that they understand to be the sum-total of the extreme Calvinist idea of the sovereignty of God. Fatalism is a pessimistic philosophy that strongly suggests that everything that happens, including all decisions in life, is controlled by God. Every action, including one's salvation, or not, has been predetermined by God. One is either predestined for heaven or hell. That the atonement was limited to only the predestined elect whose calling of salvation was irresistible. Traditionalists envision the Calvinist concept of the sovereignty of God as though man is a pre-programmed computer without a will to decide or to change anything. They question how God can hold men and women accountable for their actions if it was ultimately predestined by God in which they have no control. To this, the Traditionalists ask, "If this is true, how can God be a God of justice?" Since God demands that sin has consequences one needs to remember that God is righteous. Therefore, He acts in conformity to His law while administering His kingdom according to His laws. His justice is His official righteousness, as well as His requirement that all individuals adhere to His standard as well. God's judgment means that He administers His law fairly without favoritism or partiality. Each person is responsible for his or her actions, not that of others, or their station in life. In human judgment each is to receive what is due to them, whether good or bad, based upon His holy laws. [165]

To clarify the Traditional view, I will quote one of my favorite writers, A. W. Tozer after he suggests that he is neither an Arminian nor a Calvinist:

> God's sovereignty is the attribute by which He rules His entire creation, and to be sovereign God must be all-knowing, all-powerful, and absolute free. The reasons are these:

> Were there even one datum of knowledge, however small, unknown to God, His rule would break down

at that point. To be Lord over all creation, He must possess all knowledge. And were God lacking one infinitesimal modicum of power, that lack would end His reign and undo His kingdom; that one stray atom of power would belong to someone else and God would be a limited ruler and hence not sovereign.[166]

Tozer views God's sovereignty and man's free will as being compatible with each other.

God sovereignly decreed that man should be free to exercise moral choice, and man from the beginning has fulfilled that decree by making choice between good and evil. When he chooses to do evil, he does not thereby countervail the sovereign will of God but fulfills it, inasmuch as the eternal decree decided not which choice the man should make but that he should be free to make it. If in His absolute freedom God has willed to give man limited freedom, who is there to stay His hand or say, "What doest thou?" Man's will is free because God is sovereign. A God less than sovereign could not bestow moral freedom upon His creatures. He would be afraid to do so.[167]

The Arminians' View of the Sovereignty of God: One of the best sources of Arminian Theology is written by the Arminian, Roger E. Olson. While Calvinists claim that Arminians deny God's sovereignty, Olson attests that classical Arminians do teach God's sovereignty; they just interpret it differently than the Calvinist. Jacob Arminius suggests that God has the right and the power to do whatever He wills. There were no limitations to God by creation but only God's character, which is love and justice. Arminius stated, "God can indeed do what He wills with His own; but He cannot will to do with His own what He cannot rightfully do, for His will is circumscribed within the bounds of justice." Arminius was not suggesting that God is limited to human justice. Nonetheless, He did suggest that God's justice cannot be foreign to the best understanding of justice, especially as communicated in God's Word or it would just be an empty meaning. Arminius acknowledged that God has all rights and power to do whatever He wished to accomplish with any creature, However, God's character as supreme love and justice makes certain acts of God inconceivable.[168]

Arminians rejected divine determinism (the belief that all that happens is inflexibly caused and fixed) [169] since he felt that it leads inevitably to God being the author of sin. Nevertheless, many Arminians would be surprised to learn that Arminius affirmed the doctrine of God's providential sovereignty. He suggests that God is the cause of everything but evil. It could only happen if God permits it. Evil is not authorized by God. God permits it "designedly and willingly," but not efficaciously.[170]

The Calvinists' View of the Sovereignty of God: Calvinists, also known as the Reformed Faith, teach that God's sovereignty is absolute, unconditional, and unlimited. All things in the realm of the natural, including one's salvation, have been predetermined by God. God saves only those whom He wills to save and there is no power able to frustrate God's power in saving the sinner He wills to save. The five points of Calvinism hinge on the sovereignty of God.

The Extreme Calvinists hold to the fatalism view of the sovereignty of God. Most other forms of Calvinism suggest the determinism view. Norman Geisler explains, "*Determinism is the view that all human actions are caused by another, not by one's self. Hard* determinism as defined by Gregg Allison, "embraces coercion: people are constrained in their decisions and actions."[171] Therefore, according to Norman Geisler, determinism does not allow for any free choice at all. *Soft* determinism as defined by Allison accounts for significant human freedom: causal conditions decisively prompt people to decide and act in accordance with their will."[172] Therefore Geisler suggests that the term posits [suggests or assumes] free choice but sees it as completely controlled by God's sovereign power."[173] Notice that hard determinism provides no freewill and is somewhat akin to fatalism as if people are pre-programmed robots. Soft determinism provides the illusion of free will, but in reality offers no free will, since all outside experiences and actions in the life of an individual are designed by God to manipulate all of one's inner actions and personal decisions of that which have been predetermined by God.

THE FOREKNOWLEDGE OF GOD

According to Millard Erickson, the simplest definition of God's divine foreknowledge is God's prescience or foresight concerning future events. He further states that it is the doctrine that God knows from eternity all that will ever happen.[174] In its pure form it means to know beforehand.

The Traditionalist Philosophical Theological View of the Foreknowledge of God: I will begin this section, as I did in the last by, quoting a few Church fathers concerning the fore-knowledge of God:

> God is in every country, and in every place, and is never absent, and there is nothing done that he did not know...The power of the Word [has] in itself a faculty to foresee future events, not as fated [prede-termined], but as taking place by the choice of free agents. **Tatian** (120 – 180 AD) [175]

Anselm (1033 – 1109 AD) a theologian during the Middle Ages states:

> If something is going to occur freely, God, who foreknows all that should be, foreknows this very fact. And whatever God foreknows shall necessarily happen in the way in which it is foreknown. So it is necessary that it shall happen freely, and there is therefore no conflict whatsoever between a fore-knowledge which entails a necessary occurrence and a free exercise of an uncoerced will. For it is both necessary that God foreknows what shall come to be and that God foreknows that something shall freely come to be. [176]

There is a difference of opinion between the Free Grace Traditionalists and the Romans Five Traditionalists concerning the foreknowledge of God. Both groups believe that God knows all that will happen, every decision, every thought, and every action before it takes place. However, the Free Grace group believes in self-determinism; that "all" human actions are not caused by anything or anyone but one's self. They believe that God predetermined His actions concerning everyone based upon what He foreknew, what each would freely do, or how each would freely respond in life. They believe that God does not predetermine one's action; He only predetermines His responses to them; which becomes fixed in the future.

God indeed allows a person to freely express his or her free will, especially when it relates to salvation. It should be noted that when discussing salvation that God initiated a plan and expects each individual to conform to His plan. The work of the Holy Spirit is to influence the unregenerate to conform and without His work, no one would be able to accept Christ. This plan of salvation was predestined before the foundation of the world. It is up to everyone to comply with God's plan. Therefore, under the working of the Holy Spirit each may choose to accept God's terms or to reject the plan of God and continue to be under the wrath of God. Nonetheless, God already knew the outcome.

But no man or woman experiences self-determinism in all life's events. God is sovereign and at times He still intercedes in one's life through particular acts. There are occasions when God, through His foreknowledge, has determined certain events and actions within one's life or the history of one's country. It seems to me that God has determined factors for and against those who bless or curse His people. How often has God interceded to protect His people who obeyed His word? And, how often has He chastised His people when they disobeyed Him and allowed the enemy of the people of God to experience victory? Sometimes God allows chastisement by removing the hedge (Heb. *Halo*) around His people, as He did Job, and allows Satan to be Satan. God does not initiate evil, yet He sometimes allows Satan to fulfill his desire to destroy. God sometimes initiates a somewhat "soft Determinism" to get a believer's attention when he or she lives outside His will by controlling events in such a way to bring an erring believer to repentance. Unlike full self-determinism, the believer still can refuse God which could result in sickness or even death (1 Cor. 11: 27 -32). This is a reaction to the free action of a believer living a sinful life resulting in the chastisement referred to by Paul (Heb. 12: 5 – 11).

There is evidence of "hard determinism" as a reaction of God protecting His obedient people such as Moses parting the Red Sea. Some may question the event when God hardened Pharaoh's heart. I believe that this too was a reaction of God to protect His people. Pharaoh was a lost soul. However, by him denying the Hebrews' freedom through the first nine plagues and the parting of the Red Sea God was able to demonstrate His power and when the people of other lands heard what God had done, they became afraid. God demonstrated His supernatural power when He caused the Hebrew people to cross over the Jordan River on dry ground while he held back the waters (Jos. 3 & 4). These acts of supernatural power frightened the enemies of God's people (Jos. 5; 1).

The Arminian Philosophical Theological View of the Foreknowledge of God: Robert E. Picirilli, an Arminian, affirms that the future is completely foreknown by God "and yet is, in principle and practice, "open" and "undetermined." He clarifies with the next sentence, "In other words, the person who makes a moral choice is free either to make that choice or to make a different choice."

Picirilli continues that "holding to this kind of "indetermination" [The view that human actions are not caused by anything.

They are simply unknown]...is considered to be necessary to affirm the reality of both God's omniscience (infallible foreknowledge) and human freedom." Picirilli further suggests that Arminians do not attempt to explain how both realities can be correct at the same time, nor do they think that it requires explaining.[177]

The reader must realize that when Robert Picirilli used the terms "open" and "undetermined" in conjunction with future actions and events, he was implying that the future is not fixed. A minority of modern Arminians (open Theists) have redefined foreknowledge to mean that God knows all that is possible to be known and that the future free acts of moral agents cannot be known. This view is referred to as the "limited foreknowledge" view.[178] This view questions the infinite omniscience of God; that God knows everything past, present, and the future.

The Calvinist Philosophical Theological View of the Foreknowledge of God: The meaning of the Calvinist view of the foreknowledge is found in a Calvinist Dictionary. It is defined as "God's knowledge of all future possibilities, contingencies, and actualities." It further states John Calvin's definition, "All things always were, and perpetually remain under his eyes, so that to his knowledge there is nothing future or past, but all things are present" ([Calvin's] Institute 3.21.5).[179] John Calvin believed that the future was fixed and could not be changed. That all world or individual actions and decisions were inflexibly caused and fixed by God. Often a Calvinist will interpret the word "foreknowledge" as "foreordained," which is a synonym of the word "predestination."[180]

PREDESTINATION

Predestination means to predetermine, to foreordain by divine decree. The question at hand is, what dynamics did God employ when determining the salvation of future believers and eternal hell for others? Some suggest that God elects some as believers or reproves others to an eternal hell based on foreseen faith or unbelief (His foreknowledge). Others suggest that God pre-determined that certain ones should be saved because of His unconditional election (they have no say-so in the matter), by determining that Christ only died for the pre-chosen elect.

The Arminian Philosophical Theological View of Predestination: Roger Olson, an Arminian, states that "what Arminians deny is not predestination but *unconditional* predes-tination [salvation that's not dependent upon foreknowledge, virtue, or faith], they embrace conditional predestination based upon God's foreknowledge of who will freely respond positively to God's gracious offer of salvation and the prevenient enable-ment to accept it [The idea that God restores each individual to the point where there is sufficient ability to believe]."[181]

The Calvinist Philosophical Theological View of Predestination: Most Calvinists deny that humans have any ability to choose. They believe God does not respond to one's action but is the very cause of all decisions and actions of humankind and that of salvation. Therefore, each action or decision has been pre-determined by God.

The Traditional Philosophical Theological View of Predestination: Traditionalists have adopted a foreknowledge view of predestination. This view suggests that from the very beginning of time that God knew how each human would live and act. God knew in advance whether one would accept Christ as Savior and who would reject Him. God knew humanity's free choices before each was made. The difference between the Romans 5 and the Free Grace Traditionalists is that God foreknows those who would believe "in Christ." He also predestinated new believers "in Christ" to be adopted sons and part of the elect. The electing, predestination, and adoption of all regenerated individuals occurs "in Christ." This means that a person is saved when he or she believes due to the drawing of the Holy Spirit. Therefore, God's choice of each one's eternity was made established on what He knew each one would freely choose concerning their salvation. Those who freely chose Him He predestinates "in Christ" and elect all who would respond favorably by faith to the call of the Holy Spirit. God chose the elect in advance since, with foreknowledge, He knew who would freely choose His Son and that He would place "in Christ" to fulfill his or her salvation.

The question at the beginning of this chapter was "What was the extent of the atonement?" The Calvinists insist that Christ only died for the elect, those who were preselected by God to save for the only reason known by God. The Arminians and Traditionalists insist that Christ died for all humanity and will save whoever receives His free gift of salvation. In chapter ten, I will discuss how the opposing philosophical-theological groups view the call of salvation and its importance and acceptance.

Part Four

How One Experiences Authentic Salvation

No one can come to Me unless the Father who sent Me draws him. And I will raise him up at the last day...And He said, "Therefore I have said to you that no one can come to Me unless it be granted to him by My Father...And I, if I am lifted up from the earth, will draw all *peoples* to Myself." John 6:44, 65; 12:32

Part four consists of one chapter that emphasizes that one's salvation is initiated by the work of the Holy Spirit while leaving the recipient the free will to chose.

CHAPTER TEN

The Call and Acceptance
of Salvation

No one can come to Me unless the Father who sent
Me draws him. And I will raise him up at the last
day...And He said, "Therefore I have said to you that
no one can come to Me unless it be granted to him
by My Father...And I, if I am lifted up from the earth,
will draw all *peoples* to Myself." John 6:44, 65; 12:32

During my childhood, the neighborhood boys played ball.
Often a mother would call out for her son to come home
for supper; this was before cell phones. When one mother would
call-out from one end of the neighborhood another mother
would hear and would face toward where the boys were playing
and called out to the son of the first mother, and so forth, until
the son was aware that his mother was calling and it was time
for him to stop playing and go home to eat supper. There were
times when the game was so exciting that the boy did not want
to stop playing when he was called. He would have to make a
choice to either heed the call of his mother or to act as though
he never heard the call and ignore it. This is similar to what I

will discuss concerning the call, conversion, and regeneration regarding salvation.

There are various opinions concerning the call and acceptance of salvation. This is why I wrote the last chapter to identify diverse interpretations concerning the extent of the atonement. With this background, I will establish how these interpretations embellish the opinions of God-fearing people concerning their belief of the meaning of the call and the acceptance of salvation. First, I will define the implications of the biblical word "call." Second, I will discuss the conflicting interpretations of the word "call" when applied to salvation. Lastly, I will discuss the biblical meaning and importance of the "call" to salvation.

When one looks up the word "call" he or she will find the following implications: To speak loudly as to be heard; To make a request or demand; To communicate by telephone; to make a brief visit; a command or request to be present; and many other implications.[182] The biblical word "call" like the regular English word, has many implications. Millard Erickson provides some of the implications such as, "a summons to salvation" or "a special position of service;" "a call that comes through the inner-working of the Holy Spirit;" "a call that is efficacious (having the power to produce the desired result) in a favorable response by the one called."[183]

Greek scholar, William Mounce defines both "call," "called," and "calling," by suggesting the adjective of the Greek word *kaleo* means to call, invite, appeal, or summon. This term is not only applicable to salvation but a life of service for Christ and others (1 Cor. 7:15; Eph. 4:1, 4; 1 Thess. 2:12; 4:7). The Greek *kletos* denote believers who have been called by God, such as to a Christian vocation (Rom. 1:1; 1 Cor. 1:1). Lastly, the Greek word *klesis* is a reference to God summoning people to Himself (Rom. 11:29; Phil. 3:14).[184]

Bruce Demarest suggests that the "calling in Scripture involves a God-given summons to salvation." He further suggests that some Christians distinguish between a general external call and a special internal call of the Spirit for salvation. The general external call, he discloses, is a presentation of the gospel with an invitation to repent of sins and trust Christ. It is a true who-so-ever-will invitation. Nonetheless, according to Demarest, some suggest that the general invitation is often met with indifference and rejection; thereby ineffectual. The inner and effectual call, he claims, provides salvation through a secret wooing of the Spirit (1 Cor. 1: 9, 26). This is an internal operation of the Holy Spirit that illumines the darkened mind, softens the stubborn will, and inclines the reluctant sinner to seek God. This internal call of the Spirit opens the sinner's heart, providing the individual both the desire and the ability to repent of sins and to have faith in Christ Jesus.[185]

It is important to bear in mind that the apostle John refers to the call as a drawing from God (John 6: 44; 12: 32). On one hand, some believe this inner call is irresistible while on the other hand others believe the call can be resisted by the individual.

When we combine all the biblical implications of the word "call" from the above information we observe the following:

- It is a summons, invitation, drawing, or an appeal to salvation.

- It may be a summons to a special position or vocation of service such as preaching, evangelizing, or some other form of ministry.
- It is a special inner working of the Holy Spirit that illuminates the darkened-mind, softens the rebellious will, and inclines the reluctant sinner to seek God.
- It can be efficacious.
- It can be a general external call with a gospel presentation with an invitation to repent.
- It is a wooing of the Holy Spirit.

During my early Christian life, it never occurred to me that there were diverse interpretations regarding the call to salvation. Throughout the first decade of my salvation I, like many I knew, just assumed that the call was a supernatural working of the Holy Spirit inviting the non-believer to salvation. I had never heard of Arminian or Calvinist theology. However, during my last three decades, I attended Seminary and later taught for two Bible colleges having the opportunity to study in detail both the Arminian and Calvinist views. I found myself convinced of some views of each and rejecting some of each. I have to acknowledge that there were times in which I changed my views as I continued to study. A major surprise was the divergence of views concerning the call of the salvation of the Arminians, the Calvinists, and the Traditionalists.

The Arminian View of the Call of Salvation: Classical Arminians believe that the call of salvation is followed by prevenient grace. Classical Arminians use the term "depravity," but more in a moral sense. The term total depravity is often understood that man's total nature is depraved with an inability to repent or exercise faith on his, or her, own accord. Therefore, any universal invitation to salvation makes little sense to their thinking. On the other hand, the Arminian view of moral depravity refers to one's immorality, their bent toward sin. Millard Erickson suggests that along with the Arminians denying total depravity they adopted the concept of "prevenient grace." Prevenient grace is often assumed as God's grace given to all humans indiscriminately. Arminians understand it as God sending sunshine and rain upon all. It is considered as the basis of goodness found in humans everywhere. Henry Thiessen explains it thus: "Since mankind is hopelessly dead in trespasses and sins and can do nothing to obtain salvation, God graciously restores to all men sufficient ability to choose the matter of submission to Him. This is the salvation-bringing grace of God that has appeared to all men."[186]

Progressive Arminians have eliminated the idea of depravity all together. Olson shares that Charles Finney denied original sin, except as a misery that has fallen on the majority of humanity and is passed on through bad examples. Finney taught that everyone has the ability and responsibility apart from any assistance of prevenient grace. He believed that a person could respond through enlightenment and persuasion to freely accept the forgiving grace of God through repentance and obedience to the moral government of God. Finney further wrote, "There is no degree of spiritual attainment required of us that may not be reached directly or indirectly by right willing," and "The moral government of God everywhere assumes and implies the liberty of the human will, and the natural ability of men to obey God."[187]

Classical Arminians understand the call of salvation as a Holy Spirit summons, or drawing, to initiate one's salvation and since each has a measure of prevenient grace he or she has the choice to receive or reject the call. Progressive Armenians, on the other hand, have a weak view of the call. They propose that one may freely decide to receive salvation through enlightenment and persuasion with little effort of the work of the Holy Spirit.

The Calvinist view of the Call of Salvation: Calvinists differentiate what they refer to as the general call (external) and the effectual call (inner call). They suggest that the general call is addressed to all sinners without distinction. It provides the truth and the terms of the gospel with a promise that all who receive Christ by faith will receive eternal life. Calvinists further believe that the general call will not impact the internal change in sinners that is necessary for one to exercise repentance and faith.

They believe that the effectual call accomplishes much more of the work than that of the general call. They believe that this call is initiated by the Holy Spirit only to the elect who were chosen before the foundation of the earth without any condition on their behalf. The effectual call is the inner call of the Holy Spirit that effects (making a change) by regenerating the spiritually dead sinner by enlightening their mind, renewing their will, and by providing them the gifts of repentance and faith. All who experience the inner call (effectual) will be saved. There is no choice. They first receive regeneration so that they may later experience repentance and faith.[188]

The Traditionalist View of the Call of Salvation: Since I have interviewed and read from those whom I would place in the traditional view, I will share the following consensus information regarding the call of salvation. Traditionalists agree with the

Calvinist concerning the total depravity of humankind. They emphatically agree that there is zero amount of righteousness in any man or woman that would allow them to come before the throne of grace in prayer searching for salvation and desiring fellowship with God. Many of them either oppose the Arminians' view of prevenient grace while some have no opinion on the matter and others have never even heard of it.

Traditionalists agree with the classical Arminians and the Calvinists that one's salvation is first initiated by the calling, or drawing, of the Holy Spirit. This drawing is caused by Christ who has the right to rule His kingdom. Jesus stated that He would draw all men to Himself (John 12:32). Jesus accomplishes this draw of humankind through the Holy Spirit. Traditionalists insist that anyone who experiences the outward (general) call also experiences the inner call. They view this call as a supernatural work of the Holy Spirit that illuminates the mind to spiritual understanding and enables men and women to understand the divine work of redemption (1 Cor. 2: 6 – 16). During the time-lapse of this act when the individual is experiencing this call, or drawing, he or she has the spiritual ability to experience conversion (repentance and faith) and almost simultaneously regeneration when God's free offer of salvation is accepted; or it may be refused. The period of the calling may last for minutes or days and without this calling, one would never have the ability to repent and exercise faith.

The apostle Paul emphasizes the importance of the call as he includes it in the five stages of salvation (Rom. 8: 28 – 30).

> And we know that all things work together for good
> to those who love God, to those who are the called

according to His purpose. For whom He foreknew, He also predestined to be conformed to the image of His Son, that He might be the firstborn among many brethren. Moreover, whom He predestined, these He also called; whom He called, these He also justified; and whom He justified, and these He also glorified.

Paul explains that each believer is called to conform to the image of God's Son. This image begins with the imputed righteousness of Christ and continues throughout the sanctification process. The first stage of the process begins with the foreknowledge of God; God foresaw who would obediently accept His divine plan of salvation. During the second stage, God predetermined His elect based upon His foreknowledge. Although God knew each individual's future decision, He continues to offer His call. This call would be rejected by some (God already knew they would reject Him, but as a just God He provided a call anyway). Nonetheless, the call is obediently accepted by many. Once accepted, the call became an effectual call (it was life-changing) and the salvation of the elect is actualized the moment he or she accepts the call by believing (agreeing with God) and God placing the believer "in Christ." The fourth stage of salvation is when God justified the believer by restoring him or her to the state of righteousness in God's sight. The last stage of salvation is the glorification of the believer. It involves the continuation of the sanctification process and the removal of spiritual defects in the believer's lifestyle.

To be "called" guarantees that one will have the opportunity to hear the gospel, which is not irresistible, and obediently accept it or disobediently reject it. Nonetheless, all saved believers have experienced the call and have obediently accepted it and therefore are referred to as "the called."

The call is the work of the Holy Spirit as He illuminates the heart and conscience of an individual which enables the person to understand the divine work of redemption (John 16: 8 – 12; 1 Cor. 2: 6 – 16). This call is completed by the two processes of drawing the person to Christ and to convict that person of sin.

The apostle John refers to this drawing of the Holy Spirit in John 6:44 and 12: 32. The Biblical Greek word *helkuo* means "to draw" or "to induce to come." [189] Calvinists often interpret this word as an irresistible drawing to go along with their idea of an irresistible call. Nonetheless, many scholars disagree with this interpretation. A. T. Robertson suggests that the words used in John 6:44 mean the same as drawing a net with fish, or a sword [note that there is resistance with both]. John 12:32, he suggests is like drawing with moral authority.[190] William Barclay provides the best description:

> Only those accept Jesus whom God draws to him. The word which John uses for *to draw* is *helkiein*... The interesting thing about the word is that it almost always implies some kind of resistance. It is the word for drawing a heavy laden net to the shore (John 21: 6, 11). It is used of Paul and Silas being dragged before the magistrates in Philippi (Acts 16: 19). It is the word for drawing a sword from the belt or from its scabbard (John 18:10). Always there is this idea of resistance. God can draw men, but man's resistance can defeat God's pull.[191]

It is imperative to understand that this drawing of God, with His illumination of the heart and conscience, initiates the salvation process. Liberals and progressive Arminians seem to overlook this most important experience. Because of this misunderstanding, many are living with false hope of salvation. One's salvation is eternal when it is initiated by the Holy Spirit, not by one's self or by man.

The apostle John provides a better understanding of the convicting power of the Holy Spirit in John, chapter sixteen. Jesus has informed His followers that He had to go away (16:5); nonetheless, He would send them a Helper (The Holy Spirit, 16: 7). Then Jesus states:

> And when He has come, He will convict the world of sin, and of righteousness, and of judgment: of sin, because they do not believe in Me; of righteousness, because I go to My Father and you see Me no more; of judgment because the ruler of this world is judged. John 16: 8 -12

Conviction is the act of the Holy Spirit persuading one through a sense of guilt and shame of his or her sinful nature with the undertaking of leading to repentance. Glenn McCoy suggests that a study of the above passage of Scripture yields the following results:

> First, the conviction of sin is the result of the Holy Spirit awakening humanity to a sense of guilt and condemnation because of sin and unbelief. Second, more than a mental conviction is intended. The total person is involved. This can lead to action based on

> a sense of conviction. Third, the conviction results in
> hope, not despair. Once individuals are made aware
> of their estranged relationship with God, they are
> challenged and encouraged to mend that relation-
> ship. The conviction not only implies the exposure
> of sin (despair) but a call to repentance (hope).[192]

True conviction results in a contrite heart, humility, and a strong
sense of guilt and shamefulness. David adds that this experience of the heart is not only contrite but that of a broken spirit
(Ps. 51:17). When the Holy Spirit calls a sinner, He first draws
them to God and then He convicts them of their sin.

Once a person has experienced the "call" of the Holy Spirit
to salvation he or she must decide to accept or reject God's
free offer of salvation; if accepted it will lead the unregenerate
individual to conversion and spiritual regeneration and God
placing the individual in Christ. There are diverse opinions concerning the order of conversion and regeneration. Some believe
that both happen simultaneously, others believe that conversion
must come first so that the individual may experience salvation,
while some believe that one must be first regenerated before he
or she may respond to conversion in his or her life. Following
is an overview of conversion and regeneration.

Conversion

Referring to conversion David Mapes explains, "Conversion is
what man is called upon to do. It has two distinguishable but
inseparable aspects which are like the positive and negative
poles of a magnet. The negative is repentance and the positive is
faith."[193] Conversion is the action of a person turning to Christ.

It includes renunciation of sin (repentance) and the acceptance of Christ as Lord and Savior (faith). I will provide more information regarding repentance and faith later. Jesus affirmed the need for conversion when stating, "Unless you are converted and become as little children, you will by no means enter the kingdom of heaven" (Matt. 18:3). Conversion is conceivable for any male or female who approaches God with simple trust as a child coming before his or her parents.

Calvinists insist that regeneration is before conversion. They suggest that since man is totally depraved that it is impossible for the elect to respond to the gospel call without first experiencing regeneration. Believing that all men and women are dead to God and are insensible or unresponsive to God just as if they were a dead person. Therefore, according to the Calvinist, the elect must first be made alive to God (regenerated) to respond to Him. Nonetheless, the Scriptures reveal that this conversion takes place before regeneration. "But as many as received Him, to them He gave the right to become children of God, to those who believe in His name" (John 1:12); note how belief precedes regeneration. Peter states, "If therefore God gave them the same gift as He gave us when we believed on the Lord Jesus Christ" (Acts 11:17). Paul suggests that conversion comes before regeneration with the following, "Knowing that a man is not justified by the works of the law but by faith [part of conversion] in Jesus Christ, even we have believed in Christ, that we might be justified by faith in Christ and not of the works of the law" (Gal. 2:16). Paul's reply to the Philippian jailor, "Believe on the Lord Jesus Christ and you will be saved" (Acts 16:31). David Mapes suggests how those who are dead in trespasses and sin can respond to God while totally depraved:

While man is dead in trespasses and sins, this does not mean that he is insensible to God. But, rather, that the person is separated from God. If all lost people really are insensible to God, then we should not find any verses in the Bible where God carries on a conversation with a lost person. But this is not the case. Several passages do exist where God speaks to lost people. For example, Genesis 4: 6 – 16 God converses with Cain on two occasions. Cain appears to be able to hear God and to respond to Him so that the idea of "dead" meaning insensible does not stand up under scrutiny. See also the account of Abimelech in Genesis 20: 3 – 7; Balaam in Numbers 22-23; and many other instances in Scripture. Therefore, God (the Holy Spirit) can speak to (illuminate) unsaved people while they are dead in trespasses and sin and bring them to a state of conviction at which time they may surrender their life to the Lord.[194]

Conversion has a divine side as well as a human side by representing the infiltration of divine grace into the human resulting in the resurrection from spiritual death to eternal life. The individual is active in his or her conversion, but as we shall discover passive in his or her regeneration. When I refer to the individual being active, I am not suggesting that one has the power to procure their salvation. I am suggesting that one is only active based on grace, only through the power of grace. Through this power of grace, one can decide his or her salvation once the inward eyes are open to the reality of their sinful life and the necessity of God's fellowship through the Spirit's free offer of salvation. Walter Elwell states: "Conversion is the sign but not the condition of our justification, whose sole source is the free unconditional grace of God."[195] The evidence of this grace of God is present when the sinner repents and by faith places his or her trust and life in the hands of God who positions the repented sinner "in Christ" completing his or her salvation. Earlier I referred to the two aspects of conviction: repentance and faith. I will discuss them in greater length at this time.

Repentance: Before one may truly comprehend the term "repentance" he or she must understand the biblical background for its requirement. All humankind's mind and nature is enmity against God (Rom. 8:7; Eph. 2: 15-16). The biblical word enmity (*echthra*) is defined as hatred or hostility.[196] This is not to suggest that all non-believers are holding their fists toward heaven and cursing God. Enmity is humankind's rebelliousness toward God and His will as their inclinations or orientations are gratified by self-motivation and depraved nature. Men and women may sometimes present themselves as religious or moral but only for psychological or selfish reasons. All unsaved human beings possess enmity against God because all are sinners (Rom. 3:23). Therefore, before one can come to God, he or she must have a change of mind and nature resulting in a change of direction.

In defining repentance D. L. Moody states, "Man is born with his face turned away from God. When he truly repents, he is turned right toward God; he leaves his old life."[197] A. W. Tozer references the essence of repentance, "To move across from one sort to another is the essence of repentance: the liar becomes truthful, the thief, honest."[198] Clark Palmer defines repentance as "Change of Mind; also can refer to regret or remorse accompanying a realization that wrong has been done or to any shift or reversal of thought. In its biblical sense repentance refers to a deeply seated and thorough turning from self to God. It occurs when radical turning to God takes place, an experience in which God is recognized as the most important fact of one's existence."[199]

Millard Erickson provides a richer explanation by first relating that repentance is based upon the feeling of godly sorrow for one's sin. He points to two Hebrew words that are often used in Scripture relating to repentance. The first Hebrew word is *nacham* which came to mean "to lament (to cry out or wail) or to grieve." When referring to an emotion of consideration of others, it suggests compassion and sympathy. When used in consideration of one's character or deeds, it means "to rue (regret or deplore)" or "to repent."

The second Hebrew word that he refers to is *shub*. This word is the most common word that denotes the genuine repentance that humans are expected to display. Erickson states that "it stresses the importance of a conscience morals separation, the necessity of forsaking sin and entering into fellowship with God." He provided an example of the meaning by quoting 2 Chronicles 7:14: "If My people who are called by My name will humble themselves, and pray and seek My face, and turn from their wicked ways, then I will hear from heaven, and will forgive their sin and heal their land."

Erickson continues by referring to two major New Testament Greek words; *metameloman* and *metanoeo*. The first word, *metameloman*, suggests a feeling of care, concern, or regret. It stresses the emotional aspect of repentance (Note Matt. 21:29 – 32; Matt. 27:3; Heb. 12:17). Erickson suggests that the second word *metanoeo* means "to think differently about something or to have a change of mind."[200] Erickson further suggests that there is a difference between simple regret and true repentance:

> Repentance is a godly sorrow for one's sin together with a resolution to turn from it. There are other forms of regret over one's wrongdoings that are based on different motivations. If we have sinned and the consequences are unpleasant, we may well regret what we have done. But that is not true repentance. That is mere penitence. Real repentance is sorrow for one's sin because of the wrong done to God and the hurt inflicted upon Him. The sorrow is accompanied by a genuine desire to abandon that sin. There is regret over the sin irrespective of sin's personal consequence.[201]

The Scriptures insist that repentance is a prerequisite for salvation. There can be no conversion without repentance in deed and attitude. Anything less is nothing but cheap grace (easy believism) and is unacceptable to God.

Faith: While repentance is the negative aspect of true conversion, faith is the positive aspect. During repentance, the non-believer turns away from sin, while in faith he turns to Christ. Repentance and faith are inseparable; you cannot have one without the other. Therefore, true repentance cannot exist apart from faith or faith from repentance. It has been said that repentance is faith in action and faith is repentance in rest.[202]

There are different types of faith. There is natural faith which is a belief or confidence possessed by all humanity which varies in degrees that are established upon measurable testimony, life's experiences, and upon considered evidence. This faith of intellect or experience is insufficient to meet God's requirement for salvation. This natural faith may divulge the existence of God, but not the ability to believe in Him (as Lord and Savior). Satan and his demons know that God exists, but they do not trust in Him. Tragically, many only possess a natural faith rather than a spiritual saving faith in Christ who are living with false hope of salvation.

Spiritual saving faith, according to Henry H. Bancroft, "is that belief or confidence possessed by regenerated believers in varying degrees which rest upon the knowledge of God and His will as obtained through revelation and personal experiences." [203] I need to clarify this statement. When one exercises his or her faith while obtaining their salvation that faith must be full. Nevertheless, after one has experienced salvation there are times when that faith may vary (more later). Bruce Demarest sheds light on spiritual saving faith by suggesting that it is a multidimensional reality:

- Faith involves the knowledge of Christ (John 20:31) revealed in the gospel Scriptures which are a message of a rational foundation and truth. The term "belief" best captures the aspect or meaning of faith. Nonetheless, knowledge of the truths of the good news (gospel) presented in Scripture by itself does not save (John 2: 23 -24).

- Faith that saves requires a personal acceptance of the truth of the gospel (Luke 24: 25; 2 Thess. 2:13). One must not only understand the truth but also agree to the truth of the gospel without reservation from the heart.

This includes the acceptance of the truth of Jesus' deity (John 1:1), His sacrificial death upon the cross (1 Cor. 15:3), and His resurrection from the dead (Rom.10:9).

- Authentic salvation includes unreserved trust in and a commitment to Christ Jesus as a personal Savior (2 Tim. 1:2). This trust and commitment result in the believer counting the cross of discipleship. The evidence of true faith is obedience in the life of the believer (Rom. 1:5) and good works (1 Thess. 1:3) that bless others and glorify God.[204]

William Mounce offers a little more comprehensive description. The noun for the Greek word "faith" is *pistis,* which means belief, trust, or confidence. He proceeded to provide the following example of the use of the word:

- Faith, which is saving, can refer to the act of believing (Mark 11:22). Most often it refers to faith in, or believing in, Jesus Christ (Acts 3; 16; Gal. 3:26; Eph. 1:15). This faith in Christ assures that he or she may approach God (Heb. 10:22). This faith in Christ protects the believer against the enemy since it is a part of the armor of God (Eph. 6:6). The writer of Hebrews defines this faith as "Now faith is the substance of things hoped for, the evidence of things not seen" (Heb. 11; 1).

- Degrees of faith may vary from believer to believer after salvation. Faith may be weak (Rom. 14:1), it can be possessed in differing measures (Rom. 12: 3, 6), and can grow (2 Cor. 10:15; 2 Thess. 1:3). Faith may be tested and possibly strengthened when faced with the trials of life (1 Thess. 3:2 – 10). The successful testing of faith will result in perseverance (Jas. 1:3).

- Faith can refer to Christian doctrine or a collection of beliefs (Jas. 2:17; Phil. 1:27; 1 Tim. 1:13; Tit 2:2). Sometimes it refers to the Christian religion as a whole as in Paul's exhortation to the Corinthians to "stand firm in the faith (1 Cor. 6: 13).

- Faith can denote a certainty of belief (Mk. 11:23) or an assurance of proof such as an assurance that God will send Jesus back to judge the world by raising Him from the dead (Acts 17: 31).[205]

I explained previously in this chapter that faith is not considered "works" but rather simply believing or agreeing with what God says (Rom.4: 1 – 4). However, it should be noted that God's grace and saving faith go hand in hand. "For by grace you have been saved through faith, and that not of yourself; it is the gift of God (Eph. 23:8). Previously Paul's message has been: you were dead in trespasses and sin, but God is rich in mercy and has made the believers alive together with Christ (Eph. 2: 1 – 5). Paul suggests God's purpose was to exhibit His grace (Eph. 2: 6 – 7). This same grace is reiterated throughout this section as the basis for salvation (Eph. 2: 7 – 8). Grace is received by men and women "through faith" (Eph. 2:8). Paul previously stated that the righteousness from God comes through faith in Jesus Christ to all who believe (that is saving or believing faith; Rom. 3:22).

The nature of saving faith is a heart response to hearing or reading the gospel message. Paul reveals this in Romans 10: 9

– 10, "That if you confess with your mouth the Lord Jesus and believe in your heart that God has raised Him from the dead, you will be saved. For with the heart one believes unto righteousness, and with the mouth, confession is made unto salvation." Millard Erickson affords additional elements as to the nature of saving faith when explaining John 1:12, "But as many as received Him, to them He gave the right to become children of God, to those who believe in His name." Erickson suggests that this verse was very significant to the Hebrew people who regarded one's name as virtually equivalent to the person. To believe in or in the name of Jesus was to place one's trust in Him. Whereas he concluded that the type of faith necessary for salvation involves both believing "that" and believing "in"; assenting to the facts and trusting in a person.[206] Therefore, saving faith is an acceptable response to believing that: (1) what the Bible reveals about God is true, (2) that all men and women are unrighteous sinners and in need of Christ as Savior, (3) that Christ is God, born of a virgin, died on the cross, and three days later raised from the grave to make atonement for sin, and (4) that one must place his or her faith in Him for salvation. Saving faith is also the accepting response to believe "in" Christ as Savior and "in" Christ as Lord meaning that Christ is the Master and you are the servant who obeys His will and Word.

Paul reminds the reader that it is "not of yourselves, it is the gift of God, not of works, lest anyone should boast" (Eph. 2: 8 – 9). The question is what was Paul referring to; was it grace or faith? Calvinists suggest that Paul was referring to faith as the gift of God. Nevertheless, John Calvin himself did not: "He [Paul] does not mean that faith is the gift of God, but that salvation is given to us by God."[207] Paul is referring to salvation by grace as the gift of God. Salvation is a gift of God. There is nothing within the sinner that has inclined God to choose us. There is nothing one may do to gain righteousness other than to depend on the imputed righteousness of Christ. Therefore, without God's grace, there would be no salvation. Without God's grace, there would be no saving faith provided where a lost unregenerate sinner could ever experience spiritual regeneration and have fellowship and peace with God.

Regeneration

Gregg Allison suggests regeneration as:

> The mighty work of God by which unbelievers are given a new nature, being born again. Regeneration is particularly ascribed to the Holy Spirit (John 3: 3 – 8) working through the gospel (James 1:18; 1 Pet. 1: 23 – 25). It is both (1) the removal of one's old sinful nature, and the imparting of a new nature that is responsive to God. Unlike conversion, which is the human response to the gospel, regeneration is completely a divine work, to which human beings contribute nothing.[208]

Bruce Demarest suggests that:

> Regeneration brings about radically new outcomes for those who believe. The new birth...imparts to the soul a new spiritual nature (Ephesian 4: 24; 2 Peter 1:4), and unites the life to Christ (Galatians 2:20; Hebrews 3:14). By imparting a new nature, Holy Spirit regeneration infuses into the soul renewed intellectual, volitional [making conscious choices],

> moral, emotional, and relational powers that initiate
> the renewal of *imago Dei*- being made in the image
> of God – in the Christian's through the process of
> lifelong sanctification.[209]

Let me take a moment and address Gregg Allison's and Bruce Demarest's references to the new nature received when one experiences regeneration. I do not know if they were referring to the ontological nature of man or to the propensity (inclination) of an individual to act in one way or another. Therefore, it is important to clarify the nature of man that has experienced a change. When I am referring to the ontological nature of a man or woman, I am referring to his or her being. Ontology refers to that which is real, that of being. In chapter three, I discussed the dichotomy of men and women. Each one is made up of the material (flesh or body) and the immaterial (spirit) when joined together they form a soul (human being). The nature of a man = body + spirit. It requires both parts to make up the single nature of man. Therefore, the nature does not equal just the spirit. One's spirit is not something that can be touched since it is the immaterial part of the human ontological nature. A living human being exhibits a certain behavior, which, unfortunately, is also called the nature. Hence, to distinguish this use of the word "nature" from the ontological nature, this nature could be called behavioral or psychological nature.

When the Scripture speaks of the "new man," it is referring to the behavioral nature, not the ontological nature. Regeneration does not affect the component parts of the ontological nature (body + spirit), but it does affect the behavior of the person (i.e. the behavioral nature). Every person born receives a corrupted ontological nature, which results in bad behavior. Regeneration does not change the ontological nature since a person, who is saved, continues to sin. Nonetheless, a person's thought processes (behavioral nature) do change due to the indwelling of the Holy Spirit. The Holy Spirit makes us alive to God and changes the way we think and act. He works in us both to will and to do His good pleasure (Rom. 1:5; Phil. 2:13). In Romans 5, Paul shows that God, through grace, has provided the "free gift" of salvation to every person who believes. God's provision of salvation brings the person into a relationship with Himself and frees the new believer from the bondage of sin.

Note Romans 6:3 -5, "Or do you not know that as many of us *as were* baptized into Christ Jesus were baptized into His death. Therefore, we were buried with Him through baptism into death, that just as Christ was raised from the dead by the glory of the Father, even so, we also should walk in newness of life. For if we have been united together in *the likeness* of His death, certainly we also shall be *in the likeness* of His resurrection" (italics is mine). Now I will explain this text by first asking the reader a question. When you experienced your salvation, did you physically die like our Lord? The answer of course is a resounding "no!" There are many instances where the Holy Spirit used literary devices to reveal His word. One of the devices is that of using metaphors. A metaphor is the use of a word or phrase that should not be interpreted literally, but rather a literary device of a vivid comparison that expresses or represents something about the subject. Paul was metaphorically speaking about the death of the new believer. Christ's death was itself a "death to sin." Paul states, "We have been united together *in the* likeness of His death." A believer's nature should reflect Christ's death to sin. Douglas Moo writes concerning the death of Christ to sin, "So close is this association with Christ's death that we may be said to have been "buried with Him." Burial both sets the seal on death and prepares for that which is to follow: living a new life patterned after the resurrection of Christ."[210] One's original nature never ceased to exist; it was not annihilated. The person is filled with the Holy Spirit of God who changes our behavior from hostility or enmity toward God to one that consists of the Spirit and His illumination and now has fellowship with God. Although the believer's nature is no longer totally depraved, it still experiences the inclination or propensity to sin. Paul encourages the believer to overcome his or her "old man," one's former lifestyle. The believer is no longer the slave to sin but rather should be the slave to righteousness. Paul further urges the believer not to allow sin to reign in his or her mortal bodies and not to present the members of his or her body as instruments to sin. God's people producing fruits of righteousness accomplishes this. Later, in Galatians chapter 5, Paul provides a list of unrighteous fruits and a list of righteous fruits. Later, in the next chapter when I discuss the topic of sanctification, I will present more information regarding the new man.

David Mapes suggests that "regeneration is a supernatural work that God does to the repentant person which restores a relationship with God lost by Adam (See Ezek. 36:27). "And I will put my Spirit within you, and cause you to walk in my statutes, and ye shall keep my judgments, and do them." The regenerated person is no longer at enmity with God because of his permanently changed mind."[211]

Greek scholar William Mounce suggests that the basic Greek word for regeneration is *palingenesia*. Nonetheless, in the New Testament, the concept is much larger than this one word. He states that often the word refers to the "new birth" (John 3:

3 – 5) and the "new creation" (2 Cor. 5: 17; Gal. 6:15). He further explains that in conversion the believer is made new, brought from death to life (Eph. 2: 1 – 5), by the power of God's Holy Spirit.[212]

Biblical support confirming the meaning of regeneration is found in John's gospel chapter three; and Paul's epistle such as 2 Corinthians 5: 17.

In John chapter three, Jesus claims that the unregenerate man or woman must be born again (another term for regeneration, verse 3). Nicodemus responds with the following question, "How can a man be born when he is old? Can he enter a second time into his mother's womb and be born?" (v.4). Over the next several verses Jesus answers this question by comparing the difference between the fleshly physical birth to spiritual birth. The physical birth begins when the water breaks while the spiritual birth is accomplished by the infilling of the Spirit (v.5). Jesus immediately re-emphasized this statement by stating, "that which is born of the flesh is flesh, and that which is born of the Spirit is Spirit" (v.6). David Mapes' suggests, "To be born of the Spirit means that the Holy Spirit now takes up residence in the person or indwells the person. I believe that when a person is saved, nothing about that person changes. The person now in Christ is a new creation because he is indwelt by the Holy Spirit who causes us both to will and to do God's good pleasure."[213] All humans possess *bios*, or biological life. Nonetheless, born again believers possess a *zoe* life, a new spiritual life. Spiritual regeneration is a new beginning and a relationship with God. Everyone is born by water, nonetheless, only those who have been reborn with the Spirit will have fellowship with God and spend eternity with Him in heaven.

Paul states, "Therefore, if anyone is in Christ [an aspect of true regeneration], he is a new creation; old things have passed away; behold, all things are new" (2 Cor. 5:17). Authentic regeneration will cause a change in one's life and nature. He or she is a new creature; the old things of their life have passed away.

Paul Enns suggests two major results of regeneration:

> *A new nature.* The result of regeneration is the impartation of "divine nature" (2 Pet. 1:4). The believer has received a "new self" (Eph. 4:24), a capacity for righteous living. He is a "new creature" (2 Cor. 5:17).

> *A new life.* The believer has received a new mind (1 Cor. 2:16) he or she might know God; a new heart (Rom 5:5) that he may love God (1 John 4:9); and a new will (Rom. 6:13) that he may obey God.[214]

When we consider the above definitions of regeneration, we can summarize the following:

- Regeneration is the supernatural work of God particularly ascribed to the Holy Spirit in which the new believer contributes nothing.

- It results in the new believer no longer experiencing enmity with God but rather being born anew by removing the old sinful nature being replaced with a new nature responsive to God.

- It brings forth a radical new outcome and imparts to the soul a new spiritual nature.

- Holy Spirit regeneration infuses into the soul renewed intellectual, volitional, moral, emotional, and relational powers that initiate the renewal of *imago Dei*- being made in the image of God.

- Regeneration begins the sanctification process starting with the new believer as a child of God and the maturing process thereafter until the believer is in heaven with Christ.

- The Scriptures provide additional words to ascribe regeneration such as "born again," "the new birth," or "new creation."

I desire that this chapter helps the reader to understand that one's salvation is initiated by the call of the Holy Spirit, that during this event the non-believer is convicted of his or her sinful life, and the realization that the work of Christ on the cross provides the only hope of salvation. The Holy Spirit encourages the individual to have faith (to accept as true) that Christ died on the cross, He was buried for our sins, and was raised on the third day. And if the individual would place their faith, not only in the truth but in Christ Jesus and make Him Savior and Lord, he or she would experience regeneration. This regeneration experience will result in the righteousness of Christ imputed to them so that he or she will have a relational fellowship with God while standing before Him justified and righteous. Once the believer has experienced the regeneration of the Holy Spirit, he or she discovers many benefits. We will discuss these benefits in the next chapter.

Part Five

The Results of Authentic Salvation

Blessed be the God and father of our Lord Jesus Christ, who has blessed us with every spiritual blessing in the heavenly places in Christ, just as He chose us in Him before the foundation of the world that we should be holy and without blame before Him in love, having predestined us to adoption as sons by Jesus Christ to Himself, according to the good pleasures of His will, to the praise of the glory of His grace by which He made us accepted in the Beloved. In Him we have redemption through His blood, the forgiveness of sins, according to the riches of His grace which He made to abound toward us in all wisdom and prudence, having made known to us the mystery of His will, according to His good pleasures which He purposed in Himself, that in the dispensation of the fullness of times He might gather together in one all things in Christ, both which are in heaven and which are on earth – in Him. In Him also we have obtained an inheritance, being predestined according to the purpose of Him who works all things according to the counsel of His will, that we who first trusted in Christ should be the praise of His glory. In Him you also trusted after you heard the word of truth, the gospel of your salvation; in whom also, having believed, you were sealed with the Holy Spirit of promise, who is the guarantee of our inheritance until the redemption of the purposed possession, to the praise of His glory. Eph. 1: 3–14

Part five consists of two chapters that disclose all the wonderful changes and blessings of the Holy Spirit that are experienced immediately at salvation as one is placed "in Christ." The writer follows up by disclosing the continuing work of the Holy Spirit after the experience of authentic salvation that empowers the believer to be an obedient vessel for Christ.

CHAPTER ELEVEN

The Blessings of Salvation

Blessed be the God and father of our Lord Jesus
Christ, who has blessed us with every spiritual
blessing in the heavenly places in Christ, just as He
chose us in Him before the foundation of the world
that we should be holy and without blame before
Him in love, having predestined us to adoption as
sons by Jesus Christ to Himself, according to the
good pleasures of His will, to the praise of the glory
of His grace by which He made us accepted in the
Beloved. In Him we have redemption through His
blood, the forgiveness of sins, according to the riches
of His grace which He made to abound toward us
in all wisdom and prudence, having made known to
us the mystery of His will, according to His good
pleasures which He purposed in Himself, that in
the dispensation of the fullness of times He might
gather together in one all things in Christ, both
which are in heaven and which are on earth – in
Him. In Him also we have obtained an inheritance,
being predestined according to the purpose of Him
who works all things according to the counsel of
His will, that we who first trusted in Christ should

> be the praise of His glory. In Him you also trusted
> after you heard the word of truth, the gospel of your
> salvation; in whom also, having believed, you were
> sealed with the Holy Spirit of promise, who is the
> guarantee of our inheritance until the redemption of
> the purposed possession, to the praise of His glory.
> Eph. 1: 3–14

The new believer's salvation is initiated by a call of the Holy Spirit. With the exercise of free will, he or she undergoes conversion (repentance and faith) and immediate regeneration by the Holy Spirit when God places the individual "in Christ." Precisely at that moment the new believer's life and nature (behavior, not ontological) begin to transform as he or she experiences several immediate blessings of the salvation gained when positioned "in Christ." Throughout the rest of this chapter, I will endeavor to share and explain the following immediate blessings received at salvation, such as union with Christ, forgiveness of sin, adoption into the family of Christ, justification, and sanctification.

The New Believer's Union with Christ

Union with Christ, Gregg Allison suggests, is the mighty work of God as He joins His people in an eternal covenant with His Son who completed their salvation on the cross. Through the union, the believer identifies with Christ's death, burial, resurrection, and ascension (Rom. 6:1 – 11; Eph. 2:6). Through this union, God communicates all His blessings of salvation such as grace, regeneration, redemption, eternal life, justification, and sanctification. He furthers defines it as Christ dwelling in those whom He is united, and they, in turn, dwell in Him (John 15: 1 – 5; Gal. 2: 20).[215]

This union between Christ and believers was the predetermined plan and purpose of God. Paul establishes this, "Just as He chose us in Him before the foundation of the world, that we should be holy and without blame before Him in love" (Eph. 1:4). This union commences the moment the Christian is made alive (spiritually quickened) together with Christ, which is the opposite of spiritual death, as Paul suggests, "even when we were dead in trespasses, made us alive together with Christ" (Eph. 2:5). Paul explains, in First Corinthians chapter twelve, that all believers are baptized by the Holy Spirit to make up one body, which is Christ. He further reports that each member has a particular function within the body for which to serve. God receives each one that has been made alive in the Spirit and engrafts him or her into this life-union with Christ.

Paul explains the transfer of federal headship during the initiation of the union with Christ, which is the judicial aspect of one's union (Rom. 5: 12 – 21). Under the headship of Adam, all human beings suffer the guilt and nature of sin. The result of the new union with Christ (the second Adam) is His imputation of our sins to Himself and the imputation of His righteousness to the new believer. Thereby, in a legal sense, the believer is no longer under the headship of Adam but rather under Christ. He is the believer's representative, he or she possesses all the assets of Christ.

The union with Christ is a spiritual union authored by the Holy Spirit (1 Cor. 6:17; 12:13). Paul explains how dynamic the spiritual union is in one's life, "I have been crucified with Christ; it is no longer I who live, but Christ lives in me; and the life which I now live in the flesh I live by faith in the Son of God, who loved me and gave Himself for me" (Gal. 2: 20). He also clarifies how Christ must be revealed throughout the life of the believer, "If then you were raised with Christ, seek those things which are above, where Christ is, sitting at the right hand of God. Set your mind on things above, not on things on the earth. For you died, and your life is hidden with Christ in God" (Col. 3: 1 – 3).

Henry Thiessen suggests four consequences of this union; First, union with Christ speaks to the eternal security of the believer (John 10:28 -30) in which there is nothing that can separate the believer from the love of God, which is in Christ Jesus (Rom. 8:38). Second, union with Christ speaks to fruitfulness (John 15:5). Paul provides a list of fruits of the Spirit that should be a characteristic of the believer (Gal. 5: 22; Rom. 6:22; 7:4; Eph. 5:9). Third, union with Christ means endowment for service (1 Cor. 12: 4 – 30).And Last, the Union with Christ means fellowship with God. The believer is placed into God's confidence and made acquainted with His purposes and plans (Eph. 1:8).[216]

In Christ, God Forgives Sin

Billy Graham once stated, "In these days of guilt complexes, perhaps the most glorious word in the English language is forgiveness." [217] Forgiveness is something that we all seek, but in many cases is hard to receive. Many will tell you that they forgive you, but they never forget. Thus, there is a strain on most relationships. The glorious truth in this study is that God forgives and forgets. Oswald Chambers speaks of this truth, "The most marvelous ingredient in the forgiveness of God is that He also forgets; the one thing a human being can never do.

Forgetting with God is a divine attribute; God's forgiveness forgets."[218]

In defining forgiveness, Paul Enns states, "Forgiveness is the legal act of God whereby He removes the charges that were held against the sinner because proper satisfaction or atonement for those sins has been made."[219] He proceeds to share two of several Greek words used to describe forgiveness in the New Testament. The first word is *charizomai*, which relates to the word "grace" which means, "to forgive out of grace." It refers to the cancellation of a debt (Col. 2:13). "The context emphasizes that our debts were nailed to the cross, with Christ's atonement freely forgiving the sins that were charged against us." The second word is the most common word for forgiveness is *aphiemi*, which means, "to let go, release" or "send away." Paul spoke of this word, "In Him, we have redemption through His blood, the forgiveness of sins, according to the riches of His grace" (Eph. 1:7). Paul stresses that the believer's sins have been forgiven or sent away because of the riches of God's grace as revealed in the death of Christ.[220] Concerning the extent of God's forgiveness the Psalmist wrote, "As far as the east is from the west, so far He removed our transgressions from us" (Ps. 103: 12).

The forgiveness of sins extends after one's salvation, "If we confess our sins, He is faithful and just to forgive us our sins and to cleanse us from all unrighteousness" (1 John 1:9). Confession is the admission of sin and guiltiness. It is a sincere acknowledgment of the wrongdoing of the act before God. Since the believer is in Christ, he or she is expected to forgive others as God forgives us (Matt. 6: 14 – 15; Col. 3:13). To choose not to forgive is a serious sin (Matt. 18: 34 –35).

In Christ, the Believer is Adopted into the Family of God

Through His redeeming act, God takes the sinful people who were once alienated and separated from His fellowship and bestows positive favor as He embraces each as a treasured child into His family through the Spirit's working act of adopting them as sons and daughters, by whom God is referred to as "Abba! Father!" (John 1:12; Rom. 8: 14 – 16; Gal. 4: 4 – 7; 1 John 3:1). Thereby, all who are adopted into this family are brothers and sisters in the Lord, united with one another (Gal. 3: 26 – 28) and fellow heirs with their brother Jesus Christ (Rom. 8:17). Note Galatians 4: 1 – 7:

> Now I say that the heir, as long as he is a child, does not differ at all from a slave, though he is a master of all, but is under guardians and stewards until the time appointed by the father. Even so we, when we were children, were in bondage under the elements of the world. But when the fullness of the time had come, God sent forth His Son, born of a woman, born under the law, that we might receive the adoption as sons. And because you are sons, God has sent forth the Spirit of His Son into your hearts, crying out, "Abba Father!" Therefore, you are no longer a slave but a son, and if a son, then heir of God through Christ.

The apostle Paul employs a Roman background to describe the biblical meaning of this new status of adoption in Christ. Paul Enns provides a great summary of Paul's explanation:

The word *adoption* (Gr. *Huiothesia*) means, "placing as a son" and describes the rights and privileges as well as the new position of the believer in Christ. The word is taken from a Roman custom where, in a legal ceremony, the adopted son was given all the rights of a natural-born son. In this rite, four things happened. "[a] The adopted person lost rights in his old family and gained all the rights of a fully legitimate son in his new family. [b] He became heir to his new father's estate. [c] The old life of the adopted person was completely wiped out. For instance, legally all debts were canceled; they were wiped out as if they had never been. [d] In the eyes of the law the adopted person was literally and absolutely the son of his new father."[221]

In Christ, the Believer is Justified

During my early seminary years, I attended a course taught by my advisor and later close friend, Dr. Roebuck Burch. One day he wrote the word "justify" on the board. He proceeded by instructing the students to take out a pen and a paper since he was about to define the word. We thought that this was going to be an exceedingly academic definition when he stated, "When God looks upon me clothed in the righteousness of His Son, He sees me 'just-if-I' had not sinned." Speaking of justification, Henry Smith states, "He hides our unrighteousness with His righteousness. He covers our disobedience with His obedience. He shadows our death with His death that the wrath of God cannot find us."[222] Lastly, Thomas Watson reminds us, "God does not justify us because we are worthy, but by justifying us makes us worthy."[223]

The major emphasis of justification, Paul Enns suggests, involves two main aspects. "It involves the pardon and removal of all sins and the end of separation from God (Acts 13: 39; Rom. 4: 6 – 7; 5: 9 – 11; 2 Cor. 5:19). It also involves the bestowal of righteousness upon the believing person and a title to all the blessings promised to the just." [224]

Justification is a declarative act of God. This means that justification is not based upon anything that an individual may do. The believer is legally "declared" righteous. Justification does not make one upright or cause one to live a life of perfection. It only means that one is declared righteous, or not guilty, since his or her sins were pardoned, and the penalty of sin has been settled through the atoning bloodshed on the cross. Paul clarifies this truth when stating,

> Being justified freely by His grace through the redemption that is in Christ Jesus, whom God set forth as a propitiation by His blood, through faith to demonstrate His righteousness, because in His forbearance God had passed over the sins that were previously committed to demonstrate at this present time His righteousness that He might be the just and the justifier of the one who has faith in Jesus"(Rom. 3: 24 – 26)

In Christ, the Believer is Sanctified

Millard Erickson provides a simple, but vague, definition of sanctification, "The divine act of making the believer holy – that is, bringing the person's moral condition into conformity with the legal status established in justification."[225] Alan Cairns suggests that the verb "sanctification" has two meanings: 1) to consecrate, or set apart for a sacred purpose (John 10: 36). 2) To purify or make holy (John 17: 17; 1 Cor. 6: 11; Heb. 13: 12).[226] The first meaning is the experience of salvation, while the other is experience throughout one's Christian life. Spiros Zodhiates provides additional insights when referring to the Greek word *hagiazo*, which is from the word *hagios* (holy). There is a connection between one of the meanings of the word holy and the word sanctification. They both suggest cleanliness and purity. To make clean in a moral sense, to consecrate (to dedicate or revere), devote, or set apart from the common to a sacred use since, in the Jewish ritual, this was one great object of the purification. It further speaks of a person as being set apart by God and sent by Him for the performance of His will (John 10: 36; 17:17).[227] Therefore, the reader may read a Scripture verse relating to "holy" and notice that it may be a synonym of the word "sanctification."

When one examines the doctrine of sanctification, he or she soon discovers that the doctrine is divided into the following three stages: positional sanctification, progressive sanctification, and perfection or final sanctification.

Positional Sanctification: It is my understanding that all believers are positionally sanctified (set apart) unto God when declared justified and holy at regeneration and each identified as a saint. The reader should note that the act of justification only declares the regenerated individual righteous; it does not make him or her righteous. This is the work of sanctification. Tragically, there are those whose denomination suggests that one may experience salvation and sanctification may come later, if at all. They feel unfulfilled while seeking some emotional or psychological experience. The truth of the matter is that they experienced positional sanctification at the moment of regeneration.

Positional sanctification speaks of the believer's instantaneous standing before God. Note Paul's comments to the Corinthians, "To the Church of God which is at Corinth, to those who are sanctified in Christ Jesus" (1 Cor. 1:2), But of Him you are in Christ Jesus, who became for us wisdom from God – and righteousness and sanctification and redemption" (1 Cor. 1: 30). The reader may find more enlightenment of sanctification when the apostle Paul reveals his shame of the believers in Corinth for suing one another and behaving much like those who were unbelievers (1 Cor. 6: 4 – 10). He reminds them whom they are (set apart for the purposes of God) and how each is supposed to behave when he writes, "And such were some of you. But you were washed [regenerated], but you were sanctified, but you were justified in the name of the Lord Jesus and by the Spirit of God" (6: 11). Did you notice that Paul had written his epistle to all the saints and that all had experienced sanctification? No believer residing in the Corinth Church was without sanctification. Paul explains that each one experienced regeneration, justification, and sanctification simultaneously, which provides more evidence that positional sanctification begins at regeneration; it is not something that the believer must seek.

Because of the believer's regeneration, justification, and sanctification Paul further employs, "Or do you not know that your body is the temple of the Holy Spirit [holy dwelling, set apart for the service of God] who is in you, whom you have from God, and you are not your own? For you were bought with a price;

therefore, glorify God in your body and in your spirit, which are God's" (6: 19 – 20).

Sanctification, like union with Christ, begins the journey of changing the life and standing of the regenerated individual when his or her federal headship was transferred during the initiation of the union with Christ (Rom. 5: 12 – 21). Since the believer has "been crucified with Christ," he or she no longer should live life as his or her own, but for Christ who lives within (Gal. 2: 210). Since Christ is the believer's federal head, He (Christ) must be exhibited throughout the life of the believer. As Paul previously stated, "If then you were raised with Christ, seek those things which are above, where Christ is, sitting at the right hand of God. Set your mind on things above, not on things on the earth. For you died, and your life is hidden with Christ in God" (Col. 3: 1 – 3). Therefore, this change of headship and a new position in Christ sets the believer apart (sanctified) from this world economy.

The moment salvation is experience the Spirit not only changes their standing by placing the individual "in Christ" but now indwells them. He, the Spirit, sets the believer apart as a holy vessel for the sacred purpose of fulfilling God's will. Positional sanctification is the beginning of the believer's progressive sanctification as he or she matures in the Lord.

Progressive Sanctification: Unlike positional sanctification, which stresses the believer's standing with God, progressive sanctification stresses the believer's walk with God. In discussing the progressive sanctification of the believer, John MacArthur states:

> Though the believer enjoys this decisive victory over the dominion of sin as a result of union with Christ, his heart and life are not totally purified. Though the penalty of sin is paid for and the power of sin is broken, the presence of sin still remains in the believer's flesh and therefore must continually be put to death. Thus, the sanctification that begins definitively at regeneration necessarily continues throughout the entirety of the Christian life. This continuous aspect of sanctification is called progressive sanctification.[228]

The constant, progressive nature of sanctification is authenticated by the Scripture's frequent challenge to the regenerated believer to live a life of holiness (present tense), a life that is continuously changing from the old to the spiritually new. This is what Paul was implying when he commanded the Christians to "Not be conformed to this world but be transformed by the renewal of your mind" (Rom. 12: 2). Paul is expressing the idea that the believer should not conform, or carry-on, with the secular worldview of the society, but rather change his or her lifestyle, beliefs, and ideologies that were acquired from the same society. The New Testament Greek word "transform" is *metamorphoushe*, meaning to continue to change. It is the idea of transformation and refers to an invisible process in Christians that takes place, or begins to take place, during this life.[229] The author of Hebrews instructs the believer to "Pursue [strive for] peace with all people, and holiness, without which no one will see the Lord" (Heb. 12: 14). The Greek word for "pursue" is *diokete*, meaning to continually strive or pursue. Although the apostle Paul was positionally sanctified and strived for spiritual maturity, he admitted that his perfection or ultimate sanctification was still incomplete.

> Not that I have already attained, or am already perfect; but I press on, that I may lay hold of that for which Christ Jesus has also laid hold of me. Brethren, I do not count myself to have apprehended, but one thing I do, forgetting those things which are behind and reaching forward to those things which are ahead, I press toward the goal for the prize of the upward call of God in Christ Jesus. Phil. 3: 12–14

Previously I quoted Romans 12: 2, however, to completely understand Paul's message we need to take a look at verse one, "I beseech you therefore brethren, by the mercies of God, that you present your bodies a living sacrifice, holy, acceptable to God, which is your reasonable service." The word "beseech" speaks of imploring, demanding, and even pleading that the believer would present his or her body as a living sacrifice. One may find a meaning to Paul's appeal from Romans 6: 12 and 13, "Therefore, do not let sin reign in your mortal body, that you shall obey it in its lusts. And do not present your members [hands, eyes, mouth, feet, etc.] as instruments of unrighteousness to sin, but present yourself to God as being alive from the dead, and your members as instruments of righteousness to God." When the believer presents himself or herself properly then they will live a life of holiness that is acceptable to God. Paul understood that for one to be obedient to his pleading it would take an intentional sacrifice of one's selfish fleshly desires, feelings, and affections.

Paul encouraged the Christians in Ephesus to transform the old man (the old affections) into the new man. This is progressive sanctification, " That you put off concerning your former conduct, the old man which grows corrupt according to the deceitful lusts, and be renewed in the spirit of your mind, that you may put on the new man which was created according to God, in true righteousness and holiness" (Eph. 4: 22 – 23). The old man is a reference to the lifestyle of an unregenerate man or woman under the headship of Adam before who allows the world (society) to conform his or her actions, beliefs, and lifestyle. The new man is one whose headship is Christ and is in constant conformity to a Christ-centered lifestyle. This transformation championed by Paul is not to be understood as a list of do's and don'ts. It is accomplished through the renewal of one's mind (Rom. 12:2; Eph. 4: 23) and the strengthening of the might of the inner man (Eph. 3: 16).

David Mapes clarifies this concept:

> The essence of sanctification is not to stop living your life and let God somehow live through you in some mystical way. Rather, sanctification means that you allow God, the Potter, to shape your thinking to the point that what you do is the will of God. The driving influence on our life is the indwelling of the Holy Spirit, who causes us both to do His will and do His good pleasure.[230]

The question that one may ask is "how does one gauge the change in a person's affections. Jesus stated that you should know by the fruits one bears (Matt. 7: 16). The fruits of the flesh (old man) is the works of adultery, fornication, uncleanness, lewdness, idolatry, sorcery, hatred, contention, jealousies out-burst of wrath, selfish ambitions, dissensions heresies, envy, murder, drunkenness, revelries, and the likes (Gal. 5; 19 – 21). Most believers understand that he or she must at times, or continually, intentionally combat the pressure or temptation of certain sinful fruits of the flesh. The way to gain victory over the "old man" and live for the "new man" is to intention-ally transform, by walking in the Holy Spirit (Gal. 5: 16), his or her lifestyle will evidence spiritual fruit, such as; love, joy, peace, longsuffering, kindness, goodness, faithfulness, gentle-ness, self-control. Thus, Paul concludes that such actions will result in the crucifixion of the flesh with its passions and desires (Gal. 5: 22 – 25). Thereby living a changed and holy lifestyle before God and within the society, he or she abides.

While the discussion that the Christian has been set apart for the holy service of God and how he or she must go through a transition to grow into a spiritually mature individual to be effective, I find the following quote from John Dagg most clarifying:

> Regeneration is the beginning of sanctification, but the work is not completed at the outset. A new affec-tion [propensity of feeling] is produced in the heart, but it does not govern without opposition. The love of the world, the love of self, and all the carnal appe-tites and passions, have reigned in the heart; and the power of habit gives them controlling influence, which is not readily yielded. Hence arises the war-fare of which every regenerate man is conscience: the flesh lusting against the Spirit, and the Spirit against the flesh. In this struggle, the carnal propensities

often threaten to prevail, and they would prevail, if God did not give a supply of the Spirit of Jesus Christ. "Without Me," said Jesus, "ye can do nothing." If severed from the living vine, the branches are sapless, fruitless, dead. But "he that is joined to the Lord is one Spirit;" and the Spirit of life from Christ, the head, flows through all the members of his body, and gives and preserves vitality. This Spirit in them lusteth against the flesh, and enables them to carry on their warfare, and gives them final victory; "He that hath begun a good work in you, will perform it until the day of Jesus Christ."[231]

The apostle Paul wrote much concerning the progressive sanctification of the believer in Romans, chapter six. I refer to the chapter as the sanctification chapter (I urge the reader to read Romans 9 after he or she completes this chapter). Nonetheless, Paul understood the struggle of the warfare with the flesh as he wrote.

For what I am doing, I do not understand. For what I will to do, that I do not practice; but what I hate, that I do. If then, I do what I will not to do, I agree with the law that it is good. But now, it is no longer I who do it, but sin that dwells in me. For I know that in me (that is, in my flesh) nothing good dwells; for to will is present with me, but how to perform what is good I do not find. For the good that I will to do, I do not do; but the evil I will not to do, that I practice. Now if I do what I will not to do, it is no longer I who do it, but sin that dwell in me. Rom. 7: 15 – 20

The means of progressive sanctification is somewhat understood as man and God working together (Phil. 2: 12 – 13). By that, I suggest that God's work is the primary work (1 Thess. 5:23; Heb. 13: 20 – 21). The believer's work is the secondary one, which is passive since each regenerated person depends on God for sanctification. Throughout the New Testament, the believer is encouraged to strive, to present, to yield, to be holy, etc. meaning that they play a part in sanctification. One does not depend on one's self and expect spiritual changes. Each must make an intentional effort with the help of the Holy Spirit who blesses the effort made. John Murray clarifies this working process:

> God's working in us is not suspended because we work, nor our working suspended because God works. Neither is the relation strictly one of co-operation as if God did His part and we did ours so that the conjunction or coordination of both produces the required results. God works in us and we also work. But the relation is that *because* God works, we work. All working out of salvation on our part is the effect of God's working in us.[232]

When I served as a pastor, I would sometimes preach a message that hit me as much as it did those who were listening. I experienced the same while writing this section dealing with progressive sanctification. I believe that most who read this may agree that we all fall short. This is why I think there should be a follow-up to this section dealing with the question, "What spiritual disciplines should I partake in to help me become the spiritually mature individual that God would have me be?" To provide the answer I am sharing some practical spiritual disciplines I found to be most helpful in one's journey to seek spiritual maturity:

- **Apply what God has Revealed**: Often the Spirit will reveal the truth and the individual will ignore it. Whenever the Spirit has revealed truth, he or she should apply it to their life.

- **Chastity** (1 Cor. 6:18): Chastity is a discipline since all of our inclinations draw us toward sexual immorality. We must discipline ourselves so that we might flee it and pursue pure thoughts and actions. Chastity does not necessarily mean celibacy, although celibacy is a calling for some. It means freely enjoying God's good gift of sex within the bonds of marriage, as God created it to be (1 Cor. 7: 1 – 5). Nevertheless, unless we are married, chastity requires abstinence (Acts 15: 20).

- **Confession** (Pro. 28:13): Confession is an admission of sin followed by repentance. It can be private between you and God, or between you and an individual, or it could be public to all.

- **Evangelism and Disciple-Making** (Matt. 28:19): One must actively seek out opportunities to share the gospel, baptize new believers, and teach them how to obey God's Word.

- **Fasting** (Phil. 3:19): The abstaining from food for spiritual reasons. It is a time to focus on spiritual dependence on God to sustain us.

- **Fellowship** (Acts 2:42; Phil. 4: 6 – 7; Heb. 4: 16; James 4:2; 1 John 1:9): This is more than a social activity, but being united as a body of believers, encouraging one another in a common goal.

- **Giving** (Acts 20:35): We should be willing to share our resources, tithes, and treasurers with others and be helpful to those in need.

- **Keep the Precepts and Commandments of God** (John 15:10; 1 John 5:3).

- **Prayer** (Heb. 4:16): Prayer is how one communicates with God, when we talk, He listens. The believer may find additional benefit when praying to God by listening for His quiet still voice.

- **Reading and Meditating on the Word** (Ps. 1: 2 – 3; 19: 7 – 11; James 1: 23 – 25). This is somewhat different from studying God's Word in that the believer finds spiritual encouragement and richness from God's Word and the Holy Spirit speaks to him or her (1 Sa. 30: 6).

- **Rest** (Matt. 11:28): In this life of technology, we seem to be more preoccupied than ever before. God instituted the discipline of rest in the creation. We must maintain a balance of when to work and when to rest so that we may be more responsive.

- **Service** (Col. 3: 23 – 24): We are to serve not only our Savior but also one another. This often takes humility.

- **Study** (2 Tim. 3:16): Only through instruction from God's Word can one understand the ways and the will of God. The theology and practice of every spiritual discipline are rooted in Scripture.

- **Worship** (1 Chron. 16:29): Worship is more than attending a service and singing. It means to respond to God's worthiness, His infinite worth in one's life.

The goal of progressive sanctification is that the believer is conformed to the image of Christ (Rom. 8:29), not to look like Him, but to be like Him. The reward for progressive sanctification in this life is not only spiritual blessings but that the believer's fellowship and relationship with God are so strong through his or her spiritual maturity that he or she " may prove what is that good and acceptable and perfect will of God" (Rom. 12:2;b). Every believer is responsible to mature spiritually. It is an on-going journey. He or she should never think that they have arrived at perfection; this will never happen in this lifetime, but only when one stands before the One who gave His life for us face-to-face. Then we will be like Him!

Perfection (Final or Ultimate Sanctification): Sanctification begins at regeneration and increases throughout one's life. Nonetheless, at some point, the believer's sanctification will be brought to completion at the end of his or her life. Paul wrote, "For now [in this lifetime] we see in a mirror, dimly but then [in heaven after death] face to face" (1 Cor. 13:12). Speaking of mirrors I am reminded, " But we all with unveiled face, beholding as in a mirror the glory of the Lord, are being transformed into the same image from glory to glory, just as by the Spirit of the Lord" (2 Cor. 3:18). Paul explains that the believer will continue their transformation in an effort that he or she is transformed into Christlikeness (Rom. 8:29; Phil. 3: 12 -14; 1 John 3:2). When the believer continually focuses on Christ the Spirit transforms him or her into His image. The more that the believer grows in the knowledge of Christ, the more He (Christ) is revealed in their life (Phil. 3: 12 -14). The perfection of one's sanctification is complete the day when the believer will see Christ face-to-face. The apostle John stresses that this proportional relationship continues until sanctification is perfected in glorification, "Beloved, now we are children of God; it has not yet been revealed what we shall be, but we know that when He is revealed, we shall be like Him, for we shall see Him as He is" (1 John 3: 2). At this time, all believers will be conformed to, or bear, His image (Rom. 8: 29: 1 Cor. 15: 42 -49).

Concerning the perfection of the body and spirit John MacArthur shares the following:

> Yet for all who have died in faith before the return of Christ, the perfection of sanctification comes in two stages: The soul is fully sanctified at death, while the body awaits its perfected sanctification at the Second Coming of Christ. When believers pass from this present life, their spirits are separated from their bodies (2 Cor. 5:8) and enter the presence of the Lord (Phil.1:23). Thus, the author of Hebrews speaks of the glorified citizen of heaven as "the spirits of the righteous made perfect" (Heb. 12:23). They are glorified in the sense that sanctification is complete, but it is specifically their spirits that experience this perfection since their bodies undergo the corruption that is tied to sin and death. However,

the Lord Jesus does not provide half a salvation. He has purchased the redemption not of men's souls alone but also of their bodies (Rom. 8:23). For this reason, says Paul, we eagerly wait for Christ's return from heaven, when He "will transform our lowly body to be like His glorious body, by the power that enables Him even to subject all things to Himself (Phil. 3: 20 – 21). The believer's perishable, inglorious, weak natural body will be raised from the dead and transformed into an imperishable, glorious, powerful spiritual body (1 Cor. 15: 42 – 44; cf. 15: 22 – 23). This is glorification, the final aspect of salvation.[233]

What we do know is that the saints will be like Him, not look like Him. All saints will have the same glorified body that will exist for eternity and possess the communicable attributes as Him. Other truths concerning the saints' perfected sanctification are as follows:

- The saints resurrected bodies will include both body and soul.
- The saints resurrected bodies will be eternal.
- The saints resurrected bodies will not experience present limitations.
- The saints resurrected bodies will be glorified, both body and spirit.

We may assume that the privileges that we enjoy partially during this life will then be ours fully and completely.

Sanctification is often a neglected doctrinal truth of the Scriptures. However, most Christians could experience a spiritual revival and experience the riches of His blessings they understood it and implemented it within their lives Sanctification is one of many works of the Holy Spirit. I will discuss several other works of the Holy Spirit in the next chapter.

CHAPTER TWELVE

The Work of the Holy Spirit At Salvation

> But when the Helper [Holy Spirit] comes, whom I
> shall send to you from the Father, the Spirit of truth
> who proceeds from the Father, He will testify of Me.
> John 15: 26

While attending a worship service some time back, I witnessed an event that caused me to cringe. The service was somewhat awkward and non-moving; evidence that the music director spent little, if any, time in prayer and preparation. All at once, from the front of the church, a middle-aged woman stood while stomping her feet, clapping her hands, and with a brash voice urged the church to help her "get the Spirit moving;" as if the Holy Spirit could be conjured up like a false pagan god. Surprisingly, many of those in the congregation began to stamp their feet and clap to the rhythm of the music. I have to admit that the atmosphere did improve and the service was a little easier to endure from a secular and fleshly point-of-view since the action increased the adrenaline flow of the congregants who confused their adrenaline flow as that of the moving of the Holy Spirit. Nonetheless, their actions were not significant to the actual moving or illumination of the Holy Spirit. Now I will stop here for the moment to make a point. I am not against emotional displays during the worship service. During my study in Church history, I noted that the style of worship often changes from time to time; often these styles come and go in cycles. I am an older person. I still remember the late 50s and 60s when the Baptist Church worship was very formal, quiet, and rigid producing an atmosphere that younger adults would suggest was compatible with that of a funeral service. On the other hand, some churches place more importance on the experience of worship than the truth or doctrines of the Scriptures. Their focus is on the performance of that which increases adrenaline flow, and some go so far as to choreograph much of their worship service; thereby placing their reliance on the spirit and capability of man rather than the Holy Spirit. The way I understand it is that what I experienced as a young man shifts completely to one side of the pendulum scale of the style of worship. On the other hand, some of the modern-day ideas of the style of worship shift completely to the other side. I honestly believe that true worship is found somewhere in the middle. I say all this to make the point that there is often a misunderstanding of the Holy Spirit and His wonderful work. Therefore, I will address what He is, who He is, and His work.

I will share with the reader a little review of what and who the Holy Spirit is before addressing in detail His work. A. W. Tozer defines the "what" of the Holy Spirit:

> The Holy Spirit is a Being dwelling in another mode of existence. He has no weight, nor measure, nor size, nor any color, no extension in space, but He, nevertheless, exists as surely as you exist.

227

> The Holy Spirit is not enthusiasm. I have found
> enthusiasm that hummed with excitement, and the
> Holy Spirit was nowhere to be found there at all,
> and I have found the Holy Ghost when there has
> not been much enthusiasm present...He is Himself
> a Person, with all the qualities and powers of per-
> sonality. He is not matter, but He is substance...The
> Holy Spirit has will and intelligence and feeling and
> knowledge and sympathy and ability to love and to
> see and think and hear and speak and desire the
> same as any person has.[234]

The Holy Spirit is the Third Person of the Trinity. He is divine
in the same sense, as are the Father and the Son. The Holy Spirit
is the fulfillment of the promise made by Jesus that after His
departure He would send a Helper or Comforter (John 15: 26)

The work of the Holy Spirit has many facets, such as; convicting
nonbelievers of sin (John 16: 7 – 11), the regeneration of those
who by faith accept Christ as Savior and Lord (John 3: 1 – 8),
and the sanctification of the believer, which has been previously
discussed. Nonetheless, I will address the immediate work of the
Holy Spirit in the regeneration of the believer, such as His baptism, His indwelling, His sealing, and His filling. Finally, I will
share the indwelled Holy Spirit's continuous work in the life of
the believer such as His prayer for them, His illumination of the
Scripture, His conviction of sin, and His provision of gifts.

The Holy Spirit's Work in Baptizing the Believer:

Henry Thiessen provides the following short explanation of the
Baptism of the Spirit:

Christ baptizes believers in the Spirit into the body of Christ (Matt. 3:11; Mark 1:8; Luke 3:16; John 1:33; Acts 1;5; 11:16). Paul writes, "For by one Spirit we were all baptized into one body, whether Jew or Greeks, whether slaves or free, and we were all made to drink of one Spirit" (1 Cor. 12:13). This baptism takes place at the moment of salvation. The rite of water baptism symbolizes Spirit baptism (Rom. 8:16; cf. Gal. 4:6).[235]

David Mapes provides a subsequent simple definition, "The baptism of the Holy Spirit may be defined as the operation of the Holy Spirit in which He brings the believer into union with Christ and all other believers."[236]

Denominations somewhat disagree as to the meaning of the baptism of the Holy Spirit. John MacArthur provides clarification by suggesting that "The *expectation* of Spirit baptism appears in all four Gospels and Acts 1. The *experience* of Spirit baptism began in Acts 2, as recalled in Acts 11. The *explanation* of Spirit baptism came later, in Corinthians 12." [237] I will address all three points.

The Expectation of Spirit Baptism: The reader must understand that before the First Advent of Christ and the day of Pentecost the Holy Spirit's work in the life of an individual was much different. The day of Pentecost was a transition between the old covenant work and ministry of the Holy Spirit and His new covenant work and ministry. Although the Holy Spirit was at work throughout the Old Testament, His work in the lives of individuals was somewhat a general work of lesser power. To this Wayne Grudem states:

There are several indications of a less powerful and less extensive work of the Holy Spirit in the old covenant: The Holy Spirit only came to a few people with significant power for ministry (Num. 11: 16 – 17, for example), But Moses longed for the day when the Holy Spirit would be poured out on all of God's people: "Would that all the LORD's people were prophets, that the LORD would put His Spirit upon them!" (Num. 11:29). The equipping of the Holy Spirit for special ministries could be lost, as it was in the life of Saul (1 Sam. 16:14), and as David feared that it might be in his own life (Ps. 51:11). In terms of spiritual powers in the lives of the people of God, there was little power over the dominion of Satan, resulting in very little effective evangelism of the nations around Israel, and no examples of the ability to cast out demons. The old covenant work of the Holy Spirit was almost completely confined to the nation Israel, but in the new covenant there is created a new dwelling place of God (Eph. 2:22), the church, which unites both Gentiles and Jews in the body of Christ.[238]

The Old Testament saints looked forward to a new covenant age when the work of the Holy Spirit would be considerably more powerful and widespread (Num. 11:29; Jer. 31: 31 – 33; Joel 2: 28 – 29). The transition is provided in the New Testament beginning with the four Gospels' report of John the Baptist's reference to Christ baptizing with the Holy Spirit (Matt. 3: 11 – 12; Mark. 1:8; Luke 3: 16 – 17; and John 1: 32 -34). The baptism of the Holy Spirit is sometimes confusing since different translations read differently. Some translations suggest that one is baptized "in" the Holy Spirit, others translate "with" the Holy Spirit, while even others translate "by means of" the Holy Spirit. To clarify this confusion, one should understand that the biblical Greek preposition *en* may be translated all three ways. Therefore, the appropriate word should be used as best explained in the text.

There are three baptisms referenced in the New Testament. Water baptism, in which the people of the old covenant signified as a baptism of repentance. Spirit baptism, this signified salvation, and the entrance to the universal Church, the body of Christ (1 Cor. 12: 13). Finally, fire baptism, which is a reference to the final judgment of unbelievers (Matt. 3: 12; 25:41; Luke 3:16; John 15:6; Rev. 20: 14 – 15).[239]

During the water baptism of our Lord, John the Baptist provided the expectation that Jesus would someday baptize with the Holy Spirit (John 1: 32 -34), thereby radically changing baptism completely. The old covenant symbolic water baptism of repentance would change to the new covenant of symbolizing the death, burial, and resurrection of Christ Jesus in the life of the believer (Rom. 6: 3 – 4). Christ would initiate the new spiritual baptism of the Holy Spirit some three years later after He had died and was resurrected. Right before He would ascend to heaven from the Mount of Olives, He assembled with His disciples and provided them last-minute instructions regarding the Spirit baptism mentioned by John the Baptist in which they were to wait for in Jerusalem (Acts 1: 4 – 5).

The Experience of Spirit Baptism: Ten days later, on the day of Pentecost, John the Baptist's and Christ's pronouncements were fulfilled (Acts 2:1-21). Some may ask, "How do we know that this experience was the fulfillment of their pronouncement?" Some years later Peter would travel to the Gentile household of the Roman centurion Cornelius after receiving a vision from God (Acts 10: 9 – 15). Peter was instrumental in Cornelius and his household accepting Christ. When Peter addressed the importance of accepting Christ, he repeated some of the very words of Christ when He (Christ) spoke on the Mount of Olives, the household accepted Christ and the Holy Spirit fell on them as He did on the Day of Pentecost (Acts 10: 44 – 48). Later, Peter is in Jerusalem listening to some of the leaders complaining about the acceptance of Gentiles within the church. Peter shared his testimony of the vision and the experience, then ended the conversation with the following:

> "And as I began to speak, the Holy Spirit fell upon them, as upon us at the beginning. Then I remembered the word of the Lord, how He said, 'John indeed baptized with water, but you shall be baptized with the Holy Spirit.' If therefore God gave them the same gift as He gave us when we believed on the Lord Jesus Christ, who was I that I could withstand God?"

> When they heard these things, they became silent; and they glorified God, saying, "Then God has also granted to the Gentiles repentance to life." Acts 11: 15 – 18

Many years later, the apostle Paul would return to Antioch from a mission trip to discover large dissension within the Church initiated by legalistic Jews from Judea who had taught that the males were to be circumcised (under law). The church sent

Paul and Barnabas to the Church of Jerusalem to question the council of elders (mainly Apostles) about the matter (Acts 15: 1 – 5). Again, Peter concluded the matter:

> "Men and brethren, you know that a good while ago God chose among us, that by my mouth the Gentiles should hear the word of the gospel and believe. So God, who knows the heart, acknowledged them by giving them the Holy Spirit, just as He did to us, and made no distinction between us [Jews] and them [Gentiles], purifying their hearts by faith. Now therefore, why do we test God by putting a yoke on the necks of the disciples which neither our fathers nor we were able to bear? Acts 15: 7b – 10

The assembly was convinced of God's work when Peter again reminded the Jewish believers that God has accepted the salvation of the Gentiles with the evidence of the baptism of the Holy Spirit experienced by both Jews and Gentiles.

I am reminded of a conversation that Jesus had with His disciples in the sixteenth chapter of Matthew's gospel. Jesus asked the question, "Who do men say that I, the Son of Man, am?" Some answered John the Baptist, Elijah, Jeremiah, or one of the prophets (6: 13b – 14). Peter answered correctly stating, "You are the Christ [Messiah], the Son of the living God" (16: 16). Part of the response of Christ was that He would give Peter the keys to the kingdom of heaven. To this William Hendriksen responds, "The one who has the keys (cf. Rev. 1:18; 3:7) of the kingdom of heaven determines who should be admitted and who must be refused admission."[240] William Barclay suggests, "What Jesus was expressing to Peter is that in the days to come, he will be the steward of the kingdom. And in the case of Peter, the whole idea is that of opening, not shutting, the door of the kingdom."[241] John Broadus suggests that:

> He who had the keys of a city or place determined whether any given person should enter or be shut out (Rev. 9:1; 20: 1 -3). This would suggest a general authority and control, varying in extent according to the nature of the case. There seems to be an allusion here to the high steward of the palace of David, Isa. 22: 15,22 and in Rev. 1: 18; 8:7, a similar but spiritual function is ascribed to Jesus Himself. The Talmud makes like use of the phrase.[242]

Peter held the metaphoric keys to heaven, according to Barclay. He was responsible for opening the doors to heaven and receiving authority and power. Reading the New Testament one can understand that this was not referring to individuals, but nationalities or people groups. The Scriptures refer to three distinct groups: Jews, Gentile, and Samaritans (a mix of both). Peter was a witness when the Jews received the Holy Spirit (Acts 2), he was a witness when the Gentiles received the Holy Spirit (Acts 10), and he was a witness when the Samaritans received the Holy Spirit (Acts 8). Phillip, one of the first deacons, who was also an evangelist, traveled to Samaria to share the gospel. Many believed his message and had yet to receive the Holy Spirit. When word got back to Jerusalem, Peter and John were sent to investigate. Peter laid hands on them and they received the Holy Spirit. Peter's presence legitimatized the acceptance of each group.

I want to review the first experience that took place in Jerusalem (Acts 2). To understand, one must see the event through the eyes of someone of that day and in his or her culture. But first, Pentecost was known in the Old Testament as the Feast of Weeks (Lev. 23:15; Deut. 16:9). The Greek meaning of Pentecost is "fifty." Therefore, Pentecost refers to the fifty days that had passed since the participation of the wave offering during the Passover. This holy day is celebrated at the end of the grain harvest. In the New Testament, Pentecost signaled the birth of the church age and the new work of the Holy Spirit.

In Acts, chapter two, on the day to offer first fruits, the disciples were in one accord in the upper room and experienced the Holy Spirit as the first fruits of their inheritance and the full harvest of all believers to come (2 Cor.5:5; Eph. 1; 11, 14). Then a mighty sound of rushing wind begins. Often wind is used in Scripture as a picture of the Spirit (John 3:8). Verse three is often misunderstood. There appeared to them divided tongues, as of fire. During this time there was no electricity. The light was either through sunlight or fire. Luke is describing a great radiance of bright light, not fire, but somewhat like fire (as of fire). This large radiance of light must have hovered over them than divided into smaller portions that sat upon each in attendance. Some envision the light to look like flaming human tongues. This is not the case. The reader is aware that the New Testament was written in the Greek language. The Greek word for tongue is *glossa*, which means speech or language.[243] Some readers wonder why many translations use the word tongues instead of the word languages. The answer is simple to address. Until the last few decades, the leading translation of the Bible was the King James version. In 1611 and with its major revision in 1769 the word *glossa* was interpreted as tongues since the word "language" was rarely used. A person was not asked what language he or she spoke, but what "tongue." By the 1980s when the New King James Version was translated, the word "tongue" had become so part of church speak that it was decided to continue its use. Some of the new translations use the word "language." Therefore, on the Day of Pentecost after the radiant light divided into smaller parts, each part contained a language that was given to the one in which it sat. Spiros Zodhiates provides a deeper understanding of the Greek word *glossa*. He states that the word's meaning here actually includes not only the language of others but the dialect (Acts 2:11). Concerning Acts 2:4, he states that unlike many of the other uses of the word "tongues" that the Holy Spirit inspired the writer to use the Greek words *glossais heterais*, which has the meaning of languages other than one's native tongue, languages not previously known to them.[244] As soon as they were empowered and filled with the Spirit they went into the city to witness to Jews from sixteen nations who were in the city for Pentecost. Some interpret this section of Acts as the disciples speaking the same ecstatic speech and each person heard in his or her native language. This is not the case. Note, the gift of tongues is plural, not single. The disciples supernaturally spoke a language to the listeners that were previously unknown to them (those speaking) and they spoke not only in the other people's present languages but their dialect (2: 4 – 13). Peter stood before the crowd and preached that they were witnessing the fulfillment of the prophet Joel which described the new work of the Holy Spirit (2: 14 – 21). Peter's invitation was to repent, be baptized, and receive the gift of the Holy Spirit (2: 38). This resulted in three thousand saved (2: 40).

There are some, who have read the previous texts in this section, who misunderstand this experience of the baptism of the Holy Spirit. Some believe that one may experience salvation and receive the baptism of the Holy Spirit later. Others believe that one must speak in tongues as evidence of the baptism of the Holy Spirit. I want to address both misunderstandings. Those who believe what is referred to as "the second blessing," a belief that one receives the baptism of the Holy Spirit sometime after conversion, need to understand that the previous experiences (Acts 2; 8; and 10) happened during the time of transition between the old covenant work of the Holy Spirit and His new covenant work. The previous experiences are not to be taken as a pattern for today. Simply said, the believers, who were under the old covenant of lesser empowerment from the Holy Spirit, became believers with a new covenant of empowerment from the Holy Spirit in such a way that the Christian Jewish believers, understanding the activities that Peter witnessed as a sign (1 Cor. 1:22), accepted the Samaritans (Acts 8) and the Gentiles (Acts 10 & 11) as Christian brothers and sisters. Today, the moment one is regenerated he or she immediately receives empowerment through the baptism of the Holy Spirit.

Because of the experience of tongues (languages)in Acts 2 and 10, some believers are convinced that one must speak in tongues to show evidence that he or she has been baptized in the Holy Spirit. My response to that is what about Acts chapter eight. The new converts received the power of the Spirit, but there is no mention of the gift of tongues. When I read Acts 2, I understand tongues (languages) as only a tool needed at the time by those newly empowered by the Holy Spirit to witness to the multitude. The marvelous thing that I see is not that people spoke in tongues, but that three thousand people were regenerated by the Holy Spirit. Tongues were only a gift tool for witnessing.

The Explanation of Spirit Baptism: Although the gospels and the Book of Acts recount the expectation and experience of Spirit baptism, they do not fully provide a full explanation as to its meaning or significance. The apostle Paul provides this in 1 Corinthians 12: 12–14:

> For as the body is one and has many members, but all the members of that one body, being many, are one body, so also is Christ. For by one Spirit we were all baptized into one body – whether Jews or Greeks, whether slaves or free – and have all been made to drink into one Spirit. For in fact the body is not one member but many.

The church of Corinth was experiencing great division. Paul addressed the disunity by applying the metaphor of the baptism of the Spirit in the body of Christ to deal with the situation as he often did (Eph. 1:3; 2:16; 4:4; Col. 3:15). Gordon Fee suggests that "The first paragraph sets forth the basic presupposition of the imagery (the body is one) and its urgency (but has many members). This is followed by a twofold collaboration of the metaphor, the first emphasizing diversity, the second unity."[245] This universal body of Christ in which all regenerated believers are baptized, or immersed in, is the Church (1 Cor. 12: 27).

Several thoughts come to mind when I think of the baptism of the Holy Spirit. First, the church (body of Christ), which through its immersing (baptizing) in the Spirit, is not viewed as an organization but a living organism. Like the human body, it reflects both unity and diversity, but "one body" (v. 12). This one body is made up of all ethnicities, all education levels, all economic levels, and of both genders. Second, as stated previously, the baptism of the Holy Spirit was spoken of by John the Baptist (John 1:33; Acts 1:5). Jesus assured the disciples that He would send the Spirit (John 16: 7). When Jesus was encouraging His disciples before His death, He told them He would soon leave, then made the following statement, "A little while longer and the world will see Me no more, but you will see Me. Because I live, you will live also. And that day you will know that I am in My Father, and you in Me" (John 14: 19 – 20). The baptism of the Spirit fulfilled the Words of our Lord, "you in Me!" Third, it is fitting to refer to the Church, which is formed by all regenerated believers when they were immediately immersed in the union by the Spirit, as the body of Christ since He is the head (Acts 4:11; Eph. 1:22; 4:15; 5:23; Col. 1:18). Fourth, it is significant that the Holy Spirit immerses (baptizes) us into the metaphoric body of Christ. Christ is no longer dwelling physically in a body on earth. Although there are many tasks that He wants to accomplish and since He is not physically living here, He appoints fellow believers for the task. If someone needs teaching, He will appoint someone within the spiritual body to teach. If He wants His gospel shared, He will appoint those in the body to do so. The believers, who form the body of Christ, become His hands to do His work, His mouth, to spread His gospel, and His feet to accomplish His errands. Fifth, according to John Walvoord, the baptism of the Spirit places the believer in a new position; Union with Christ. Before salvation, the individual was in Adam, partaking of Adam's nature, sin, and destiny. When the individual experienced salvation he or she was baptized by the Spirit and immediately placed in Christ. All the elements of the new believer's salvation come from this new position, such as his or her justification, sanctification, forgiveness, relationship with God, inheritance, and glorification, all are the results of this new position in Christ Jesus. A by-product of this new position is the identification with Christ in His righteousness, His death, His resurrection, and His glorification (Rom. 6: 1 – 4).[246] Finally, the baptism of the Holy Spirit should not be equated with the indwelling or filling of the Holy Spirit. They are all distinct. The Spirit baptism is permanent, it is a one-time thing that occurs simultaneously with regeneration. It is not a reversible or recurring event. Once the church went through the transition period from the old covenant to the new covenant there is not one Scripture to be found that suggests the believer will experience the spirit baptism after salvation, nor experience the event again.

The Holy Spirit's Work of Indwelling the Believer

While the baptism of the Spirit entails the regenerated believer living within the metaphoric body of Christ (the Church universal), the indwelling entails the Holy Spirit residing within the believer permanently. This work of the Holy Spirit was dramatically changed from its Old Testament concept during the birth of the Church Age on the Day of Pentecost.

There are very few occasions during the Old Testament that a saint was indwelt by the Holy Spirit; two such men were Joshua (Num. 27:18) and Ezekiel on two separate occasions (Ezek. 2: 2; 3: 24). Thus, the dwelling was not a permanent indwelling. More often, the Old Testament speaks of the Holy Spirit coming "upon" a particular person for a limited time. During each occurrence, whether by indwelling or coming upon, the idea was that the individual was empowered to accomplish a work for the Lord. Nonetheless, the characteristics of the Holy Spirit's indwelling in the Old Testament can be summarized as occasional, only applied to selective leaders in Israel, always temporary, and for empowerment for service. The work of the Holy Spirit was not the same work during the Old Testament as in the New Testament, beginning at Pentecost. There was a marked difference that we will explore in this section.

Since the Day of Pentecost, the indwelling of the Holy Spirit is provided for every believer, rather than a select few (John 7:37; Acts 11: 16 – 17; Rom. 5:5; 1 Cor. 2:12). Anyone not possessing the indwelling of the Holy Spirit has never experienced regeneration (Rom. 8:9; Jude 19). Even regenerated believers living in sin continue to be indwelt with the Holy Spirit (1 Cor. 6:19). Even though such believers are spiritually immature, their testimony is an embarrassment to both lost people and the saved, and their walk with the Lord is a disaster. In time he or she will experience the chastening of the Lord (Heb. 12: 3 – 11).

Beginning in the New Testament the indwelling is permanent. The Holy Spirit will never leave the regenerated Christian. The Lord left us a positive promise when He prayed to the heavenly Father to provide us a" Helper" when He left so that "He may abide with you forever [never leaving] – the Spirit of truth, whom the world cannot receive because it neither sees Him nor knows Him; but you know Him, for He dwells with you and will be in you [occurred at Pentecost]" (John 14: 15b – 17).

The result of the indwelling of the Holy Spirit is peace, conviction, Spirit's leading, spiritual growth, and spiritual empowerment. Jesus promised the disciples such power, "But you shall receive power when the Holy Spirit has come upon you; and you shall be witnesses to Me in Jerusalem, and in Judea, and Samaria, and to the ends of the earth. This reminds me of an old definition of witnessing, "Sharing the gospel in the power of the Holy Spirit and leaving the results to God." Therefore, the characteristics of the Holy Spirit's indwelling of the believer in the New Testament are: it transpires immediately at salvation; it is inclusive to all believers; it is a permanent indwelling; it is cohesive in the collective sense of the body of Christ (universal church), and it is an empowerment for holy living and productive service.

The Holy Spirit's Work of Sealing the Believer

The apostle Paul encouraged the Church of Ephesus with the following words, "In Him, you also trusted after you heard the word of truth, the gospel of your salvation; in whom also, having believed, you were sealed with the Holy Spirit of promise, who is the guarantee of our inheritance until the redemption of the purchased possession, to the praise of His glory (Eph. 1: 13 – 14). Paul reminded the believers that immediately after one heard the gospel and believed that he or she was sealed by the Holy Spirit, who guaranteed (or pledge) each salvation until the day of redemption. John MacArthur suggests Paul utilized two secular Greek words to develop the theme of "sealing." The first, *sphragizo,* meaning "to seal," the second, *arrabon,* meaning "a pledge." Pledge could also be interpreted as a "guarantee." Paul appropriated these two Greek words as spiritual word pictures to describe the salvation ministry of the Holy Spirit.[247]

The New Testament Greek word: *sphragizo* "seal," described the ancient practice of placing soft wax on an individual's correspondence, property, or the decree of a king, which was then stamped with an exclusive mark that distinctly identified the owner or originator. The seal that was stamped was a symbol of authority, protection, ownership, or security. On the other hand, the New Testament Greek word; "*arrabon* "a pledge or guarantee," describes a financial down payment or a deposit given in good faith with an unbreakable promise that all remaining payments would be forthcoming to complete the business transaction. It communicates the idea of a pledge, or guarantee, to inspire certainty and assurance.

The Scriptures are adamant that all regenerated believers have been sealed by the Holy Spirit. Note the recent passage, "having believed, you were sealed with the Holy Spirit of promise"(Eph. 1:13). Ephesians 4:30, "And do not grieve the Holy Spirit of God, by whom you were sealed for the day of redemption." Finally, "Now He who establishes us with you in Christ and has anointed us is God, who also has sealed us and given us the Spirit in our hearts as a guarantee"(2 Cor. 1: 21 – 22). Therefore, every believer has been sealed by the work of the Holy Spirit and this work will continue until the day of redemption. Often, the Scriptures reveal that the Holy Spirit is the agent of sealing the believer. Nevertheless, some passages such as 2 Corinthians, chapter one, verse twenty-two, suggests that God the Father works in sealing the believer and that the Holy Spirit is the seal.

The truth is that the seal, *sphragizo*, speaks to God's ownership of the regenerated believer who has been purchased with the price of the blood of Christ (1 Cor. 6: 19 – 20). The sealing of the Holy Spirit speaks to the eternal security of the believer since He protects until the day of redemption, the time of complete deliverance from sin.

The Spirit is not only God's seal of the truly regenerated believers but also God's guarantee, *arrabon* (2 Cor. 1:22; 5:5; Eph. 1:14). The guarantee that He will ultimately fulfill His promise of eternal life with a resurrected and glorified body. The sealing of the Holy Spirit is God's pledge, His down payment, and His deposit that confirms with impeccable assurance the inevitability that what God began He will complete (Phil. 1: 6; Eph. 1: 13 – 14).

The Holy Spirit's Work of Filling the Believer

There seems to be a considerable misunderstanding regarding the "filling of the Spirit." Many confuse the "filling of the Spirit" with the "feeling of the Spirit." When a believer seeks the "feeling of the Spirit," the end result is desiring an emotional euphoric adrenalin rush experience. To these believers, it is all about feelings, not maturity or service! When a believer seeks the "filling of the Spirit," the results are obedience to God, spiritual maturity, and service. It is not about experiencing feelings but that of working out one's faith! Some think of "being filled with the Spirit" as a synonym of the "baptism of the Spirit." "The baptism of the Spirit" is a one-time event that takes place with regeneration. However, the "filling of the Spirit" may be experienced on multiple occasions. Many seem to think that one may receive the Holy Spirit increasingly by degrees even suggesting that some degree of the Holy Spirit may be lost, or leak out, therefore, the believer must do what it takes to be refilled. But the truth of the matter is that every Christian not only possesses the Holy Spirit but also possesses Him in His fullness. God does not section out the Spirit.

Writing to the Christians in Ephesus, the apostle Paul implored, "And do not be drunk with wine, in which is dissipation [indulgence, debauchery]; but be filled with the Spirit." (Eph. 5:18). Some speculate the interpretation of the first part of the verse, "Do not be drunk with wine." To this Clinton Arnold suggests:

> In some of the Graeco-Roman religions, drunkenness was even seen as the means by which one could experience ecstasy and union with a god [false god]. This was most notable in the cult of Dionysus (or Bacchus), whose cultic symbol was a vine. The presence of this cult is well attested for Ephesus in literary accounts, on Ephesian coins, and many inscriptions...Because of this evidence, some interpreters have concluded that Paul's injunction warning against-drunkenness prior to his command to be filled with the Spirit was needed because some of the believers in Ephesus may have been attempting to increase their unity with God by the practice of cultic inebriation (which they may have learned in the Dionysiac cult).[248]

To better understand the second part of the verse, "but be filled with the Spirit," the reader needs to observe the background of the "filling" and "fullness" language in the Book of Ephesians. During the Old Testament or old covenant, the temple [a building] was filled with the glory of God; the *Shekinah* glory (Isa. 6: 1; Ezek. 43:5; 44:4). However, under the new covenant, the regenerated believers have replaced the physical structure of the temple as the dwelling place of God's Spirit (Eph. 2:22; 1 Cor. 3: 16 – 17; 2 Cor. 6:16). Therefore, Arnold suggests, "The Spirit of God thus inhabits the lives of believers, and Paul wants this to happen in ever-increasing measure. The previous context (Eph. 4:30) suggests that sinful behavior grieves the Spirit and by implication hinders the full reception of the Spirit."[249]

Every true believer is indwelt by the Holy Spirit. Each received the fullness of the Spirit at salvation. He or she will never experience less or more of the Holy Spirit's indwelling. Some readers may be asking the question, "How can a believer be further filled with the Spirit if he or she has all there is to have?" The answer is not that one may receive more of the Spirit, but he or she allows more of the Holy Spirit to "fill" every area of his or her life; to allow the Holy Spirit to control our thoughts and actions. The believer must decrease with his or her own fleshly, old nature, desires, and allow the Holy Spirit to increase in his or her life. When the believer is filled, he or she authenticates genuine salvation by allowing God's will to prevail to the Scripture's admonitions, teachings, and the Holy Spirit's guidance.

There are a few actions that hinder the Spirit from fully filling, or controlling, one's life: Grieving the Holy Spirit (Eph. 4:30). When one displeases God and their Christian walk does not match his or her identity in Christ. They live like a sinner when they should be living like a saint! The "grieving" of the Holy Spirit, while tragic, is most certainly forgivable. Then there is the quenching of the Spirit (1 Thess. 5:19), "quenching" suggests the suppressing of fire or the denying of power. Therefore, living as though one has no spiritual power or spiritual energized life. Thus, living a wasted life for God.

Referring back to Ephesians, chapter five, the apostle Paul points to how the Spirit can fill the lives of believers: "speaking to one another in psalms and hymns and spiritual songs, to the Lord, giving thanks always for all things to God the Father in the name of our Lord Jesus Christ, submitting to one another in the fear of God" (Eph. 5; 19 – 21). John MacArthur shares several arguments concerning the means of being filled by the Holy Spirit:

1. To be filled with the Spirit involves confession of sin, the surrender of will, intellect, body, time, talent, possessions, and desires. It requires the death of selfishness and the slaying of self-will. When we die to self, the Lord fills us with His Spirit.

2. To be filled with the Spirit is to live in the consciousness of the personal presence of the Lord Jesus Christ, as if we were standing next to Him, and to let His thoughts be our thoughts.

3. Being filled with the Spirit is walking by thought, decision by decision, act by act under the Spirit's control.

4. Not to be filled with the Spirit is to fall back into the deeds of the flesh...which are: immorality, impurity, sensuality, idolatry, sorcery, enmities, strife, jealousy, outburst of anger, disputes, dissensions, factions, envying, drunkenness, carousing, and other sins that are unpleasing to God (Gal. 5: 19 – 21). One does not have to consciously choose to accomplish the deeds of the flesh. If he or she is not living under the control of God's Word and Spirit, the deeds of the flesh are the only things one may accomplish, because the flesh is the

only resource a person has within to accomplish his or her selfish works.

5. But when one surrenders to the control of God's Spirit, he or she experiences the Holy Spirit producing amazing things within, things which are entirely of His [Holy Spirit] doing. Paul calls these marvelous blessings the fruit of the Spirit, and they are: "love, joy, peace, patience, kindness, goodness, faithfulness, gentleness, self-control" (Gal. 5: 22 – 23).[250]

Recapping the immediate work of the Holy Spirit during the regeneration experience of the believer is He baptizes the believer; meaning that He brings the believer into union with Christ and all other believers by immersing them in the meta-phoric body of Christ. He indwells the believer; meaning that He abides in His fullness within the believer forever and per-forms many other works in which I will discuss momentarily. He seals the believer, which is His stamp of ownership and His pledge to keep the believer until the day of redemption. Finally, He fills the believer, meaning that one surrenders control over his or her life to the Holy Spirit and lives out the power that God has provided for every Christian.

The Holy Spirit's Work after Regeneration

After discussing the indwelling and filling of the Holy Spirit earlier in this chapter, I felt the need to provide additional ben-efits of the indwelling by listing some of the additional works of the Spirit that He accomplishes after one experiences regen-eration since the focus of this chapter is the immediate work during salvation. I will only provide a simple overview of the following work of the Holy Spirit: I addressed the convicting of the Spirit previously.

The Holy Spirit Teaches the Believer: One of the last promises of the Savior, before His crucifixion, in the upper room was:

> I still have many things to say unto you, but you cannot bear them now. However, when He, the Spirit of truth, has come, He will guide you into all truth; for He will not speak on His own authority, but whatever He hears He will speak; and He will tell you things to come. He will glorify Me, for He will take of what is Mine and declare it to you. All things that the father has are Mine. Therefore, I said that He will take of Mine and declare it to you. John 16: 12 – 15

This work of the Holy Spirit began on the day of Pentecost and encompassed "all truth." This reference of revelation concerning Christ was based on the written Word (for we have no information about Christ except through the Word). Therefore, the Holy Spirit teaches by enlightening the conscience of the believer. This enlightenment, or illumination, is necessary because of the spiritual blindness, inexperience, and spiritual immaturity of the believer (1 Cor. 2: 10 – 16). This illumination removes the ignorance and error that hinders the understanding of spiritual truths concerning the content and meaning of Scripture, the messages and life of Christ (glorify Me; John 16: 14), and that of prophecy (things to come; John 16: 13). John discloses how the Holy Spirit teaches (illuminates) the mind of the believer, " But the anointing which you have received from Him abides in you, and you do not need that anyone teaches you, but as the same anointing teaches you concerning all things, and is true, and is not a lie, and just as it has taught you, you will abide in Him" (1 John 2: 27). This does not mean that human teachers are redundant since the Holy Spirit bestows the gift of teaching upon some saints (Rom. 12:7). One of the reasons that John wrote his epistle was to expose false teachers. Nonetheless, the Holy Spirit often employs gifted teachers to teach biblical truth. John was declaring that not the person teaching confirms the truth, but the truth will be confirmed by the Holy Spirit to the believer whose spiritual life and maturity were sufficient to hear His quiet voice (Holy Spirit). John Walvoord addresses this notion:

> To Christians who are spiritual, i.e., filled with the Spirit, it is possible for the Spirit to reveal the deep things of God. In the extended revelation of this truth in 1 Corinthians 2: 9 – 3:2, it is made clear that the deeper things of spiritual truth can be understood only by those who are spiritually qualified to be taught by the Spirit. The natural man is unable to understand even the simple truths understood by those who are Spirit-taught. The appalling ignorance of many Christians concerning the things of the Word of God is directly traceable to their carnality and failure in seeking the blessings of a life filled with the Spirit.[251]

The Holy Spirit Guides the Believer: Paul writes, "For as many as are led by the Spirit of God, these are the sons of God" (Rom. 8:14). Woodrow Kroll explains that the word "led" in the New Testament Greek is the verb *ago*, which means to guide, direct, impel, or lead away. It is utilized in Luke, chapter

4, where Jesus was led about by the Spirit in the wilderness. Kroll further suggests four conclusions concerning this verse in Romans 8:14: First, "It is obvious that to be led does not merely mean to be influenced. Jesus was not "influenced" like a sheep to the slaughter, nor was Paul "influenced" before King Agrippa. *Led* means to be moved by a force external to oneself. When we are led by the Spirit of God it is not by the suggestion but by exertion [action]. Second, the leading is not harsh but gentle. The Holy Spirit does not lead as a tyrant but as a teacher (John 14:26). Third, the leading is not sporadic or haphazard but steady and sustained. The verb *ago* implies continuous action. Finally, the leading of the Spirit is authenticating. His continuous gentle leading, the Spirit assures us that we are indeed the children of God.[252]

John Walvoord adds additional information concerning the leading (guidance) of the Holy Spirit.

> Guidance is the most important element in Christian experience, and it is essential to a life in the will of God. Guidance, while similar to the teaching work of the Spirit has a distinct character. While the teaching ministry of the Spirit in this age is directed to make clear the content of the Word of God, guidance is the application of the truths thus known to the individual problems of life. Guidance is always deductive, that is, the application of general Biblical principles to particular problems at hand. While the Word of God may reveal the purpose of God to preach the gospel throughout the world, only the Spirit of God can call an individual life to an appointed field of service. In the many details

of each life, only the Spirit of God can provide the necessary guidance.[253]

The Holy Spirit Assures the Believer: The apostle Paul encourages the believers in Rome with the following statement: "The Spirit Himself bears witness with our spirit that we are children of God" (Rom. 8:16). The Holy Spirit is not only instrumental in making each believer a child of God. He also provides an inner-conscience blessing by involving each one's own spirit in the very process of making known, or testifying, that he or she is a child of God and the salvation benefits that the position bestows. This assurance is increased with the understanding of what the Holy Spirit has accomplished for the believer. For instance, the assurance will deepen when the believer understands the meaning of being baptized, sealed, indwelt, and filled with the Spirit.

However, John Walvoord warns, "One of the important reasons why some Christians do not have the assurance of salvation is their failure to meet the conditions for the filling of the Spirit and the resultant [subsequent] ministry of the Spirit to their hearts."[254]

The Holy Spirit Prays for the Believer: There are periods in every believer's life when he or she will experience physical, mental, or even spiritual fatigue that hinders his or her walk with God, especially one's prayer life. This writer has experienced such occasions when I could not pray. During these periods in my life, I am reminded of Paul's encouragement, "Likewise, the Spirit also helps in our weakness. For we do not know what we should pray for as we ought, but the Spirit Himself makes intercessions for us with groanings which cannot be uttered" (Rom. 8:26). While referring to this verse Woodrow Kroll shared the following.

> When your whole world collapses around you and you can't even pray, the Spirit grieves with you and prays for you. But His grief exceeds yours, and He groans with feelings too deep for words. The Father searches the mind of the Spirit, interprets these groanings, and knows what His Holy Spirit is thinking as He prays in your behalf. The Spirit groans with thoughts that always concur with the will of God (v. 27).[255]

Before Jesus left for heaven, He met to encourage His disciples and stated, "But when the Helper [Holy Spirit] comes, whom I shall send to you from the Father, the Spirit of truth who proceeds from the Father, He will testify of Me. And you also will bear witness, because you have been with Me from the beginning" (John 15: 26). The Lord's atonement that was completed on the cross provided ever-lasting salvation. Nonetheless, He did not leave His believers powerless and guideless. The Holy Spirit unites all believers as a family by the process of His baptism. This same Helper seals each believer to the day of redemption, and the Helper indwells every true believer, thereby, providing the prayers, teaching, guidance, and power to all Christians who are filled with the Spirit to be faithful in accomplishing all that God purposes in one's life and assurance of his or her salvation until the day of redemption.

Part Six

The When of Authentic Salvation

> Jesus answered and said to him, most assuredly, I
> say to you, unless one is born again, he cannot see
> the kingdom of God...Most assuredly, I say to you,
> unless one is born of water and the Spirit, he cannot
> enter the kingdom of God. That which is born of the
> flesh is flesh, and that which is born of the Spirit is
> spirit." John 3: 3,5,6

Part Six consists of one chapter that provides a gospel presentation to the reader. The writer felt that if one was to write a book explaining the doctrine of salvation that he or she has not completed the work without a presentation of the gospel written about.

CHAPTER THIRTEEN

You Must Be Born Again

> Jesus answered and said to him, most assuredly, I
> say to you, unless one is born again, he cannot see
> the kingdom of God...Most assuredly, I say to you,
> unless one is born of water and the Spirit, he cannot
> enter the kingdom of God. That which is born of the
> flesh is flesh, and that which is born of the Spirit is
> spirit." John 3: 3,5,6

Whenever I read this text, I am reminded of my first sermon. At the age of fifteen, over fifty years ago, God graciously called me to proclaim His Word. I shared my calling with my family, pastor, and friends. A little over a month later, after turning sixteen, I attended our church's weekly Sunday service held on live radio. After my family and I sang the pastor stood behind the large microphone and announced that everyone was in for a treat (his words) since brother Joe McGee was going to preach his very first sermon. The problem with this announcement was that the pastor had never informed brother Joe McGee (me) that he was to bring this Sunday's message. I was almost paralyzed with fear. I could barely walk to the microphone since my legs felt like rubber. While I stood behind the microphone my mind went blank. I silently prayed that God would provide me the message. Then this passage of Scripture came to mind. My text was "You must be born again!" I began to preach what I felt was an hour, but in reality, it was probably 5 -7 minutes. I learned a valuable lesson that day to always be ready to preach. I am convinced that many new preachers choose this text simply because it is John's main focus of authentic salvation.

After writing twelve chapters explaining the details of authentic salvation, I felt the need to write one more that provides a gospel presentation from chapter three of John's gospel as well as a recap of the past chapters to properly conclude this work. In doing so I will discuss why we must be born again. What does it mean to be born again? Who provides the new birth? And, how is one born again? Lastly, I will share some information concerning the basics after one has experienced authentic salvation.

The chapter begins with Nicodemus meeting with Jesus in secret at night. Many who read this passage overlook the importance of Nicodemus's life and how such knowledge relates to the interpretation of this text. We know that he was a successful businessman when we read where Nicodemus provided for the body of Christ (John 19:39), "bring a mixture of myrrh and aloes, about a hundred pounds." Only a wealthy man could have afforded this. He was a Pharisee. They were known as a *chaburah*, or brotherhood. They entered this brotherhood by taking a pledge in front of witnesses promising that they would spend all their lives observing every detail of the law.[256] The Pharisees were extremely strict and precise regarding the law. Another distinguishing mark of the Pharisees was their commitment to "the traditions of the elders" as supplementing or amending biblical law.[257] It was to the Pharisees that Jesus proclaimed they were "like whitewashed tombs which indeed appeared beautiful outwardly [externally], but inside [internally] are full of dead men's bones and all uncleanness" (Matt. 23:27). Nicodemus was not only a Pharisee; he was a Ruler of the Jews. The word ruler is from the Greek *archon*. This is to say that he was a member of the Sanhedrin, a court of seventy members who made up the supreme court of the Jews. Although, under the Romans, their powers were limited. Nonetheless, the Sanhedrin had religious jurisdiction over every Jew.[258] Externally, one may say that Nicodemus was a religious man. However, Jesus informs him that he was inwardly deficient. Nicodemus, like many people in our lifetime, relied on the external matters for salvation, resulting in a salvation that is false (chapter one). Countless believe that participation in external religious activity is all that is needed. Nonetheless, as Nicodemus was speaking, who was importantly a man and a representative of the ruling authorities of the religions of God, Jesus interrupts him to reveal the true light by informing him that he must be born again. Nicodemus may have experienced an externally changed lifestyle. Buy, he had never experienced an internal change of the heart. Nicodemus was about to learn that authentic salvation is only achieved by the regeneration of both the internal (immaterial spirit of the person) and the external (the fleshly material lifestyle or conduct of the person).

Why Must We Be Born Again?

Jesus answered this question. "For God did not send His Son into the world to condemn [judge] the world, but that the world through Him might be saved. He who believes in Him is not condemned; but he who does not believe is condemned already because he has not believed in the name of the only begotten Son of God." (John 3:17–18). Jesus explains to the externally religious Nicodemus that anyone who does not believe that He (Jesus) is the Son of God and accept Him as their Lord and Savior is condemned already. This condemnation is the judgment of God to everlasting hell, eternally separated from God's grace and mercy.

The apostle Paul sheds more light on this subject when writing, "For all have sinned and fall short of the glory of God" (Rom. 3: 23). And, "For the wages of sin is death, but the gift of God is eternal life in Christ Jesus our Lord." (Rom. 6:23). This takes us back to Genesis 2:17. God desires to be known by His creation. Therefore, he has revealed Himself through general revelation through His creation and His creatures and His special revelation revealed by His actions, dreams and visions, the incarnation of His Son, and through the Holy Scriptures (chapter two). Motivated to be known by His creation, God created Adam and Eve with a nature that consists of immaterial (spirit) and material (flesh) aspects, thereby creating a living being (soul) that would be able to experience His presence and His fellowship (Gen. 2; 7). God created Adam in His image (Gen. 1:26). Thus providing him with the characteristics of a living nature which are the intellectual capability of the mind, the emotional capacity of feelings, the volitional (making choices or decisions) of a will, the social capacity of relationships, the moral capacity of conscience, and the causal (to cause to act) capacity of a body (see chapter three). This image furnished him with the communicable attributes of God (such as holiness, grace, love, and justice to name a few). Before the fall, Adam and Eve lived in perfection and in a constant state of righteousness, thereby being sinless (see chapter three). They lived in utter peace and tranquility in the Garden of Eden. God provided for all their needs and happiness. However, God shared a restriction with them, "But of the Tree of knowledge of good and evil you shall not eat, for in the day that you eat of it you shall surely die" (Gen. 17). This was not a temptation but rather a test of their dedication and obedience. Nonetheless, it was Satan who made this into temptation by suggesting that they would become like God. Adam and Eve failed God. This became known as the Fall (chapter four). This Fall affected both the material and immaterial aspects of Adam and Eve (Chapter three and four). They had to experience the consequences of their immoral activities such as sin and death.

As stated previously in this book by Millard Erickson is that sin is "any act or disposition that fails to completely fulfill or measure up to the standards of God's righteousness. It may involve an actual act of transgression of God's law or failure to live up to His norms." [259] There are many Hebrew and Greek words that describe sin. I will only discuss two Greek words that are clarified by Greek scholar, William D. Mounce. The first Greek word is *hamartano*. Mounce explains that this word "gives the sense of missing the mark, losing, or falling short of the goal" (Rom. 3:23). He furthers explains that generally the meaning "refers to sins or sinning against oneself or another person" (Luke. 17: 3 – 4; Matt. 18: 15 – 21; Acts 25: 8; 1 Cor. 6:18). The second Greek word is *hamartia*, which is normally translated as "sin." It refers to the transgression of the law. Thereby, *hamartia* is used to denote one's sin against God. "Apart from the atoning blood of Jesus Christ, *hamartia* results in death" (Rom. 6:23). [260] Adam and Eve sinned against God.

Immediately after Adam and Eve sinned against God by eating the forbidden fruit, they experienced the consequences. Their eyes were opened and for the first time, there was a recognition of nudity. This was part of the new knowledge that was gained. Their former healthy relationship had become something unseemly, shameful, and embarrassing. Their innocence was lost, but more importantly, they lost their righteous standing before God. They were no longer perfect; their communicable attributes had been sullied. Their nature was now sinful and depraved. This in turn negatively affected their relationship with God. A relationship that neither Adam nor Eve could ever repair on their own.

This moment of disobedience is often referred to as "original sin." In one sense original sin refers to the first sin committed by Adam. However, the consequence of Adam's original sin is also humanities consequence since it also incorporates the sinful state and condition of all humankind because of each one's relation with Adam, who is seen as the federal head, or headship, of the entire human race. Federal headship means that the action of the representative is determinative for all members united under him or her. Therefore, when Adam sinned, he represented all humanity, resulting in his sin (disobedience) being imputed (crediting something to someone that comes from another) to all his descendants (1 Cor. 15: 21 -22; Rom. 5:12 – 21). Adam's sinful and depraved nature was imputed to all humanity resulting in the inability to fellowship with God (Ps. 51:5; Eph. 2: 1 – 3). All unbelievers are spiritually dead and possess a darkened understanding of God. This is not to say that unbelievers cannot perform good works in society. They just cannot accomplish spiritual good or be good in terms of a relationship with God. (chapter six).

All humanity shares in Adams guilt or judgment, "for the wages of sin is death." When most think of death it is usually in the form of biology (physical death). The scripture explains that death is a form of separation. First, there is spiritual death. When Adam and Eve first ate of the forbidden fruit, they did not instantaneously die physically but experienced immediate spiritual death. They lost their innocence and righteous standing before God. They were now less than perfect and were separated from God's presence and fellowship. This is the state and standing of all unbelievers. Centuries later they both would experience physical death. This is the separation of the material body (flesh) from the immaterial (spirit). Lastly, the Scriptures share the consequence of eternal death. This is by far the most horrific death. All unbelievers will stand before the Great White Throne of God and hear their judgment; Eternal death in the everlasting fires of hell. Tragically, this death entails eternal separation from God and His mercies (Rev. 20: 11 -15). Therefore, every human being needs to experience authentic salvation. But because of everyone's depraved nature, he or she can never save themselves. All seems hopeless at this point. Later in this chapter, I will share the only hope that all who make up humankind must experience to be born again.

What Does it Mean to Be Born Again?

In His discussion with Nicodemus, Jesus was adamant that Nicodemus must be born again (John 3:3). The phrase 'born again" literally means "to be born from above." It also carries the idea of becoming a child of God through trust in God's Word. This new birth consists of a spiritual transformation or regeneration that is produced through the working of the Holy Spirit (2 Cor. 5:17; Titus 3:5; 1 John 2:29; 3:9; 4:7; 5:14-18).

Jesus continued by providing additional information of the new birth, "Most assuredly I say to you, unless one is born of water and the Spirit, he cannot enter the kingdom of God. That which is born of flesh is flesh, and that which is born of the Spirit is spirit" (John 3: 5 – 6). There are different interpretations of this verse. Some mistakenly use it to suggest that water baptism imparts salvation. This interpretation leaves out grace and is based upon works. Some interpret water as some sort of cleansing or purification. It is my understanding that any purification of one's nature happens after he or she experiences salvation, not before. Purification is not a prerequisite to experiencing salvation. During my hermeneutical studies, I found that one of the rules of interpretation is that one must examine the verses before and after any text. It seems to me that the text is comparing a new birth to the old. The difference between the flesh and the Spirit. The physical birth to that of spiritual birth. I know that some are uncomfortable discussing what happens when a woman gives birth. However, in biblical days it was part of life. Therefore, it was commonly known that a woman's water breaks before birth. I believe that Jesus was informing Nicodemus that an individual had to be born of the flesh (water) and of the Spirit to experience authentic salvation. Nicodemus had experienced the water at birth, yet he had not experienced the Holy Spirit. In the flesh, he accomplished many religious works, but to no avail since he had never experienced the Spirit.

Many who read this may be like Nicodemus; they have experienced the physical birth and are presently relying on their religious activities, but they have never experienced the saving power of the Holy Spirit, and until they do they are destined to eternal separation from God in hell.

Who Provides the New Birth?

In a previous section in this chapter, I revealed how all human-kind received Adam's depraved nature and guilt through imputation and that no one on his or her own could ever accomplish anything to acquire a relationship with God. All of humanity has no hope; each one's future is eternal damnation. But I have good news! Jesus Christ provided an escape, an intervention, but most importantly an atoning sacrifice so that any human beings may experience authentic salvation and a relationship with God. Previously I spoke of the negative aspects of imputation. But there is a positive aspect. Jesus' righteousness is imputed to all who by faith repent and believe. Believers stand before God and are declared justified, having fellowship and a relationship with Him.

John spoke of this, "For God so loved the world that He gave His only begotten Son, that whoever believes in Him should not perish but have everlasting life" (John 3;16). The apostle Paul proclaims, "But God demonstrated His love for us, in that while we were still sinners, Christ died for us" (Rom. 5:8). Why would God embrace human weakness and suffering? Why would He send His only Son? What made Christ endure mockery, shame, and pain? The answer is rooted in love!

Sin is the breaking of God's law deserving of physical, spiritual, and eternal death (Rom. 6:23) and the judgment of God's wrath. Therefore, the only hope for humankind was for Christ to make atonement by freely offering Himself to suffer and die on the cross. He accomplished this to bear the full penalty for sin in the place of all sinners who would accept His free gift of salvation. It was on the cross that Christ shed His blood to make full atonement for those who would believe. The actuality of "the blood of Christ" as a means of atonement (at-oneness) for sin has its origin in the Mosaic Law, especially in the "Day of Atonement" found in Leviticus 16 (previously discussed). Once a year, the high priest presented an offering of the blood of bulls and goats on the altar of the temple, for his and his family's sins, and that of the sins of all the people. In preparation, all things had to be cleansed with blood, for without the shedding of blood there is no forgiveness (Heb. 9:22; Lev. 17:11). The offerings were to be pure with no spot or blemishes on the outside. However, this blood offering was limited in its effectiveness and had to be offered annually again and again. Jesus' blood was perfect. Unlike Adam who had sinned and brought death into the world, Christ, the second Adam, never sinned but brought forth grace (Rom. 5). While the animal sacrifices were spotless outside, Christ was spotless on the inside; He was faultless. Therefore, the blood offered by Christ on the cross was "once and for all" and would never be shed again (Heb. 7:27).

The Crucifixion was a Roman form of capital punishment of suffering and shame that was most painful and degrading. The punishment began with the victim being scourged with a whip referred to as a cat of nine tails, consisting of leather straps in which pieces of metal and bone were attached to the ends that would rip the flesh of the body. The victim was then forced to carry the crossbeam to the execution site. A sign would be placed around the neck of the victim or fastened to the cross detailing the victim's crime. The victim would be stripped of his clothing and placed on the cross so that nails may be pounded into both his wrists and often one nail through his feet. The victim would have to force his body upward by pushing, in great agony, with his feet so that his body would rise, as to be able to breathe. In most cases, death was caused by the loss of blood circulation and coronary failure. Often this could take days before the victim would succumb to the agony. Sometimes the soldiers would break the victim's leg so that he could no longer push up to breathe to hasten their death. Christ's death on the cross paid in full the debt of sin that each individual owed. There would never be any further sacrifices for sin. Christ's resurrection from the grave is the proof that God accepted His sacrifice (Heb. 5:7). For more information read chapters seven and eight.

How is One Born Again?

One's salvation experience is initiated by a call, or summons, from the Holy Spirit (John 6:44; 12:32). This call is the work of the Spirit as He illuminates the heart and conscience that will enable the individuals to understand the divine work of redemption (John 16: 8 – 11; 1 Cor. 2: 6 – 16). This call is two-fold; it draws the individual to Christ while convicting him or her of sin. This conviction is the act of the Holy Spirit persuading one through a sense of guilt and shame of his or her sinful nature with the undertaking of leading to repentance. Previously in this book, I quoted Glenn McCoy concerning the conviction by the Holy Spirit:

> First, the conviction of sin is the result of the Holy Spirit awakening humanity to a sense of guilt and commendation because of sin and unbelief. Second, more than a mental conviction is intended. The total person is involved. This can lead to action based on a sense of conviction. Third, the conviction results in hope, not despair. Once individuals are made aware of their estranged relationship with God, they are

challenged and encouraged to mend that relationship. The conviction not only implies the exposure
of sin (despair) but a call to repentance (hope). [261]

True conviction results in a contrite heart, humility, and a strong
sense of guilt and shamefulness. David adds that this experience
of the heart is not only contrition but that of a broken spirit
(Ps. 51:17). When the Holy Spirit calls a sinner, He first draws
them to God and then He convicts them of their sin.

Once the individual has experienced the "call" of the Holy Spirit
to salvation he or she must decide to accept or reject God's free
offer of salvation. If accepted it will lead the unregenerate individual to conversion and spiritual regeneration and God by
placing the individual in Christ. Following is an overview of
conversion and regeneration.

Conversion

Previously stated in this book, David Mapes explains,
"Conversion is what man is called upon to do. It has two distinguishable but inseparable aspects which are like the positive
and negative poles of a magnet. The negative is repentance and
the positive is faith." [262] Conversion is the action of a person
turning to Christ. It includes renunciation of sin (repentance)
and the acceptance of Christ as Lord and Savior (faith). Jesus
affirmed the need for conversion when stating, "Unless you are
converted and become as little children, you will by no means
enter the kingdom of heaven" (Matt. 18:3). Conversion is conceivable for any male or female who approaches God with the
simple trust of a child coming before his or her parents.

Repentance: Millard Erickson previously explained by first relating that repentance is based upon the feeling of godly sorrow for one's sin. He points to two Hebrew words that are often used in Scripture relating to repentance. The first Hebrew word is *nacham* which came to mean "to lament (to cry out or wail) or to grieve." When referring to an emotion of consideration of others, it suggests compassion and sympathy. When used in consideration of one's character or deeds, it means "to rue (regret or deplore)" or "to repent."

The second Hebrew word that he refers to is *shub*. This word is the most common word that denotes the genuine repentance that humans are expected to display. Erickson states that "it stresses the importance of a conscious morals separation, the necessity of forsaking sin and entering into fellowship with God."

Faith: While repentance is the negative aspect of true conversion, faith is the positive aspect. During repentance, the non-believer turns away from sin, Nonetheless, in faith, he turns to Christ. Repentance and faith are inseparable; you cannot have one without the other. Therefore, true repentance cannot exist apart from faith or faith from repentance. Emery Bancroft states that "repentance is faith in action and faith is repentance in rest."[263]

Following is a better understanding of saving faith:

- Faith that saves requires a personal acceptance to the truth of the gospel (Luke 24: 25; 2 Thess. 2:13). One must not only understand the truth but also agree to the truth of the gospel without reservation from the heart.

This includes the acceptance of the truth of Jesus' deity (John 1:1), His sacrificial death upon the cross (1 Cor. 15:3), and His resurrection from the dead (Rom.10:9).

- Authentic salvation includes unreserved trust in and a commitment to Christ Jesus as a personal Savior and Lord (2 Tim. 1:2). This trust and commitment results with the believer counting the cross of discipleship. The evidence of true faith is obedience in the life of the believer (Rom. 1:5) and good works (1 Thess. 1:3) that bless others and glorify God.[264]

The nature of saving faith is a heart response to hearing or reading the gospel message. Paul explains in Romans 10: 9 – 10, "That if you confess with your mouth the Lord Jesus and believe in your heart that God has raised Him from the dead, you will be saved. For with the heart one believes unto righteousness, and with the mouth, confession is made unto salvation." Therefore, saving faith is an acceptable response to believing that: (1) what the Bible reveals about God is true, (2) that all men and women are unrighteous sinners and in need of Christ as Savior, (3) that Christ is God, born of a virgin, died on the cross, and three days later raised from the grave to make atonement for sin, and (4) that one must place his or her faith in Him for salvation. Saving faith is also the accepting response to believe "in" Christ as Savior and "in" Christ as Lord meaning that Christ is the Master and you are the servant who obeys His will and Word.

Regeneration: After faith and repentance the individual experiences regeneration. As previously noted David Mapes explains that "regeneration is a supernatural work that God does to the repentant person which restores a relationship with God lost by Adam (See Ezek. 36:27, "And I will put my Spirit within you, and cause you to walk in my statutes, and ye shall keep my judgments, and do them.") The regenerated person is no longer at enmity with God because of his permanently changed mind."[265]

Greek scholar William Mounce suggests that the basic Greek word for regeneration is *palingenesia*. Nonetheless, in the New Testament, the concept is much larger than this one word. He states that often the word refers to the "new birth" (John 3: 3 – 5) and the "new creation" (2 Cor. 5: 17; Gal. 6:15). He further explains that in conversion the believer is made new, brought from death to life (Eph. 2: 1 – 5), by the power of God's Holy Spirit.[266]

Paul Enns suggests two major results of regeneration:

> *A new nature.* The result of regeneration is the impartation of "divine nature" (2 Pet. 1:4). The believer has received a "new self" (Eph. 4:24), a capacity for righteous living. He is a "new creature" (2 Cor. 5:17).

> *A new life.* The believer has received a new mind (1 Cor. 2:16) so he or she might know God; a new heart (Rom 5:5) that he may love God (1 John 4:9); and a new will (Rom. 6:13) that he may obey God.[267] When we consider the above definitions of regeneration, we can summarize the following:

- Regeneration is the supernatural work of God particularly ascribed to the Holy Spirit in which the new believer contributes nothing.

- It results in the new believer no longer experiencing enmity with God but rather being born anew by removing the old sinful nature being replaced with a new nature responsive to God.

- It brings forth a radical new outcome and imparts to the soul a new spiritual nature.

- Holy Spirit regeneration infuses into the soul renewed intellectual, volitional, moral, emotional, and relational powers that initiate the renewal of *imago Dei*- being made in the image of God.

- Regeneration begins the sanctification process starting with the new believer as a child of God and the maturing process thereafter until the believer is in heaven with Christ.

- The Scriptures provide additional words to ascribe regeneration such as "born again," "the new birth," or "new creation."

Those who need more information concerning this chapter may find chapter ten useful. At this point in the chapter, if you feel the Holy Spirit calling you to salvation, I implore you to honor the supernatural faith supplied by the call of the Holy Spirit by repenting of your sin of unbelief and all the sins you have committed. Trust Christ as Savior and Lord. One accomplishes this through prayer. You may acknowledge that you believe what the Bible reveals about God is true, that your only hope of salvation is through the atonement that Christ provided on the cross. Acknowledge that you believe that Christ was born of a virgin, died for your sins was buried and was resurrected, and will come again. place your faith in Him and live for Him.

The Basics after Experiencing Authentic Salvation

Books have been written that provide detailed information for the new believers who have experienced authentic salvation. However, I will only present a few important suggestions that every new believer should be aware of during his or her spiritual journey:

- Begin daily Bible reading. I would begin with the New Testament, especially the Gospel of John.
- Find a conservative church to join that will provide proper discipleship that will help you mature in the Lord.
- Be obedient to the ordinance of baptism as a testimony to believers and non-believers as your decision to make Christ your Lord and Savior.
- Attend all worship and training events.
- Share your testimony with others as a witness.
- Provide God your talents, time, and tithes.

I desire that you know many things that you did not before reading this book. I desire that you know without a doubt that you have experienced authentic salvation. I challenge you to share the gospel with those you know to enable them to know Christ as Savior and Lord. God be with you!

Bibliography

Allison, Gregg R. *The Baker Compact Dictionary of Theological Terms*. Grand Rapids, Michigan: Baker Books.2016.

_____, *Historical Theology: An Introduction to Christian Doctrine*. Grand Rapids, Michigan: Zondervan. 2011

Arnold, Clinton E. *Zondervan Exegetical Commentary on the New Testament: Ephesians*. Grand Rapids, Michigan: Zondervan. 2010.

_____, *Zondervan Illustrated Bible Background Commentary*, 3 vols. Grand Rapids, Michigan: Zondervan. 2002.

Baker, Warren, and Eugene Carpenter. *The Complete Word Study Dictionary Old Testament*. Chattanooga, Tennessee: AMG Publishers. 2003.

Bancroft, Emery H. *Elemental Theology*. Grand Rapids, Michigan: Zondervan Publishing House. 1960.

Barclay, William. *The Daily Study Bible Series: The Gospel of John*, 2 vols. revised edition. Louisville, Kentucky: Westminster John Knox Press. 1975.

_____, *The Gospel of Matthew, 2 vols*. Louisville. Kentucky: Westminster John Knox Press. 1975.

Brand, Chad. gen. ed. *Holman Illustrated Bible Dictionary*, rev. Nashville, Tennessee: Holman Reference. 2015.

Broadus, John. *An American Commentary on the New Testament: Matthew*. Philadelphia: American aptist Publication Society. 1886.

Bruce, F. F. *The New International Commentary on the New Testament: The Epistle to the Hebrews*. Grand Rapids, Michigan: William B. Eerdmans Publishing Company 1990.

Cairns, Alan. gen. ed. *Dictionary of Theological Terms*. Greenville, South Carolina: Emerald House Group. 1998.

Calvin, John. *Calvin's Commentary, Galatians, Ephesians, Philippians, and Colossians*. Grand Rapids, Michigan.1965.

Campbell, Don. Wendell Johnston, John Walvoord, and John Witmer. *The Theological Workbook*. Nashville, Tennessee: Word. 2000.

Chaffer, Lewis Sperry. *Chafer Systematic Theology*. 8 vols. Dallas, Texas: Dallas Seminary Press. 1975.

Chapman, Gary. *The Five Love Languages: How to Express Heartfelt Commitment to Your Mate*.

Chicago, Illinois: Northfield Publishing. 2004.

Dagg, John L. *Manual of Theology*. Harrisonburg, Virginia: Gano Books. 1982.

Demarest, Bruce and Keith J. Matthews. gen. eds. *Dictionary of Everyday Theology and Culture*. Colorado Springs, Co. 2010.

Dorman, Ted M. *A Faith for all Christian Belief in its Classical Expression.* 2nd ed. Nashville, Tennessee: Broadman and Holman Publishers. 2001.

Duvall, J. Scott, and J. Daniel Hays. *Grasping God's Word: A Hands-On Approach to Reading, Interpreting, and Applying the Bible.* 3rd. edition. Grand Rapids, Michigan: Zondervan. 2012.

Elwell, Walter A. *Evangelical Dictionary of Theology.* Grand Rapids, Michigan: Baker Books. 1984.

Enns, Paul. *The Moody Handbook of Theology.* Chicago, Illinois: Moody Press. 1989.

Erickson, Millard J. *The Concise Dictionary of Christian Theology.* Wheaton, Illinois: Crossway. 2001.

_____, *Christian Theology.* 3rd edition. Grand Rapids, Michigan: Baker Academic. 2013.

_____, *Introducing Christian Doctrine.* Grand Rapids, Michigan: Baker Academic. 2015.

_____, *What Does God Know and When Does He Know It?* Grand Rapids, Michigan: Zondervan. 2003.

Fee, Gordon D. *The New International Commentary on the New Testament: The First Epistle to the Corinthians.* Grand Rapids, Michigan: William B. Eerdmans Publishing Company. 1987.

Feinberg, John S. *No One Like Him: The Doctrine of God.* Wheaton, Illinois: Crossways Books. 2001.

Geisler, Norman L. *Baker Encyclopedia of Christian Apologetics.* Grand Rapids, Michigan: Baker Books. 1999.

_____, *The Big Book of Christian Apologetics.* Grand Rapids, Michigan: Baker Books. 2012.

_____, *Systematic Theology:* 4 volumes Minneapolis, Minnesota: Bethany House. 2005.

Graham, Billy. *The Holy Spirit.* Dallas Texas: Word Publishers.1988.

Grudem, Wayne. *Systematic Theology: An Introduction to Biblical Doctrine.* Grand Rapids, Michigan: Zondervan.1994.

Hamilton, Victor P. *The New International Commentary on the Old Testament: The Book of Genesis, Chapters 1 – 17.* Grand Rapids, Michigan: William B. Eerdmans, Publishing Company. 1980.

Hendriksen, William. *New Testament Commentary: The Gospel of Matthew.* Grand Rapids, Michigan: Baker Book House. 1973.

Horton, Michael. *The Christian Faith.* Grand Rapids, Michigan: Zondervan. 2011.

Keener, Craig S. *The IVP Bible Background Commentary: New Testament.* Downers Grove, Illinois: Intervarsity Press.1993.

Klink, Edward W. *Zondervan Exegetical Commentary on the New Testament: John.* Grand Rapids, Michigan: Zondervan. 2016.

Kroll, Woodrow. *The Book of Romans.* Chattanooga, Tennessee: AMG Publishers. 2002.

Longman, Tremper III. gen. ed. *The Baker Illustrated Bible Dictionary.* Grand Rapids, Michigan: Baker Books. 2013.

Lutzer, Erwin W. *Cries from the Cross, A Journey into the Heart of Jesus.* Chicago, Illinois: Moody Publishers. 2002.

_____, *The Serpent of Paradise: The Incredible Story of How Satan's Rebellion Serves God's Purpose.* Chicago, Illinois: Moody Press. 1996.

The MacArthur Study Bible, Copyright 1997 by Word Publishing. a division of Thomas Nelson. Inc.

MacArthur, John Jr. *The MacArthur New Testament Commentary: Titus.* Chicago, Illinois: Moody Press.1996.

_____, *The MacArthur New Testament Commentary: Ephesians.* Chicago, Illinois: The Moody Bible Institute. 1986.

MacArthur, John, and Richard Mayhue. gen. eds. *Biblical Doctrine: A Systematic Summary of Bible Truth.* Wheaton, Illinois: Crossway. 2017.

Mapes, David. *TH 6302, Systematic Theology II, Notes.* "Nature of Man." Luther Rice Seminary. Fall, 2018.

McKim, Donald K. ed. *Reformed Theology: The Westminster Handbook to Christian Theology,* Louisville, Kentucky: Westminster John Knox Press. 2001.

Manser, Martin H. The *Westminster Collection of Christian Quotations.* Louisville, Kentucky: Westminster John Knox Press. 2001.

Mathews, Kenneth A. *The New American Commentary: Genesis 1-11.* Nashville, Tennessee: Broadman and Holman. 1996.

Moo, Douglas. *The New International Commentary on the New Testament: The Epistle of Romans.* Grand Rapids, Michigan: William B. Eerdmans Publishing Company. 1996.

_____, *The NIV Application Commentary: Romans.* Grand Rapids, Michigan: Zondervan. 2000.

Mounce, Robert H. *The New American Commentary: Romans,* Nashville Tennessee: Broadman and Holman Publisher. 1995.

Mounce, William D. gen. ed. *Mounce's Complete Expository Dictionary of Old and New Testament Words.* Grand Rapids, Michigan: Zondervan. 200.

Myers, Jeff. *Understanding the Faith: A Survey of Christian Apologetics.* Colorado Springs, Colorado: Summit Ministries. 2016.

Oden, Thomas C. gen. ed. *Ancient Christian Commentary on Scripture: Old Testament: Isaiah 1-39.* Downers Grove, Illinois: InterVarsity Press. 2004.

_____, *Systematic Theology, 3 vols. Peabody,* Massachusetts: Hendrickson Publishers. 2008.

Osborne, Grant R. *Zondervan Exegetical Commentary on the New Testament: Matthew.* Grand Rapids, Michigan: Zondervan. 2010).

Olson, Roger E. *Arminian Theology: Myth and Realities.* Downers Grove, Illinois: IVP Academic. 2006.

Pennock, Michael Francis. *This is Our Faith: A Catholic Catechism for Adults.* Notre Dame, in.: Ave Marie Press. 1992.

Picirilli, Robert E. *Grace, Faith, Freewill: Contrasting Views of Salvation: Calvinism and Arminians*. Nashville, Tennessee: Randall House. 2002.

Pigeon, E. Richard and Gretchen S. Lebrum. *AMG's Comprehensive Dictionary of New Testament Words*, Chattanooga, Tennessee: AMG Publishers. 2014.

Pinnock, R Clark, Richard Rice, John Sanders, William Hasker, and David Basinger. *The Openness of God*. Downers Grove, Illinois: InterVarsity Press. 1994.

Popkin, Richard H. and Avrum Stroll. *No Nonsense Knowledge: Philosophy Made Simple*. New York, New York: Three Rivers Press. 1993.

Ratzinger, Joseph Cardinal. *Catechism of the Catholic Church*. Boston, MA: St. Paula's Book Media. 1994.

Robertson, Archibald Thomas. *Word Pictures in the New Testament. The Fourth Gospel and the Epistles of the Hebrews. 6 vols.* Grand Rapids, Michigan: Baker Book House. 1932.

Rogers, Adrian. *Adrianisms: The Wit and Wisdom of Adrian Rogers.* vol. one. Memphis, Tennessee: Love Worth Finding. 2011.

_____, *Adrianisms, The Wit and Wisdom of Adrian Rogers.* vol. two. Memphis, Tennessee: Love Worth Finding Ministries. 2007.

Rooker, Mark F. *The New American Commentary: Leviticus.* Nashville, Tennessee: Broadman and Holman Publishers. 2000.

Ryrie, Charles C. *A Survey of Bible Doctrine.* Chicago, Illinois: Moody Publishers. 1972.

_____, *Basic Theology*. Colorado Springs, Colorado: Victor Books. 1981.

_____, *The Holy Spirit*. Chicago, Illinois: Moody Publishers. 1965.

Reid, Daniel G., Robert D. Linder, Bruce L. Shelley, Harry S. Stout, and Craig A. Noll. *Concise Dictionary of Christianity in America*. Downers Grove, Illinois: Inter-Varsity Press. 1995.

Sakenfeld, Katharine Doob. *The New Interpreter's Dictionary of the Bible*. Vol. 5. Nashville, Tennessee: Abingdon Press. 2009.

Smith, Gary V. *The New American Commentary: Isaiah 1-39*. Nashville, Tennessee: Broadman and Holman. 2007.

Steele David N., and Curtis C. Thomas. *Points of Calvinism: Defined, Defended, Documented*. Phillipsburg, N. J. Presbyterian, and Reformed Publishing. 1963.

Taylor, Mark. *The New American Commentary: 1 Corinthians*. Nashville, Tennessee: Broadman and Holman Publishers. 2014.

Thiessen, Henry Clarence. *Lectures in Systematic Theology*. Grand Rapids, Michigan: William B. Eerdmans Publishing Company. 1992.

Thielman, Frank. *Zondervan Exegetical Commentary on the New Testament: Romans*. Grand Rapids, Michigan: Zondervan. 2018.

Towns, Elmer. *Twenty-First Century Biblical Commentary Series: The Gospel of John*. Chattanooga,

Tennessee: AMG Publishers. 2002.

Tozer, A. W., *How to Be Filled with the Holy Spirit.* Chicago, Illinois: Moody Publishers. 2016.

_____, *The Attributes of God. 2 vols.* Chicago, Illinois: Wing Spread Publishers. 2003.

_____, *The Knowledge of the Holy.* New York, New York: Harper Collins. 1961.

Walton, John H. *The NIV Application Commentary: Genesis.* Grand Rapids, Michigan: Zondervan. 2001.

Walvoord, John. *Jesus Christ Our Lord.* Chicago, Illinois: Moody Press. 1969.

_____, *The Holy Spirit.* Grand Rapids, Michigan: Zondervan Publishing House. 1958.

Wanamaker, Charles A. *The New International Greek Testament Commentary.* Grand Rapids, Michigan:

William Eerdmans Publishing Company. 1990.

Watts, Isaac (1674 – 1748). *Baptist Hymnal.* Nashville Tennessee: Convention Press.1956.

Webster's New Twentieth Century Dictionary. World Syndication Publishing Company. 1970.

Zodhiates, Spiros. *The Complete Word Study Dictionary: New Testament.* Chattanooga, Tennessee: AMG Publishers. 1992.

Endnotes

1   Unless otherwise noted, all Scriptures are from The *New King James Version,* Copyright 1979, 1980, 1982 by Thomas Nelson, Inc. Used by permission. All rights reserved.

2   John MacArthur, Jr. *The MacArthur New Testament Commentary: Titus* (Chicago, Illinois: Moody Press, 1996), 119.

3   William D. Mounce, gen. ed. *Mounce's Complete Dictionary of Old and New Testament Words,* (Grand Rapids, Michigan: Zondervan, 2006), 382-382.

4   Grant R. Osborne, *Zondervan Exegetical Commentary on the New Testament: Matthew* (Grand Rapids, Michigan: Zondervan, 2010), 274.

5   Catholic Dictionary, https://www.catholicculture.org/culture/library/dictionary/index.cfm?id=36178.

6   Michael Francis Pennock, *This is Our Faith: A Catholic Catechism for Adults* (Notre Dame, In.: Ave Marie Press,1992), 152-154.

7   Ibid, 154-156.

8   Ibid, 157-162.

9   Ibid, 174-175.

10 Ibid, 180.

11 Ibid, 203.

12 Joseph Cardinal Ratzinger, *Catechism of the Catholic Church* (Boston, MA: St. Paula's Book Media, 1994), 289.

13 Daniel G. Reid, Robert D. Linder, Bruce L. Shelley, Harry S. Stout, and Craig A. Noll, *Concise Dictionary of Christianity in America* (Downers Grove, Illinois: InterVarsity Press, 1995), 360.

14   Roger E. Olson, *Arminian Theology: Myth and Realities,* (Downers Grove: IVP Academic, 2006), 26-27.

15   *The MacArthur Study Bible,* Copyright 1997 by Word Publishing, a division of Thomas Nelson, Inc. p.1693.

16   Richard H. Popkin and Avrum Stroll, *No-Nonsense Knowledge: Philosophy Made Simple* (New York, New York: Three Rivers Press, 1993), 230-234.

17   Millard J. Erickson, *The Concise Dictionary of Christian Theology* (Wheaton, Illinois: Crossway,2001), 176-177.

18   Bruce Demarest and Keith J. Matthews, gen. eds, *Dictionary of Everyday Theology and Culture* (Colorado Springs, Co., 2010), 200-201.

19   Millard J. Erickson, *Christian Theology,* 3rd edition (Grand Rapids, Michigan: Baker Academic, 2013), 239 – 242.

20   Erickson, Christian *Theology,* 241.

21   Erickson, *Christian Theology,* 238.

22   Chad Bland, gen. ed. *Holman Illustrated Bible Dictionary,* rev. (Nashville, Tennessee: Holman Reference, 2015), 1351.

23   Norman L. Geisler, *Baker Encyclopedia of Christian Apologetics* (Grand Rapids, Michigan: Baker Books, 1999), 27.

24   Gregg R. Allison, *The Baker Compact Dictionary of Theological Terms* (Grand Rapids, Michigan: Baker Books, 2016), 90.

25   John MacArthur and Richard Mayhue, gen. eds. *Biblical Doctrine: A Systematic Summary of Bible Truth* (Wheaton, Illinois: Crossway, 2017), 160-161.

26   John S. Feinberg, *No One Like Him: The Doctrine of God* (Wheaton, Illinois: Crossways Books, 2001), 233-375, Norman Geisler, *Systematic Theology: God Creation.* Vol. 2 (Minneapolis, Minnesota: Bethany House, 2003), and Millard J. Erickson, *Christian Theology,* 3rd. edition (Grand Rapids, Michigan: Baker Academic, 2013), 254-271.

27   Gregg R. Allison, *The Baker Compact Dictionary of Theological Terms* (Grand Rapids, Michigan: Baker Books,2016), 42.

28   Erickson, *Christian Theology,* 233 – 253.

29 Charles C. Ryrie, *Basic Theology* (Colorado Springs, Colorado: Victor Books, 1981), 36.

30 Gregg R. Allison, 151-152.

31 Paul Enns, *The Moody Handbook of Theology* (Chicago, Illinois: Moody Press, 1989), 195.

32 Paul Enns, 194.

33 John S. Feinberg, *No One Like Him: The Doctrine of God* (Wheaton, Illinois: Crossway Books, 2001), 339-342. And Don Campbell, Wendell Johnston, John Walvoord, and John Witmer, *The Theological Workbook* (Nashville, Tennessee: Word, 2000), 161-163.

34 Millard J. Erickson, *Introducing Christian Doctrine* (Grand Rapids, Michigan: Baker Academic, 2015), 99.

35 Chad Bland, gen. ed. *Holman Illustrated Bible Dictionary*, rev. (*Nashville*, Tennessee: Holman Reference, 2015), 1672.

36 Douglas Moo, *The New International Commentary on the New Testament: The Epistle of Romans* (Grand Rapids, Michigan: William B. Eerdmans Publishing Company, 1996), 100-103.

37 John MacArthur and Richard Mayhue, gen. eds. *Biblical Doctrine: A Systematic Summary of Bible Truth* (Wheaton, Illinois: Crossway, 2017), 185.

38 Spiros Zodhiates, *The Complete Word Study Dictionary: New Testament* (Chattanooga, Tennessee: AMG Publishers, 1992), 66.

39 Spiros Zodhiates, *The Complete Word Study Dictionary: New Testament* (Chattanooga, Tennessee: AMG Publishers, 1992), 99-100.

40 Gary V. Smith, *The New American Commentary: Isaiah 1-39* (Nashville, Tennessee: Broadman and Holman, 2007), 309-315.

41 Thomas C. Oden, gen. ed. *Ancient Christian Commentary on Scripture: Old Testament, Isaiah 1-39* (Downers Grove, Illinois: InterVarsity Press, 2004), 120-123.

42 Gregg R. Allison, *The Baker Compact Dictionary of Theological Terms* (Grand Rapids, Michigan: Baker Books, 2016), 103-104.

43   Warren Baker and Eugene Carpenter, *The Complete Word Study Dictionary Old Testament* (Chattanooga, Tennessee: AMG Publishers, 2003), 876.

44   Kenneth A. Mathews, *The New American Commentary: Genesis 1-11* (Nashville, Tennessee: Broadman and Holman, 1996), 128. And Baker, 161.

45   Millard J. Erickson, *Christian Theology*, 3rd edition (Grand Rapids, Michigan: Baker Academic, 2013), 463.

46   Erickson, 464.

47   John MacArthur and Richard Mayhue, *Biblical Doctrine* (Wheaton, Illinois: Crossway, 2017), 412-413.

48   Erickson, *Christian Theology*, 465-467.

49   Erickson, *Christian Theology*, 461-463.

50   Erickson, Christian *Theology*, 460.

51   MacArthur, 412-413.

52   Wayne Grudem, *Systematic Theology: An Introduction to Biblical Doctrine* (Grand Rapids, Michigan: Zondervan, 1994), 442-443.

53   John H. Walton, *The NIV Application Commentary: Genesis* (Grand Rapids, Michigan: Zondervan, 2001), 130-131.

54   MacArthur, 413-414.

55   Erickson, *Christian Theology*, 471.

56   Millard J. Erickson, *Introducing Christian Doctrine*, (Grand Rapids, Michigan: Baker Academic, 2015), 197-198.

57   Ibid, 197.

58   Kenneth A. Matthews, *The New American Commentary: Genesis 1-11:26* (Nashville, Tennessee: Broadman and Holman Publishers, 1996), 196.

59   Matthews, 196.

60   MacArthur, 418-419.

61   Victor P. Hamilton, *The New International Commentary on the Old Testament: The Book of Genesis, Chapters 1 – 17* (Grand Rapids, Michigan: William B. Eerdmans, Publishing Company, 1980), 159. And Warren Baker and Eugene Carpenter, *The*

Complete Word Study Dictionary: Old Testament (Chattanooga, Tennessee: AMG Publishers, 2003), 758-759.

62   MacArthur, 418-419.

63   MacArthur, 417 – 418 and David Mapes, *TH 6302, Systematic Theology II, Notes*, "Nature of Man." Luther Rice Seminary, Fall, 2018.

64   Lewis Sperry Chaffer, *Chafer Systematic Theology*, vol.2 (Dallas, Texas: Dallas Seminary Press, 1975), 181.

65   David Mapes, *TH 6302, Systematic Theology II, Notes*, "Nature of Man." Luther Rice Seminary, Fall, 2018.

66   Daniel L. Akin, gen. ed. *A Theology for the Church* (Nashville, Tennessee: Broadman and Holman Academic, 2007), 347.

67   David Mapes, *TH 6302, Systematic Theology II, Notes*, "Nature of Man." Luther Rice Seminary, Fall, 2018. Quoting from Friedrich Oehler, *Theology of the Old Testament*, rev. ed. (Grand Rapids, Michigan: Zondervan, 1978), 151.

68   David Mapes, *TH 6302, Systematic Theology II, Notes*, "Nature of Man." Luther Rice Seminary, Fall, 2018.

69   Charles A. Wanamaker, *The New International Greek Testament Commentary* (Grand Rapids, Michigan: William Eerdmans Publishing Company, 1990), 205 – 207.

70   Chad Brand, *Holman Illustrated Bible Dictionary* (Nashville, Tennessee: Holman Reference, 2015), 647 – 648 and Walter A. Elwell, *Evangelical Dictionary of Theology* (Grand Rapids, Michigan: Baker Books, 1984), 443.

71   Spiros Zodhiates, *The Complete Word Study Dictionary: New Testament*, (Chattanooga, Tennessee: AMG Publishers, 1992), 1135.

72   Adrian Rogers, *Adrianisms: The Wit and Wisdom of Adrian Rogers.* Vol. 1 (Memphis, Tennessee: Love Worth Finding, 2011), 110.

73   Chad Brand, gen. ed. *Holman Illustrated Bible Dictionary* (Nashville Tennessee: Holman Reference, 2015), 1545. And Katharine Doob Sakenfeld, *The New Interpreter's Dictionary*

of the Bible. Vol. 5 (Nashville, Tennessee: Abingdon Press, 2009), 516.

74 Martin H. Manser, The *Westminster Collection of Christian Quotations* (Louisville, Kentucky: Westminster John Knox Press, 2001), 371 – 372.

75 Martin H. Manser, 35.

76 Gary Chapman, *The Five Love Languages: How to Express Heartfelt Commitment to Your Mate* (Chicago, Illinois: Northfield Publishing, 2004).

77 Victor P. Hamilton, *The New International Commentary of the Old Testament: The Book of Genesis, Chapters 1 – 17* (Grand Rapids Michigan: William B. Eerdmans Publishing Company, 1990), 171.

78 Much of the information from Genes 3: 1-6 was from Hamilton, 187 – 191.

79 Norman L.; Geisler, *The Big Book of Christian Apologetics* (Grand Rapids, Michigan: Baker Books,2012), 139.

80 Geisler, *The Book of Christian Apologetics,* 139.

81 Jeff Myers, *Understanding the Faith: A Survey of Christian Apologetics* (Colorado Springs, Colorado: Summit Ministries, 2016), 361 -362

82 Jeff Myers, *Understanding the Faith: A Survey of Christian Apologetics* (Colorado Springs, Colorado: Summit Ministries, 2016), 361 -362.

83 Martin H. Manser, *The Westminster Collection of Christian Quotations,* (Louisville, Kentucky: Westminster John Knox Press, 2001), 345.

84 Manser, 345.

85 Millard J. Erickson, *The Concise Dictionary of Christian Theology,* (Wheaton, Illinois: Crossway, 2001), 181 – 182.

86 Gregg R. Allison, *The Baker Compact Dictionary of Theological Terms* (Grand Rapids, Michigan: Baker Books, 2016), 194.

87　William D. Mounce, *Mounce's Complete Expository Dictionary of Old and New Testament Words* (Grand Rapids, Michigan: Zondervan, 2006), 656 – 657.

88　Millard J. Erickson, *Christian Theology*, 3rd Edition (Grand Rapids, Michigan: Baker Academic, 2013), 519.

89　Millard J. Erickson, *Christian Theology*, 517 – 519.

90　Millard J. Erickson, *Christian Theology*, 520.

91　Millard J. Erickson, *Christian Theology*, 519 – 526.

92　Millard J. Erickson, *Christian Theology*, 526 – 528.

93　Millard J. Erickson, *Christian Theology*, 515 – 530.

94　Victor P. Hamilton, *The New International Commentary on the Old Testament: The Book of Genesis, Chapters 1 – 17* (Grand Rapids Michigan: William B. Eerdmans Publishing Company, 1990), 192 – 212.

95　Erwin W. Lutzer, *The Serpent of Paradise: The Incredible Story of How Satan's Rebellion Serves God's Purpose* (Chicago, Illinois: Moody Press, 1996), 16.

96　Manser, 63.

97　John MacArthur and Richard Mayhue, *Biblical Doctrine* (Wheaton, Illinois: Crossway, 2017), 836.

98　Manser, 63.

99　William D. Mounce, *Mounce's Complete Expository Dictionary of Old and New Testament Words* (Grand Rapids, Michigan: Zondervan, 2006), 404 – 406 and Spiros Zodhiates, *The Complete Word Study Dictionary: New Testament* (Chattanooga, Tennessee: AMG Publishers, 1992), 703 – 704.

100　Millard J. Erickson, *Christian Theology*, 940 – 941.

101　Greg R. Allison, *The Baker Compact Dictionary of Theological Terms*, 217.

102　John MacArthur and Richard Mayhue, gen eds. *Biblical Doctrine*, (Wheaton, Illinois: Crossway, 2017), 462.

103　Paul Enns, *The Moody Handbook of Theology* (Chicago, Illinois: Moody Press, 1989), 311 and John MacArthur and Richard

Mayhue, gen eds. *Biblical Doctrine* (Wheaton, Illinois: Crossway, 2017), 462.

104 John MacArthur and Richard Mayhue, 462.

105 Paul Enns, *The Moody Handbook of Theology* (Chicago, Illinois: Moody Press, 1989), 311 – 312 and John MacArthur and Richard Mayhue, 462–463.

106 John MacArthur and Richard Mayhue, 463.

107 Paul Enns, *The Moody Handbook of Theology*, 312 and John MacArthur and Richard Mayhue, 463–464.

108 John MacArthur and Richard Mayhue, 464.

109 Paul Enns, *The Moody Handbook of Theology* (Chicago, Illinois: Moody Press, 1989), 312.

110 John MacArthur and Richard Mayhue, 464 – 465.

111 Clinton E. Arnold, *Zondervan Illustrated Bible Background Commentary*, vol. 3 (Grand Rapids, Michigan: Zondervan, 2002), 33 and Craig S. Keener, *The IVP Bible Background Commentary: New Testament* (Downers Grove, Illinois: Intervarsity Press, 1993), 424.

112 MacArthur and Richard Mayhue, 465.

113 William D. Mounce, *Mounce's Complete Dictionary of Old and New Testament Words*, (Grand Rapids, Michigan: Zondervan, 2006), 440.

114 David Mapes, Systematic Theology II. Luther Rice Seminary.

115 Tremper Longman III, gen. ed. *The Baker Illustrated Bible Dictionary* (Grand Rapids, Michigan: Baker Books, 2013), 710.

116 Wayne Grudem, *Systematic Theology* (Grand Rapids, Michigan: Zondervan, 1994), 495.

117 Gregg R. Allison, *The Baker Compact Dictionary of Theological Terms* (Grand Rapids, Michigan: Baker Books, 2016), 212.

118 Bruce Demarest and Keith J. Matthews, gen eds. *Dictionary of Everyday Theology and Culture* (Colorado Springs, Co.: Navpress, 2010), 23.

119 Martin H. Manser, *The Westminster Collection of Christian Quotations* (Louisville, Kentucky: Westminster John Knox Press, 2001), 13.

120 George R. Allison, *The Baker Compact Dictionary of Theological Terms* (Grand Rapids, Michigan: Baker Books, 2016), 28.

121 David Mapes, *Systematic Theology Course II*, Week 6, "Atonement." Luther Rice Seminary, 2019.

122 Ibid.

123 Ibid.

124 Ibid.

125 Millard J. Erickson, *Christian Theology*, 3rd Edition (Grand Rapids, Michigan: Baker Academic, 2013), 735

126 Erickson, 735.

127 Erickson, 735 – 736.

128 Mark F. Rooker, *The New American Commentary: Leviticus* (Nashville, Tennessee: Broadman and Holman Publishers, 2000), 236.

129 Chad Brand, gen. ed. *Holman Illustrated Bible Dictionary* (Nashville, Tennessee: Holman Reference, 2015), 145 – 146.

130 Martin, H. Manser, *The Westminster Collection of Christian Quotations* (Louisville, Kentucky: Westminster John Knox Press, 2001), 61.

131 Grant R. Osborne, *Zondervan Exegetical Commentary on the New Testament: Matthew* (Grand Rapids, Michigan: Zondervan, 2010), 1030.

132 F. F. Bruce, *The New International Commentary on the New Testament: The Epistle to the Hebrews*, (Grand Rapids, Michigan: William B. Eerdmans Publishing Company, 1990), 338.

133 Martin H. Manser, *The Westminster Collection of Christian Quotations* (Louisville, Kentucky: Westminster John Knox Press, 2001), 153.

134 Martin H. Manser, *The Westminster Collection of Christian Quotations* (Louisville, Kentucky: Westminster John Knox Press, 2001), 153

135 Millard J. Erickson, *The Concise Dictionary of Christian Theology* (Wheaton, Illinois: Crossway, 2001), 82.

136 Erwin W. Lutzer, *Cries from the Cross, a Journey into the Heart of Jesus* (Chicago, Illinois: Moody Publishers, 2002), 15 – 17.

137 *Adrianism, The Wit and Wisdom of Adrian Rogers* vol. two (Memphis, Tennessee: Love Worth Finding Ministries, 2007), 174.

138 Isaac Watts (1674 – 1748), *Baptist Hymnal* (Nashville Tennessee: Convention Press, 1956), 94.

139 Millard J. Erickson, *Christian Theology*, 3rd ed. (Grand Rapids, Michigan: Baker Academic, 2013), 741.

140 Erickson, 741.

141 *Webster's New Twentieth Century Dictionary* (World Syndication Publishing Company, 1970).

142 MacArthur, John and Richard Mayhue, *Biblical Doctrine* (Wheaton, Illinois: Crossway, 2017), 528.

143 David Mapes, *TH6302: Systematic Theology II.* "Week Six: The Atonement." Course taught at Luther Rice Seminary, 2019.

144 MacArthur, 528.

145 David Mapes. *TH6302: Systematic Theology II.* "Week Six: The Atonement." Course taught at Luther Rice Seminary, 2019.

146 Ibid.

147 MacArthur, 530.

148 MacArthur, 531.

149 Spiros Zodhiates, *The Complete Word Study Dictionary: New Testament* (Chattanooga, Tennessee: AMG Publishers, 1992), 692.

150 J. Scott Duvall and J. Daniel Hays, *Grasping God's Word: A Hands-On Approach to Reading, Interpreting, and Applying the Bible,* 3rd Edition (Grand Rapids, Michigan: Zondervan, 2012), 137.

151 J. Scott Duvall and J. Daniel Hays, *Grasping God's Word, 139 – 140.*

152 Ibid, 146.

153 David N. Steele and Curtis C. Thomas, *Points of Calvinism: Defined, Defended, Documented* (Phillipsburg, N. J.: Presbyterian and Reformed Publishing, 1963), 13.

154 David Mapes, *Systematic Theology II,* Week Seven" Luther Rice Seminary, Fall, 2019.

155 Steele and Curtis, 15.

156 Most of the information came from Steele and Curtis, 16 -19.

157 Much of the following information for this section was from the notes of David Mapes *Systematic Theology II course,* "lessons seven and nine." Luther Rice Seminary. Fall, 2019.

158 William D. Mounce, *Mounce's Complete Dictionary of Old and New Testament Words* (Grand Rapids, Michigan: Zondervan, 2006), 61.

159 William D. Mounce, *Mounce's Complete Dictionary of Old and New Testament Word,* (Grand Rapids, Michigan: Zondervan, 2006), 440.

160 Millard J. Erickson, *The Concise Dictionary of Christian Theology* (Wheaton, Illinois: Crossway, 2001), 187.

161 Martin H. Manser, *The Westminster Collection of Christian Quotations,* (Louisville, Kentucky: Westminster John Knox Press, 2001), 142.

162 Ted M. Dorman, *A Faith for all Christian Belief in its Classical Expression,* 2nd ed. (Nashville, Tennessee: Broadman and Holman Publishers, 2001), 49.

163 Ted M. Dorman, *A Faith for all Christian Belief in its Classical Expression,* 2nd ed. (Nashville, Tennessee: Broadman and Holman Publishers, 2001), 49.

164 Gregg R. Allison, 212.

165 Millard J. Erickson, *Introducing Christian Doctrine,* 99-100.

166 A. W. Tozer, *The Knowledge of the Holy (New York, New York: Harper Collins, 1961), 108.*

167 Tozer, 110 – 111.

168 Roger E. Olson, *Arminian Theology: Myths and Realities* (Downer Grove, Illinois: IVP Academic, 2000), 119 – 120.

169 Millard J. Erickson, *The Concise Dictionary of Christian Theology*, 49.

170 Olson, 120 – 121.

171 Gregg R. Allison, *The Baker Compact Dictionary of Theological Themes* (Grand Rapids, Michigan: Baker Books, 2016), 61.

172 Allison, 61.

173 Norman Geisler, *Systematic Theology: Sin, Salvation*, vol. 3 (Minneapolis, Minnesota: Bethany House, 2004), 84.

174 Milliard J. Erickson, *The Concise Dictionary of Christian Theology* (Wheaton, Illinois: Crossway, 2001), 69.

175 Ibid. 69.

176 Gregg R. Allison, *Historical Theology: An Introduction to Christian Doctrine* (Grand Rapids, Michigan: Zondervan, 2011), 215.

177 Robert E. Picirilli, *Grace, Faith, Freewill: Contrasting Views of Salvation: Calvinism and Arminianism* (Nashville, Tennessee: Randall House, 2002), 60.

178 Ibid, 60 – 61.

179 Donald K. McKim, ed. *Reformed Theology: The Westminster Handbooks to Christian Theology* (Louisville, Kentucky, Westminster John Knox Press, 2001), 84.

180 Ibid 85.

181 Roger E. Olson, *Arminian Theology: Myths and Realities* (Downer Grove, Illinois: IVP Academic, 2000), 19.

182 *Webster's New Explorer Encyclopedic Dictionary* (Springfield, Massachusetts: Merriam- Webster, 2006), 253.

183 Millard J. Erickson, *The Concise Dictionary of Christian Theology* (Wheaton, Illinois: Crossway, 2001), 28.

184 William D. Mounce, gen. ed. *Mounce's Complete Dictionary of Old and New Testament Words* (Grand Rapids, Michigan: Zondervan, 2006), 92 – 94.

185 Bruce Demarest and Keith J. Matthews. Gen. ed. *Dictionary of Everyday Theology and Culture* (Colorado Springs, Colorado: NavPress, 2010), 38 – 39.

186 Millard J. Erickson, *Christian Theology*, 3rd Edition (Grand Rapids, Michigan: Baler Academic, 2013), 852.

187 Roger E. Olson, *Arminian Theology: Myths and Realities* (Denver Grove, Illinois: IVP Academic, 2006), 27.

188 Alan Cairns, gen. Ed. *Dictionary of Theological Term* (Greenville, South Carolina: Emerald House Group, 1998), 71.

189 Spiros Zodhiates, *The Complete Word Study Dictionary* (Chattanooga, Tennessee: AMG Publishers, 1992), 568.

190 Archibald Thomas Robertson, *Word Pictures in the New Testament. Vol. 4: The Fourth Gospel and the Epistles of the Hebrews* (Grand Rapids, Michigan: Baker Book House, 1932), 109.

191 William Barclay, *The Daily Study Bible Series: The Gospel of John*, vol. One, revised edition (Louisville, Kentucky: Westminster John Knox Press, 1975), 220.

192 Glenn McCoy, Chad Brand, gen ed. *Holman Illustrated Bible Dictionary*, Revised (Nashville, Tennessee: Holman Reference, 2015), 336 – 337.

193 David Mapes, *Systematic Theology II*, "Week Eight." October 2019.

194 David Mapes, *Systematic Theology II*, Notes "Week Eight." October 2019.

195 Walter A. Elwell, *Evangelical Dictionary of Theology*, Grand Rapids (Michigan: Baker Books, 1984), 273

196 Spiros Zodhiates, *The Complete Word Study Dictionary: New Testament* (Chattanooga, Tennessee: AMG Publishers, 1992), 692.

197 Martin H. Manser, *The Westminster Collection of Christian Quotes*, (Louisville, Kentucky: Westminster John Knox Press, 2001), 316.

198 Ibid.

199 Chad Brand, gen. ed. "Clark Palmer," *Holman Illustrated Bible Dictionary:* Revised (Nashville, Tennessee: Holman Reference, 2015), 1344.

200 Millard J. Erickson, *Christian Theology*, 3rd edition (Grand Rapids, Michigan: Baker Academic, 2013), 866 – 868.

201 Millard J. Erickson, *Christian Theology*, 3rd edition (Grand Rapids, Michigan: Baker Academic, 2013), 868.

202 Emery H. Bancroft, *Elemental Theology* (Grand Rapids, Michigan: Zondervan Publishing House, 1960), 205.

203 Bancroft, 207.

204 Bruce Demarest and Keith J. Matthews. Gen. ed. *Dictionary of Everyday Theology and Culture* (Colorado Springs, Colorado: NavPress, 2010), 141 – 142.

205 William D. Mounce, *Mounce's Complete Expository Dictionary of Old and New Testament Words* (Grand Rapids, Michigan: Zondervan, 2006), 232 – 233.

206 Millard J. Erickson, *Christian Theology*, 870.

207 John Calvin, *Calvin's Commentary, Galatians, Ephesians, Philippians, and Colossians* (Grand Rapids, Michigan, 1965) 145.

208 Gregg R. Allison, *The Baker Compact Dictionary of Theological Terms,* (Grand Rapids, Michigan: Baker Books, 2016), 181.

209 Bruce Demarest and Keith J. Matthews, gen. eds. *Dictionary of Everyday Theology and Culture (*Colorado Springs, Colorado: NavPress, 2010), 326.

210 Douglas Moo, *The New International Commentary on the New Testament, The Epistle to the Romans* (Grand Rapids, Michigan: William B. Eerdmans Publishing Company, 1996), 354.

211 David Mapes, *Systematic Theology II.*

212 Mounce, 569.

213 Mapes, notes.

214 Paul Ennes, *The Moody Handbook of Theology,* (Chicago, Illinois: Moody Press, 1989), 340.

215 Gregg R. Allison, *The Baker Compact Dictionary of Theological Terms* (Grand Rapids, Michigan: Baker Books, 2016), 216.

216 Henry Clarence Thiessen, *Lectures in Systematic Theology* (Grand Rapids, Michigan: William B. Eerdmans Publishing Company, 1992), 284.

217 Martin H. Manser, gen. ed. *The Westminster Collection of Christian Quotations* (Louisville, Kentucky: Westminster John Knox Press, 2001), 114.

218 Manser, 113.

219 Paul Enns, *The Moody Handbook of Theology*, (Chicago, Illinois: Moody Press, 1989), 325.

220 Enns, 325.

221 Enns, 329.

222 Manser, 217.

223 Mansor, 217.

224 Paul Enns, *The Moody Handbook of Theology*, 326.

225 Millard J. Erickson, *The Concise Dictionary of Christian Theology* (Wheaton, Illinois: Crossway, 2001), 175.

226 Alan Cairns, *Dictionary of Theological Terms* (Greenville, South Carolina: Emerald House Group, 1998), 325.

227 Spiros Zodhiates, *The Complete Word Study Dictionary: New Testament*, (Chattanooga, Tennessee: AMG Publisher, 1992), 69 – 71.

228 Spiros Zodhiates, *The Complete Word Study Dictionary: New Testament*, (Chattanooga, Tennessee: AMG Publisher, 1992), 69 – 71.

229 Spiros Zodhiates, *The Complete Word Study Dictionary* (Chattanooga, Tennessee: AMG Publishers, 1992), 969.

230 David Mapes, Sys*tematic Theology II* notes, Luther Rice Seminary, 01/13/2020.

231 John L. Dagg, *Manuel of Theology* (Harrisonburg, Virginia: Gano Books, 1982), 285 – 286.

232 john MacArthur and Richard Mayhue, *Biblical Doctrine: A Systematic Summary of Bible Truth* (Wheaton, Illinois: Crossway, 2017), 640.

233 Ibid, 636.

234 A. W. Tozer, *How to be filled with the Holy Spirit* (Chicago, Illinois: Moody Publishers, 2016), 9 – 11.

235 Henry Clarence Thiessen, *Lectures in Systematic Theology* (Grand Rapids, Michigan: William B. Eerdmans Publishing Company, 1992), 255.

236 David Mapes, *Systematic Theology II notes,* Luther Rice Seminary, 2020.

237 John MacArthur and Richard Mayhue, *A systematic Summary of Biblical Truth: Biblical Doctrine* (Wheaton, Illinois: Crossway, 2017), 353.

238 Wayne Grudem, *Systematic Theology* (Grand Rapids, Michigan: Zondervan, 1994), 770.

239 MacArthur, 354.

240 William Hendriksen, *New Testament Commentary: The Gospel of Matthew* (Grand Rapids, Michigan: Baker Book House, 1973), 650.

241 William Barclay, *The Gospel of Matthew,* vol. 2 (Louisville. Kentucky: Westminster John Knox Press, 1975), 145.

242 John Broadus, *An American Commentary on the New Testament: Matthew* (Philadelphia: American Baptist Publication Society, 1886), 361.

243 Spiros Zodhiates, *The Complete Word Study Dictionary: New Testament,* (Chattanooga, Tennessee: AMG Publishers, 1992), 375.

244 Ibid, 375.

245 Gordon D. Fee, *The New International Commentary on the New Testament: The First Epistle to the Corinthians* (Grand Rapids, Michigan: William B. Eerdmans Publishing Company, 1987), 601.

246 John Walvoord, *The Holy Spirit* (Grand Rapids, Michigan: Zondervan Publishing House, 1958), 142.

247 John MacArthur, 358.

248 Clinton E. Arnold, *Zondervan Exegetical Commentary on the New Testament: Ephesians* (Grand Rapids, Michigan: Zondervan, 2010), 348.

249 Ibid, 350.

250 John MacArthur, *The MacArthur New Testament Commentary: Ephesians* (Chicago, Illinois: The Moody Bible Institute, 1986), 251 – 254.

251 John F. Walvoord, *The Holy Spirit,* (Grand Rapids, Michigan: Zondervan Publishing House, 1958), 220.

252 Woodrow Kroll, *The Book of Roman,* (Chattanooga, Tennessee: AMG Publishers, 2002), 127 – 128.

253 Walvoord, 221.

254 Walvoord, 222.

255 Kroll, 138.

256 William Barclay, *The Gospel of John,* vol. 1 (Louisville, Kentucky: Westminster John Knox Press, 1975), 120.

257 Edward W. Klink, *Zondervan Exegetical Commentary on the New Testament: John* (Grand Rapids, Michigan: Zondervan, 2016), 193.

258 William Barclay, 123.

259 Millard J. Erickson, *The Concise Dictionary of Christian Theology* (Wheaton, Illinois: Crossway, 2001), 181 – 182.

260 William D. Mounce, *Mounce's Complete Expository Dictionary of Old and New Testament Words* (Grand Rapids, Michigan: Zondervan, 2006), 656 – 657.

261 Glenn McCoy, Chad Brand, gen. eds. *Holman Illustrated Bible Dictionary,* Revised (Nashville, Tennessee: Holman Reference, 2015), 336 – 337.

262 David Mapes, *Systematic Theology II,* "Week Eight." October 2019.

263 Emery H. Bancroft, *Elemental Theology* (Grand Rapids, Michigan: Zondervan Publishing House, 1960), 205.

264 Bruce Demarest and Keith J. Matthews, gen eds. *Dictionary of Everyday Theology and Culture,* (Colorado Springs, Colorado: NavPress, 2010), 141 – 142.

265 David Mapes, *Systematic Theology II.*

266 Mounce, 569.

267 Paul Enns, *The Moody Handbook of Theology* (Chicago, Illinois: Moody Press, 1989), 340.

CPSIA information can be obtained
at www.ICGtesting.com
Printed in the USA
FSHW020838040121
77328FS

9 781662 803376